OWNING UP

Owning Up

PRIVACY, PROPERTY, AND BELONGING IN U.S. WOMEN'S LIFE WRITING

Katherine Adams

OXFORD
UNIVERSITY PRESS
2009

OXFORD
UNIVERSITY PRESS

Oxford University Press, Inc., publishes works that further
Oxford University's objective of excellence
in research, scholarship, and education.

Oxford New York
Auckland Cape Town Dar es Salaam Hong Kong Karachi
Kuala Lumpur Madrid Melbourne Mexico City Nairobi
New Delhi Shanghai Taipei Toronto

With offices in
Argentina Austria Brazil Chile Czech Republic France Greece
Guatemala Hungary Italy Japan Poland Portugal Singapore
South Korea Switzerland Thailand Turkey Ukraine Vietnam

Published by Oxford University Press, Inc.
198 Madison Avenue, New York, New York 10016

www.oup.com

Library of Congress Cataloging-in-Publication Data
Adams, Katherine, 1964–
Owning up: privacy, property, and belonging in U.S. women's
life writing / Katherine Adams.
p. cm.
ISBN 978-0-19-533680-1
1. Autobiography—Women authors. 2. Women authors, American—Biography—History
and criticism. 3. American prose literature—Women authors—History and
criticism. 4. American literature—Women authors—History and criticism. 5. American literature—
19th century—History and criticism. 6. Privacy in literature. 7. Privacy—Philosophy.
8. Privacy—United States—History—19th century. I. Title.
PS366.A88A32 2009
810.9'492072—dc22 2008041036

1 3 5 7 9 8 6 4 2
Printed in the United States of America
on acid-free paper

ACKNOWLEDGMENTS

This book owes far more than I can adequately express here to the generosity of my friends, colleagues, teachers, and family. For intellectual and professional guidance along the way I am greatly indebted to Susan Stanford Friedman, Susan K. Harris, Glenn Hendler, Jacques Lezra, the late Nelly McKay, Shirley Samuels, and Craig Werner. A special thanks goes to Bruce Burgett, who generously supported the project from its dissertation-era origins to its completion as this book. His encouragement, incisive commentary, and intellectual example were immensely important at every stage.

I gratefully exploited the skills and sympathy of many readers while finishing *Owning Up*. The project was nourished in its early development by the input of friends and fellow dissertators at the University of Wisconsin–Madison, including Emily Hall, Jim Neighbors, Lisa Schriebersdorf, Erin Smith, and especially Cristine Varholy. Further along, it benefited greatly from the expertise of Mary Chapman, Greg Eiselein, Melissa Homestead, Nancy Isenberg, Mark Brewin, Bob Fanuzzi, Sean Latham, Caroline Levander, Marc Roark, and Cindy Weinstein.

Carole Chabries and Jean Lutes read and reread draft upon draft, providing extraordinary intellectual and emotional support. I can never thank them enough for their kindness, wisdom, and fortitude.

My heartfelt gratitude goes to Dean Tom Benediktson and my colleagues in the English Department at the University of Tulsa. Laura Stevens and Lars Engle deserve a special thanks for their unstinting generosity as readers, advisors, and friends. At Oxford University Press I thank Shannon McLachlan for her enthusiasm and faith in this book.

Several institutions and organizations provided timely material support. I am deeply grateful to the P.E.O. Sisterhood and the University of Wisconsin–Madison Department of English for dissertation fellowships. I thank the University of Tulsa for three Faculty Development Summer Fellowships and a junior sabbatical. The American Council of Learned Societies and the Mellon Foundation have my eternal gratitude for a Junior Faculty Fellowship.

For their relentless moral support, even in the face of great whinyness, I thank Ray Adams, Mary Cantrell, Susan Chase, Beth Clary, Nancy Eggen, Johnny Geren, Cheryl Gordon, Cathy Halverson, Holly Helm Hill, Don Hubbard, Grant Jenkins, Connie Keller, Elana Newman, Gordon Taylor, Nelly Vanzetti, and Sandy Vice. My gratitude and love go to my parents and siblings: Bob, Ruth, Abigail, Robert, and Bill Adams.

To Nathan Halverson I owe every kind of thanks there is. His humor, intellect, love, endurance, and sense of perspective made this book possible.

CONTENTS

OWNING UP

CHAPTER ONE

Introduction

IMPERILED PRIVACY

I sell the shadow to support the substance.
—Sojourner Truth

As the nineteenth century drew to a close, American privacy was in crisis. Or so declared Samuel D. Warren and Louis D. Brandeis in an 1890 issue of the *Harvard Law Review*, announcing that "enterprise [has] invaded the sacred precincts of private and domestic life" and "gossip...has become a trade."[1] These developments, the lawyers explain, threaten not only to dispossess the individual of his most cherished entitlement, but also to corrupt collective values and relations:

> Man...has become more sensitive to publicity, so that solitude and privacy have become more essential to the individual; but modern enterprise and invention have, through invasions upon his privacy, subjected him to mental pain and distress, far greater than could be inflicted by mere bodily injury. Nor is the harm wrought by such invasion confined to the suffering of those who may be the subjects of journalistic or other enterprise. In this, as in other branches of commerce, the supply creates the demand. Each crop of unseemly gossip, thus harvested, becomes the seed of more, and, in direct proportion to its circulation, results in the lowering of social standards and of morality. (77)

Titled "The Right to Privacy: The Implicit Made Explicit," Warren and Brandeis's essay marks the first attempt to establish privacy as a category of immunity under U.S. law. It was provoked in part by the unauthorized intrusions of journalists at the wedding of Warren's daughter.[2] But, as the authors correctly point out, they were far from alone in their complaint. Legal scholars, society columnists, politicians, and even amateur gardeners were publishing similar protests against the forces of invasion, exposure, and consumption that they, too, characterized as dangerous to both the individual and the culture at large. Indeed, in comparison to their contemporaries, Warren and Brandeis might be judged conservative. They predict only an erosion of social standards while others foresee the demise of intellectual public discourse, the atrophy of citizenship, even the decline of democracy itself. According to *Scribner's Magazine*, the assault on privacy signifies nothing less than "the great future battle of the world between the two systems of Socialism and Individualism," and the *North American Review* warns that, without preventative action, "civilization . . . must deteriorate . . . crushed by brutality and vulgar indecency."[3]

Amid this outcry on its behalf, privacy itself remains curiously elusive. Although defended as the very foundation of democratic civilization, it is seldom invoked directly or concretely. Where explicit references do occur they prove slippery. Warren and Brandeis classify privacy as an "intangible entitlement" that transcends physical being; it is a dimension of the self susceptible to "pain and distress far greater than could be inflicted by mere bodily injury" (77); and for *Nation* editor E. L. Godkin, privacy is a "kingdom of the mind, that inner world of personal thought and feeling in which every man passes some time."[4] In accounts such as these, privacy seems without substance or even location—Godkin's spatial metaphor notwithstanding, his words are typical in framing privacy not as a site of physical enclosure or solitude, but as a privileged relation to one's extracorporeal self. Used at the start of the nineteenth century primarily to describe the legal and material status of private ownership, the term *privacy* had since come to name a condition of inviolable, psychospiritual selfhood that Warren and Brandeis famously define as "the right to be let alone." In this new aspect, privacy is not just immaterial but insistently antimaterial—imagined in opposition to an embodied public's "morbid hunger" and "insatiable appetite" and posed against the forces of "enterprise," "trade," "industry," and "commerce" named throughout the "The Right to Privacy" (77).[5] Here privacy obtains in the negation of corporeal and economic contingency. It is that which modern man has lost to a world where anything and everything might become a commodity. This helps to explain privacy's peculiar status as both central and absent in the writings of end-century alarmists. For although privacy represents utopian democratic value—the freedom and equality of the autonomous individual—it does so only retrospectively, in the wake of loss. Thus, the writer who imagines a "snake of inquisitiveness" that comes "crawling to the threshold and peering through the keyhole" gets it exactly right: by the end of the nineteenth century privacy has become a kind of American Eden, remembered only after the Fall.[6]

From a twenty-first-century perspective, this nineteenth-century panic narrative may sound familiar, or even prophetic. Certainly it resonates with our own postlapsarian lament for something sacred that we recall as privacy. The outrage expressed more than a century ago over "personal journalists" and corrosive public appetites closely resembles the tone of moral distaste adopted by critics like Neal Gabler and Richard Schickel in response to the present-day obsession with celebrity lives, political exposé, confessional blogging, and reality television.[7] Even the twenty-first-century affliction of identity theft seems to find antecedent in nineteenth-century portrayals of an alienated selfhood that proliferates alarmingly across the print public sphere—think here of Warren and Brandeis's grotesquely self-propagating "crop of unseemly gossip" (77). In this light, the privacy crisis of the 1880s and '90s might seem—as it claims—to mark the beginning of the end, the early deterioration of something that formerly made us human and whole as individuals, civilized and democratic as a nation.

Such a reading mistakes nostalgia for historiography. As scholars have long since demonstrated, U.S. privacy has always been porous to civic and state intrusions, always overlapped with zones of public and semipublic activity, and always received its form and meaning from the material culture of production, property, and exchange.[8] Warren and Brandeis do not name a novel state of affairs. Nor do they and their contemporaries voice a new complaint. Representations of privacy at risk are in evidence from the earliest encodings of personal life as something separate from political and economic activity—as when an 1827 literary critic describes himself reading a British novel and "wincing to have the veil of domestic privacy thus rudely torn asunder"; or when, in 1845, the *Democratic Review* rebukes "the impertinent curiosity of penny-a-liners, who, like the insects that feed upon the brain of the dead elk, make a commodity of the private lives of men"; or when an 1870 editorial complains that "now [the personal journalist] infests the country...taint[s] the social atmosphere, and develop[s] in us all a moral disease."[9] Across the century, writers conceptualize privacy in terms of violation and loss. More, they stage this loss in the present tense. Wistfully, the 1870 piece recalls that "our great-grandfathers suffered from [the invasive journalist]. But they did not suffer him. They scourged him out of their paths." Ten years later, yet another writer announces that the press has lately "burst its proper barriers" and taken up "the aspersion of private character, and the invasion of domestic privacy."[10] The effect of this continually renewed alarum is to constantly reaffirm the very thing it marks absent: each new iteration gestures back toward an originary and inviolable selfhood. In fact, this recursive, threat-driven production of privacy is so common and conventionalized by 1873 that the writer of a regular column on language defends the term *undisprivacied* as perfectly good English. According to the columnist, the word is not a neologism. Not only does it have precedent in the term *disprivacied*, it also functions distinctly from *privacied* in that "there is in disprivacied a suggestion of an active and unpleasant taking away of privacy, and that therefore undisprivacied means one who has escaped that injury from those who are willing to inflict it."[11] The double negative of privacy becomes so palpable in the U.S. imaginary that it warrants a place in the grammar. Thus, when Warren and Brandeis sound the alarm in 1890 they do so not to protect or mourn privacy, but to produce it—in a particular guise, and toward a particular purpose. Nostalgia is a productive discourse, and alarmist nostalgia even more so. By gazing longingly into the past for something that never was, writers like Warren and Brandeis generate very real effects in their own moment. This book investigates the nature and purpose of these effects in early U.S. culture.

Owning Up focuses on the figure of imperiled privacy in the five decades from 1840 to 1890 in order to understand its role within discourses of national identity and belonging. What are we to make of this recurring narrative that reinforces a fantasy of originary self-unity, autonomy, and democratic freedom, even as it reports the vulnerability or outright loss of these same entitlements? What interests are served by this gesture that simultaneously enfranchises and disenfranchises its subjects? What forms of identification does it encourage and proscribe? What modes of action and passivity does it provoke? And how does all of this change in conjunction with the nineteenth century's vast economic, social, and political upheavals? To explore these questions, among others, I analyze biographical and autobiographical writing by and about five nineteenth-century U.S. women: Margaret Fuller, Sojourner Truth, Harriet Beecher Stowe, Elizabeth Keckley, and Louisa May Alcott. This archive represents a significant departure from those consulted in previous scholarship on U.S. privacy, which typically focuses on fiction by canonical white male authors—Poe, Hawthorne, Melville, and James in particular—and on meanings symbolized by such un-self-reflecting white female characters as Madeline Usher, Hepzibah and Phoebe Pyncheon, and Verena Tarrant.[12] By turning to women's life writing I am able to examine privacy discourse at its most self-conscious. For these are texts that both enact and confront the public circulation of private matters. As a genre devoted specifically to the marketing of privacy, life writing might be seen as an agent of invasion and exposure. Yet it also routinely thematizes its own transgressive function, ruminating upon the uncouth and uncanny nature of what Sojourner Truth refers to as "selling the shadow." The result is a metadiscourse that both generates and investigates public privacy. Nineteenth-century life writers are preoccupied with the same matters that concern Warren and Brandeis: they explore the dangers of self-alienation, dependence, and existential dispossession; and they ponder the impact of published privacy upon audiences—its power to constitute publics, and to erode social boundaries. This is especially true of the writers discussed in this book, who make particularly self-conscious use of a self-conscious genre. As black and white women they symbolized privacy, but did not possess it. Although white women and African American writers made bids for the entitlement of privacy throughout the nineteenth century, they did so against the grain of its logic and—insofar as their attempts reproduced that logic—at risk of reinscribing their own marginalization. In order to appropriate the authority of privacy, the writers discussed here must negotiate and revise it from within. In doing so, they reveal its structure and purpose, its function as a badge of power and belonging in nineteenth-century U.S. culture.

Owning Up seeks to shift current understandings of nineteenth-century American privacy and its role within national and democratic imaginaries. While previous studies have concentrated chiefly on how privacy discourse suppresses the interdependence of private life with political and economic activity, I am interested in representations that emphasize such affiliations and acknowledge the nonintact, nonenclosed nature of privacy. I interpret these as sites of normative privacy production rather than critique, looking at how such references to privacy's public exposure introduce concepts of privacy into public circulation to promote and organize modes of identification. This approach is useful, in part, for what it reveals about the relationship between republicanism and liberalism in nineteenth-century political culture. Unsurprisingly, previous studies of privacy have tended to reassert the notion of a linear shift from republicanism to liberalism, wherein private life is said to replace public-political activity as the locus of democratic freedom and identity.[13] My argument troubles this account by demonstrating that in privacy discourse both paradigms of political value and identification work simultaneously, sometimes contradictorily, sometimes complementarily. I show that liberal and republican understandings of privacy coexist in political discourse, so that seemingly incompatible concepts—of freedom and dependence, enfranchisement and deprivation, transcendence and contingency, amelioration and oppression—circulate concurrently under the same sign. Building upon recent studies of U.S. sentimentalism, I explore the ways that nineteenth-century Americans recognized privacy as a public production, and thought of it in conjunction with the classically republican concerns of public good and political association.[14] The first part of the book looks at privacy in the antebellum context of Romantic nationalism, where it stands as an endangered source of communal value and national unity. Later chapters trace the changes that eventually give rise to the liberal ethos of Warren and Brandeis. But, as we shall see, even their narrative of beleaguered individuality emerges in alliance with concerns about damaged public discourse and political virtue. Even at the height of laissez-faire liberalism, it would seem that majoritarian logic conditions the minoritarian priorities of privacy discourse.

Over the past decade, scholars such as Shirley Samuels, Bruce Burgett, Glenn Hendler, and Peter Coviello have greatly expanded our understanding of how the meanings encoded as private, personal, or presocial in the nineteenth-century United States were mediated by publicity.[15] Yet most studies of privacy qua privacy have remained oddly resistant to the idea that, as Lauren Berlant and Michael Warner put it, "there is nothing more public than privacy."[16] Even some of the best recent work in this area continues to treat privacy as a place or condition that is somehow separable from, "eclipsed by," or even intolerant of publicity.[17] *Owning Up* assumes that experiences of privacy and interiority are always accessed via public mediation and subject to public negotiation. This is not to disregard the struggles for civil and political liberties–the so-called privacy rights to religious, reproductive, and sexual freedoms—that ground themselves in contested claims to private liberal subjectivity. Indeed, this study is centrally concerned with the unequal distribution of privacy as both a material privilege and the symbolic basis of legal and political personhood. I aim, however, to counter the notion that such entitlements could ever be—as Milette Shamir advocates in her important study *Inexpressible Privacy*—"nontradable" or "publicly nonnegotiable," and to investigate the hegemonic uses of such arguments.[18] Where Shamir worries that the "politics of exposure" and political exposé "reduce the self to sheer alienability," I hold that the badge of inalienable private selfhood is only ever acquired through strategies of self-display and public circulation.[19] From this premise, it becomes clear not only that publicity is the scene of privacy's production, but also that privacy discourse is a place where battles are waged for public authority and national belonging—in both the nineteenth century and the twenty-first. To explore both dynamics, I focus on how early American women writers manipulated rhetorics of exposure and invasion to create privacy meanings for their own use.[20] I also trace such strategies into recent contexts, where privacy crises ranging from welfare reform and gay marriage to bioslavery and presidential sex scandals perform similar work.

Owning Up focuses particularly on images and narratives that generate privacy effects from contexts of national emergency. As Shamir likewise notes, the nineteenth-century discourse on privacy was not exclusive to the United States; in fact, Warren and Brandeis draw widely from British common law and legal commentary. Yet nineteenth-century Americans incessantly posed privacy as a nationalist cause, and in ways designed to promote—as well as to define and delimit—both individual and communal identification.[21] Spectacles of national privacy constitute the publics they pervade, not just in reciprocally defining opposition but also as symbols around which publics take form through varying modes of identification.[22] Privacy, of course, was closely aligned with the ideals of democratic individuality and self-determination, and desire for it was regarded as a form of patriotism: as the architect Andrew Jackson Downing put it, "the love of country is inseparably connected with love of home... strengthening [a man's] patriotism, and making him a better citizen."[23] However, privacy was also thought crucial to the well-being of the nation as a whole, and often made to stand *for* the national whole as an imagined location of transcendent unity.[24] Here the importance of privacy's "intangible" and antimaterial status begins to become apparent, for this characterization removes privacy into a space of abstract universal entitlement, somewhere beyond differences in power and privilege. Arguing for a privacy tort in 1896, John Gilmer Speed conducts privacy into the founding statement of U.S. democracy—"The ancients included it in that declaration which expressed the pledge of their lives and honors to defend the inalienable rights of 'life, liberty, and the *pursuit of happiness*' "—and classifies it as an "inchoate right," an implicit originary principle destined to be articulated as law.[25] Here and elsewhere, privacy is made the alpha and omega of democracy, the lost origin and receding horizon of America's social contract. This formula would later be echoed by the 1965 Supreme Court decision *Griswold v. Connecticut*, in which Justice William O. Douglas famously locates privacy as the ghostly foundation of democratic freedoms—an entitlement not directly named within, but "older than the Bill of Rights," a "penumbra" that frames Constitutional freedoms.[26]

Two lines of inquiry shape this book's investigation into nineteenth-century American privacy crises. Both concern how such crises produce privacy as negation—as an ideality made cogent by the story of its loss. The first set of questions focuses on how its back-formation inflects the values and meanings invested in privacy. How, I ask, do recurring reports of imperiled privacy help to frame democratic freedom as a condition of self-protection versus engagement, as resistance instead of critique? How does the trope of prepolitical entitlement displace and then stand *as* a form of political obligation? By pursuing these questions, *Owning Up* traces the genealogy of a discourse on political identity that Wendy Brown charges with "abstracting us from social and political context, by masking the powers which construct, stratify, and injure us"; and that, as Lauren Berlant has influentially argued, finds its current image of "modal-citizenship" in the perfectly blank innocence of the fetus.[27] More, this book calls attention to an underacknowledged aspect of how liberalism idealizes passivity, by showing that such an ideal paradoxically requires active, often violent, cultivation. As a negative relation rather than a positive location, the threatened entitlement of privacy resides not in a stable exteriority to political and economic forces but in acts of extrication and elimination. *Owning Up* investigates the impact of privacy as a representation of democratic ideality that is not empty but rather always in the process of emptying.

This raises my second set of questions, which concern how privacy discourse delimits its own promise of universal enfranchisement. Defined by threat and requiring constant rearticulation, privacy is a powerful disciplinary concept, ideal for naturalizing hegemonic claims to putatively universal entitlements and for demonizing other "emergent" claims.[28] Thus, while "The Right to Privacy" begins by arguing for the "right to be let alone," a few pages later it revises its demand to "rights as against the world" (76, 86). Here I explore the way that privacy discourse requires and creates modes of exclusion from the belonging it promises. Why, for example, does the panic reach its highest pitch during the 1880s and '90s, when by many measures privacy is more available than ever before for people like Warren and Brandeis? In 1890, more Americans owned private homes and those occupied by the upper and middle classes were larger than at any time earlier. The rich enjoyed more distance from industry and market pressures and more insulation from urban heterogeneity. In terms of temporal and spatial isolation and the protection these afforded from strangers who might misappropriate one's "person," the possession of privacy was at an all-time high for those who most bitterly protested its loss. New technologies of invasive publicity not withstanding, then, the end-century crisis is perhaps best understood as a response to the increasing demands for change being voiced by disenfranchised groups. It should be read alongside other strategies for consolidating white, male, and capitalist privilege such as antisuffragism, lynching, Jim Crow segregation, nativism, and laissez-faire defenses of property and market liberalism. Critical legal scholar Patricia Williams succinctly defines privacy as "exclusion based on self-regard."[29] In *Owning Up* I suggest that privacy might also be understood as self-regard based on exclusion, a process of (re)claiming free and autonomous individuality against the threat of alien others.

PRIVACY AS SELF-(NON)POSSESSION

As several generations of cultural historians have shown, the material and ideological emergence of U.S. privacy corresponded to transformations in the relations of property and production. Values of individual autonomy and seclusion first became widespread with the end of European feudal systems and new opportunities for private ownership. These values gained importance with the spread of industrialization. As both property and production relocated outside of the home, personal life and family came to seem the natural locations of autonomous and authentic selfhood, imagined as both separate from and prior to economic and political activity.[30] At the same time, the growth of market economies and banking practices disrupted previous conceptions of property. Under an agrarian economy, property in land had provided a stable and naturalizing symbol of individuality and democratic self-determination. With marketization, however, property came to signify the volatile and contingent dynamics of capital, commodity, and exchange.[31] In response there emerged a new discourse on privacy as a psychospiritual domain of affect and thought, an interior selfhood that stood apart from the vagaries of economic life. Accounts of this process have differed widely and acrimoniously. Over several decades of Marxist cultural historiography, republican synthesis debates, and contending assessments of domestic ideology and sentimental culture, the nature, consequences, and extent of liberal individualism's emergence have been thoroughly examined. The timing of this transition has also been subject to disagreement, with scholars placing it as early as the 1630s and as late as the 1890s.[32] Here I will approach the shift from property to privacy not as a single or stable historical turning point, but as a recurring strategy. I propose that to fully understand the significance of privacy discourse in U.S. culture we must look beyond the illusion of inviolable and transcendent selfhood that it seems to affirm, and consider the chronic, and productive, failure of this affirmation—the impossibility of finalizing privacy's separation from material and market relations. In its utopian mode, privacy discourse suppresses the worm at its heart to promise a seamlessly unified self that exists in a space before marketization. Elsewhere, however, it emphasizes the problem of dependence on capitalist culture in ways that both amplify and assuage the anxiety of market subjects, shaping an idea of selfhood that is simultaneously structured and haunted by the threat of commodification. Nineteenth-century privacy discourse, in other words, pursues a fantasy of not being owned that is driven by fear of being owned. This paranoia focuses most literally on dehumanizing market forces. But it also informs anxiety about what legal scholars refer to as "backdoor invasion"—meaning exposure to the public eye—and even about "front door invasion," or government intervention into the individual citizen's autonomy. Both are represented as forms of being owned, whether by one's neighbors or by the state.

Warren and Brandeis and their fellow end-century alarmists illustrate the way that privacy relies on its difference from property for meaning. For, although their immediate target is print publicity, the real agents of the invasion they resent are not journalists and photographers but market commodification and capitalism. "Gossip," writes Speed, "has become a recognized trade in which large capital is invested."[33] E. L. Godkin predicts no relief "as long as money getting talent holds the field" forcing privacy to "contend...against the great commercial demand for scandal and gossip."[34] Grounding their call for privacy rights in a portrayal of encroaching market pressures, these writers mark the centrality of privacy's difference from property. They also show how the story of that (failed) difference becomes itself the condition of privacy's emergence. Their efforts demonstrate that the promise of free and originary selfhood requires articulation both with and against property, that privacy is not just opposed to but also always affiliated with problems of ownership.[35] Throughout "The Right to Privacy," Warren and Brandeis strive to establish a bright line between the "tangible" manifestations of personality—objects like letters, portraits, or photographs that they refer to as "personal property" but classify as susceptible to commodification—and the "intangible" entity of "inviolate personality" itself (75, 82). This latter is perfectly unsusceptible to appropriation by others. Indeed, as their qualifier "inviolate" dictates, it simply ceases to exist as itself once alienated from itself. From this distinction the lawyers derive their claim that privacy must be acknowledged as an entitlement not reducible to any previously recognized right, an entitlement requiring a new law that is "spiritual" rather than "material" in principle (78).[36] A number of scholars characterize this argument as an attempt to isolate privacy from property once and for all.[37] If this is the lawyers' aim, it is a self-defeating one. For, in being defined by its difference from market forces—it *is* that which cannot be appropriated by another—privacy is constantly defined in relation to them. What Warren and Brandeis attempt is by necessity as much a process of coarticulation as disarticulation—hence the way their argument repeatedly comes back to the logic and laws of ownership for analogy and contrast. Hence, too, their focus on the "evil of invasion" by market forces and the evidential injury it inflicts (76). At the very heart of Warren and Brandeis's case we find the primal wound of violated selfhood, the "heightening of sensations" that has "made it clear to men that only a part of the pain, pleasure, and profit of life lay in physical things [and that] thought, emotions, and sensations demanded legal recognition." Here is privacy as the phantom limb of the market capitalist, located only with the pain of market alienation.

To capture the double movement by which privacy, and the "inviolable personality" with which it precisely coincides, stand both with and against the idea of property, I use the term *self-(non)possession.* In a different argument this concept might be referred to simply as self-right. This is the term by which nineteenth-century Americans invoked their inalienable claim to self, recalling John Locke's distinction between those components of the self-possessed individual that can be traded (his labor and its products) and those that cannot (his "life" and "liberty").[38] My purpose, however, is to underscore the indeterminacy of Locke's distinction and the inherently unstable and dynamic nature of privacy. In particular, I am interested in how inviolable selfhood tries to balance itself between a divided self and a self so unified as to surrender self-awareness. On one side, self-(non)possession refuses any possibility of a selfhood that is divisible from itself, susceptible to appropriation and circulation, or dependent on externally determined value. It strains toward a horizon of seamless self-unity and the perfect freedom of disembedded autonomy. On the other side, self-(non)possession defends against the opposite extreme: a self so unmediated that it lacks self-mastery, self-consciousness, or any self-relation at all. This is the condition that political theorist Hannah Arendt describes as privation, where isolation from the political economy is so absolute as to reduce subjects to embodiment and deprive them of the ability to act, choose, or differentiate themselves from others.[39] Self-(non)possession is not non-self-possession. The discourse on privacy keeps tropes of property in play, nervously maintaining contact with the Lockean property-in-self that guarantees both individuation and self-awareness.

The self-(non)possessive subject is implicitly white, male, and propertied. But he does not inhabit the discourse of privacy alone, for that discourse was rooted in a market economy that required the political and economic privatization of white women and blacks—the former in the middle-class home as instruments of biological and cultural reproduction and socioeconomic stability, the latter on the southern plantation as instruments of economic production. Because property relations in nineteenth-century America were most centrally regulated by race and gender, so too were the relations and identities constituted by the discourse on privacy. To be sure, class difference is always at stake in privacy relations—whether it is being disavowed by exceptionalist representations of privacy as a universal immaterial entitlement, or reinforced by Darwinistic representations where privacy is a sign of natural aristocracy. But class is not constitutive of property or privacy in the same sense as gender and race. Nor was class constructed as a form of absolute human difference, as in the religious and pseudoscientific discourses on gender and race. Privacy discourse mimics, naturalizes, and legitimates the inequities of property by figuring white women and blacks as ontologically incapable of possessing or inhabiting privacy. Moreover, it cites this supposed incapacity constantly in the process of delineating normative self-(non)possession.

Nineteenth-century privacy discourse draws heavily upon representations of white femininity to symbolize both privacy's potential violation and its promise of universal accommodation. An editorial on "The Photographic Nuisance" offers a typical illustration. Describing the shock of discovering one's image on display without permission in the public arena, the writer notes that "those who suffer directly are usually young and lovely women. But their relatives and friends suffer deeply, if indirectly. Indeed, the public too may be said to suffer, if from no other cause, from the fear of seeing...their wives, daughters, or sisters treated in like manner."[40] Here, women bear a special, and tacitly sexualized, vulnerability to privacy invasions. But their "suffering" quickly transfers to a generalized "public" for whom women's violation "adds a new horror to life." A similar logic is at work when, following several high-profile lawsuits concerning the unauthorized sale of women's photographs, *Scribner's* announces in 1891 that "to a burlesque actress and to an English lady of title we owe the vindication of one's rights to one's person and to protection from likenesses made thereof." And we find it again, nearly a century later, when legal scholar Harry Kalven, recalling the incident that prompted the writing of "The Right to Privacy," imagines the legal entitlement to privacy as "a most marvelous tree to grow from the wedding of the daughter of Mr. Samuel D. Warren."[41] In the production of privacy, white womanhood supplies both representative victim and representative cause.

Thus, although women are named alongside men as victims of violated privacy, they do not stand on equivalent footing. Rather than having privacy women represent it for others—a function that both derives from and naturalizes their status as the legal dependents and property of men. Some of the earliest invocations of a threatened right to privacy occur in association with runaway wives; as historian Nancy Isenberg explains, "the common-law rule of recaption assumed that the wife had unlawfully seized her own body" and that a man "had a claim to privacy from state intervention" in his efforts to retrieve her (a sanction that also applied to dealings with runaway slaves).[42] Later, when Warren and Brandeis define a man's "intangible" immunities, they include, along with legal protections against "nuisance" and "fear," protections against "the alienation of a wife's affection" and "the seduction of a child" (75–76); similarly, Godkin's "kingdom of mind" comprises a man's "right to decide how much knowledge should be publicly available concerning his own thought and feeling and those of his family."[43] In these examples we can trace a development from a concept of privacy based upon property in the material being of wife and daughter, to a concept of privacy based upon the feminized, immaterial (non)property of one's self. Here again, white women represent an experience of privacy belonging both to individual citizens and to the democratic public at large: "Some people may regard this sensibility to privacy as mere selfishness," remarks the *Atlantic Monthly* in 1881; "if that is their opinion, it seems to me that one might say the same thing of the modesty of a woman."[44]

A particularly evocative illustration of feminized (non)property appears in an 1876 article calling for more privacy in residential architecture. Criticizing the ostentation of current American homes, the writer likens them to promiscuous women: they "have bad manners; they stare at you, they advertise themselves, they crowd up on the highway, they vie with each other, they are affected, proud, scornful." Having disparaged such self-prostituting designs, the writer next outlines the attractions of modesty:

> We are drawn most by negative things or qualities any way, are we not? The healthful, robust mind is positive, and seeks in nature, and mainly in art, something to awaken it and draw it out, its feminine counterpart, a condition in which its own germs of thought and feeling are unfolded and given back enlarged. How we are drawn by that which retreats and hides itself, or gives only glimpses and half views!...Such a house seems to retreat into itself, and invites the eye to follow. Its interior warmth and coziness penetrate the walls, and the eye gathers suggestions of them at every point.[45]

If showy houses seem slutty, the ideal home naturally resembles the domestic angel who inhabits it. It offers itself as a place for "retreat," "hiding," and self-discovery. This is not surprising as a characterization of either privacy or normative nineteenth-century femininity. What is interesting is that the writer presents these qualities not as the reverse of showiness, but as an alternative kind of showiness: the model home displays its lack of display, asserts the fact of its withdrawal. By withholding its charms from view, it "invites" viewers to "penetrate the walls." Most important, this feminized spectacle of privacy offers a site for masculine self-identification and transcendent (and not so transcendent) enfranchisement: gazing upon it, the viewer finds himself accommodated and "given back enlarged."

To analyze images such as these in the chapters to follow, I draw from an extensive body of scholarship on female iconography and the U.S. national imaginary. Like the allegorical figures of Columbia, Justice, Lady Liberty, and the French Marianne (and often overlapping with them), feminized spectacles of privacy circulated in public to disseminate meanings and values constitutive of masculine identity. As scholars including Lynn Hunt, Linda Kerber, Shirley Samuels, and Lauren Berlant have shown, it was precisely the middle-class woman's prepolitical status that made her eligible to represent political ideals as available for others to claim.[46] In *The Gender of Freedom*, Dillon brings such arguments to bear on the specific question of how public representations of private womanhood recursively produce what she aptly describes as the "fabulous origin" of liberal citizenship.[47] Building upon Carole Pateman's *The Sexual Contract*, Dillon reminds us that the construction of nineteenth-century women as biologically incapable of self-government was not simply a way to exclude women from (an implicitly masculine) political identity but also constitutive of that identity. Dillon emphasizes that this constitutive function was not disguised or suppressed, but overt and incessantly reinforced by images and narratives in which woman's dependent, prepolitical, and "spectacularly useless" nature is staged as an ontological foil for male sovereignty.[48] My own investigation into the iconography of private womanhood reveals a different constitutive function. Where Dillon finds a stable opposition between feminine dependence and masculine consent, I argue that images of feminized privacy represent a kind of untenable ideality that defines but also destabilizes the entitlement of masculine self-(non)possession. Like Kerber and Berlant, I find that tropes of female prepoliticality signify a perfect dislocation from the marketplace and from economic or political interests (encoded as "modesty" or freedom from sexual interest) and designate a zone of transcendent self- and collective unity. I take this analysis in a new direction by focusing on the way such values are routinely portrayed as in jeopardy. As a symbol of purity and of its potential violation, white womanhood makes a convenient focus for the crisis narrative of nineteenth-century privacy discourse. Her image projects an infinitely supple (because contentless) ideal of entitlement and belonging that is defined by its difference from—and required defense against—the enemy Other.

Sometimes, to be sure, this Other is femininity itself. For if in some cases woman's incapacity for self-possession represents utter freedom from self-interest, elsewhere it translates as a contemptible failure at self-containment—as in the theory of promiscuous architecture discussed above. Such representations do not contradict, but complement the iconic ideal of private womanhood. Thus, an 1870 editorial that begins by calling for journalistic restraint in the case of unmarried ladies concludes by deriding women's inability to distinguish between private and public modalities: "the sex differ much in this respect from men."[49] To illustrate, the writer recalls an authoress who, upon receiving a negative review, visited his office in person, "quivering with fat and indignation":

> I could hardly suppress my laughter as I saw her cheeks flaming, her eyes flashing and her mouth fairly foaming with wrath. . . . The

burden of her tirade was the denunciation of the cowardly miscreant who, incited only by enmity to her and desiring only to injure her, had written this scurrilous, lying article.[50]

Having misread literary critique as personal attack, the authoress responds in kind. She invades the quintessential space of public abstraction—a newsroom—with a self whose hyperprivatized status manifests as hyperembodiment. Indeed, it is as though she forces her way physically onto the very pages of the newspaper. The result is laughable, but also disruptive in a manner that reestablishes the need to protect the boundaries around femininity and privacy. This double bind imposed a powerful disciplinary logic against women who demanded rights to public identity and authority. Trying to assert themselves as selves, they stood as aggressors against their own symbolic value. It became necessary, and useful, to protect Woman from women.

Of course, nineteenth-century America's obsession with violated womanhood focused far more heavily on racial difference than gender normativity, and the former also underwrites the discourse of imperiled privacy. In contrast to the extensive scholarship on gender and nineteenth-century privacy, very little research exists on the role played by representations of black racial difference and slavery.[51] The persisting influence of the separate spheres paradigm, even among those historians and critics who challenge it, has tended to identify privacy with domesticity and the cult of true womanhood, and to prioritize gender as the determining structure of public/private logic. Yet the political economy that generated privacy discourse relied just as heavily upon the alienation of black labor and selfhood, and upon the narratives of absolute racial difference that justified it before and after emancipation. As with representations of white womanhood, representations of African American men and women transformed a legal denial of self-possession into a theory of biological and ontological essence. In many places these overlapped. Both blacks and white women were made to stand for the privacy values of authenticity and immediacy. Also, like the fatly indignant authoress, blacks were rendered in terms of hyperembodiment and uncontained passion. Yet, because the two groups occupied radically different positions in the political economy, they also served divergent symbolic functions in the discourse of privacy. At its most pronounced this difference consisted in the use of white women to symbolize the perfect freedom and plenitude of self-(non)possession, and the use of black men and women to symbolize threats to it.

From the Declaration of Independence forward, Americans have invoked slavery to protest alienated rights and, as the actual enslavement of African Americans took root in the national consciousness, this metaphor became linked to black racial difference. Images of black bodies were widely appropriated to represent unfreedoms other than their own—a practice Karen Sánchez-Eppler and Amy Dru Stanley have analyzed in the rhetorics of white women's and white working-class activism.[52] In nineteenth-century privacy discourse, the trope of slavery frequently represents the imagined dispossession of an individual's innermost self and the subjection of his identity to public determination. Victims of unwanted publicity imagined themselves "owned" by the reading public, or complained of journalists who made them "slave[s] to public inquiry."[53] They also used images of racial blackness to represent this unfreedom, aligning it not just with privatization—with the condition of being owned—but also with the absolute dependence of the commodity upon the fluctuating, externally determined values of the marketplace.[54] In the fullest expression of this idea, blackness comes to stand for contingency itself—that is, for the individual's location within a landscape of material and social relations that have the power to define him—and for the embodiment that thusly locates and subjects him. In this logic, whiteness and privacy both are generated from acts of transcending enslaving embeddedness. In *Intimacy in America*, Peter Coviello pursues related questions concerning the intersecting discourses of racial difference and self-possession in what he refers to as a "dream of affiliation," a mode of national belonging that is experienced as an unmediated intimacy, and represented as whiteness. Coviello argues that this racial "dream" originates in property, the most significant determinant of citizenship and belonging in early U.S. culture, and that whiteness first becomes meaningful as a state of self-propriety defined against the non-self-possession of the African slave.[55] For Coviello, this logic is corporeal. Focusing on the history of racial formation among wage laborers, he argues that whiteness emerges as an "ineradicable material property in the self" or "something securely in and of the body: it gives miraculously back to the laborer the integrity of the body whose lesser components—its skills and energies—he has bartered for pay."[56] Like Coviello, I find that white nineteenth-century Americans deploy the idea of black racial difference to stabilize an elusive distinction between the fungible and inalienable aspects of their self-ownership. But my research indicates that privacy and the whiteness it expresses are insistently *not* material, *not* of the body. Specifically, they are enacted by processes of shedding embodiment and moving beyond the embeddedness it imposes.

Focusing on the immateriality—or antimateriality—of white privacy clarifies its connection not only to black privatization, but also to the figure of black privation. I refer here to the racist belief that blacks were incapable of mastering the body and its biological drives. Here is the ultimate expression of embedded unfreedom: a subject utterly lacking interiority or agency. During the antebellum period, images of black privation circulated in justifications of slavery where it was argued that Africans lacked the self-awareness that makes one fully human and capable of self-possession, and were naturally dependent upon control by others. Antislavery activists inverted this argument, but also left its racist imagery intact, when they accused slaveholders of turning blacks into unthinking animals by denying them the conditions of individuality—literacy, self-determination, and solitude. Other reformers condemned the "irresponsible privacy" of slavery, a term referring both to the "dark and hidden iniquities" that were shielded by social denial and to the laws that prohibited blacks from testifying on their own behalf or acquiring a public voice through literacy.[57] Here, too, antislavery rhetoric emphasized a difference between having privacy—inhabiting a self-relation that occurs in separation from public culture—and being relegated to an absolute isolation that obviates self-relation and consciousness. For slavery's defenders, black privation necessitated the privatization of slavery; for its opponents, black privation resulted from slavery's privatization. Both arguments posed black subjects as bodies stripped of consciousness and political will, overpowered by their own unfreedom.

This image provided comfort to many whites, reaffirming the idea of absolute racial difference. But it also lent itself to frightening portrayals of inherently uncontained and uncontainable black embodiment. In the antebellum period it fueled fearful imaginings of a slave uprising, as well as hostile representations of free blacks as dissolute, criminal, and depraved.[58] After the war, the specter of black privation fed anxiety over how white America would cope with the newly emancipated population. It generated stark visions of a postbellum political economy overburdened by the self-insufficiency of freedpeople who threatened to spread the taint of their unfreedom to the bodies of whites.[59] At the end of the century, privation logic reappeared in social Darwinist theories on the underdevelopment of nonwhites. "Privacy," writes E. L. Godkin in 1890, is "not only unsought for but unknown in primitive or barbarous societies. The savage cannot have privacy, and does not desire or dream of it."[60] This presumed lack was again viewed as a threat to U.S. national culture which would impede national and white racial evolution. In the move from black privatization to black privation, the logic of causality shifted. Whereas early portrayals reflected the fact that black unfreedom originated in political and economic position, by the midcentury even antislavery racial theories tended to assume that black unfreedom was biologically determined. As critics including Coviello and Edmund Morgan show, this shift supported a corresponding naturalization of white freedom and privilege. It also ascribed the violence of slavery and racial reconstruction to African Americans themselves. That is, in narratives of uncontained black privation, blacks become symbols and agents of the same political and economic violence that had been inflicted upon them. Where this panic narrative intersects with discourses of miscegenation and interracial rape, it reveals how closely the logics of black privation and white feminized privacy meshed. For example, in an antislavery speech delivered before the Urban League of Philadelphia, the physician Charles Meigs begins by describing slavery as a "moral disease" infecting the national constitution, but then shifts seamlessly into a lecture on the sanctity of white womanhood and its threatened contamination by African blood.[61] Meigs's concern is still for diseased nationhood, but now the infectant is a "Melanian stream" in which "our Ario-Saxon blood . . . will assuredly disappear forever." The doctor—whose specialty, fittingly enough, was obstetrics and diseases of women—calls upon his listeners to "erase this odious blot" by restoring women to that "narrow . . . magic circle" from which all national virtue—"the will of the family; the municipality, of the very State itself"—issues forth. He warns, "Drive her out and all her sex to the primitive barbarism of our nature, leaving man alone in the world, what should, what *could* man ever afterwards do, save follow, like the lion and the tiger, his brutal instincts" (19). Meigs deploys privacy values in both feminized and racialized guise: the "magic circle" of femininity that is the origin of civilization, nation, and citizen; the "Melanian stream" of black privation that threatens to overflow its boundaries. By bringing them together, he reinscribes a story of endangered white male individuality.

SELLING THE SHADOW

Owning Up does not investigate life writing as a genre. Nor is it concerned with the problems of form and classification that frequently preoccupy scholars of biographical and autobiographical literature. Its focus lies in how the cultural practices surrounding nineteenth-century U.S. life writing helped install and naturalize the very desire for privacy they appeared to violate.[62] With this aim, the study uses not just traditional autobiographies, biographies, journals, and memoirs, but also autobiographical fiction, fictionalized biography, novels portraying the production and reception of life writing, and nineteenth-century arguments concerning the public impact of life narrative. Texts were selected for their self-reflexivity around the problem of offering private lives for public consumption. Through expressions of regret and reluctance and promises of sensational revelation, life writers developed their own highly conventionalized metadiscourse of crisis that invested their texts with the added value of privacy meanings. Harriet Jacobs's *Incidents in the Life of a Slave Girl* offers one well-known example with its prefatory apologies from both author and editor. "I trust my motives will excuse what might otherwise seem presumptuous," writes Jacobs. "I have not written my experiences in order to attract attention to myself; on the contrary, it would have been more pleasant to me to have been silent about my own history."[63] With this rhetorical gesture, the author guarantees the authenticity of her forthcoming revelations and promises us privileged access to them. She also stakes her own (non)possession of privacy by emphasizing that disclosure is her choice.[64] A more coy version of this tactic can be found in a volume of travel letters by Caroline Churchill, the prologue of which is addressed "To the Curious" but also chides, "An intelligent public can have no possible interest in one's private affairs."[65] Indeed, the strategy of opening one's life narrative with regret or remonstration becomes so ritualized as to invite satirical comment—as by the reviewer who wryly observes, "Perhaps a man who publishes his own autobiography is not the person to complain of intrusions on his privacy."[66] In this light, nineteenth-century life writing is less opposed to commentators like Warren and Brandeis than allied with them. That is, it represents another mechanism for creating privacy effects through the conceit of exposure, and for deploying these in bids for public authority and belonging.

And authority and belonging are patently at stake in these strategies of exposure and withdrawal. As the spread of industrial capitalism shifted the basis of self-sovereignty and political authority from private property to the (non)possession of privacy, it became possible to imagine a culture in which differences in material privilege mattered less. As historian Eli Zaretsky puts this, the change marked "a major social advance" toward an egalitarian understanding of citizenship; privacy, Zaretsky argues, was regarded as "the property of the masses and not just the upper-classes."[67] Whether accurate or not, this claim has proved very popular from the early 1800s into the present day, and has influenced many theories of life writing—from William Dean Howells's 1910 declaration that autobiography is "the most democratic province of literature" to recent arguments by critic Stephen Arch that the early American explosion of autobiographical writing constituted a deliberate enactment of classless equality, an insistence that all stories are equally valid and valuable currency of public authority.[68] In *The Long Revolution* Raymond Williams likewise credits the self-proprietary gesture of self-narrative with bringing social and political recognition to a wider range of players, and asserts that it also instantiated a "process of communication that is in fact a process of community."[69]

Owning Up qualifies these rather utopian accounts of early American life writing in two respects. First it demonstrates that the virtual democracy of life writing was less capacious than Howells and the others imagine. Besides the limiting material prerequisites for writing, printing, circulating, accessing, and reading texts, there was also considerable anxiety around the question of which privacies deserved publication and what public outcomes might follow. For example, an editorial that attacks the gossip industry for encroaching upon the essential freedoms of elite society also complains that this industry permits the "elevation of unimportant persons to public notice" so that readers may be "misled into supposing [an unimportant person] to be a person of some consequence."[70] Here, rather than accommodating more and more claims to democratic belonging through self-(non)possession, the economy of privacy regulates itself with warnings against burgeoning excess and eroding distinctions. In *The North American Review*, a similar article, "The Penalties of a Well-Known Name," appears immediately following a piece titled "The Servant-Girl's Point of View" in which mistresses are advised to respect their employees' privacy: "The independent, fairly well-read American girl will not sell her labor to women who insist on her giving any part of her personality but the work of her hands. She feels interference in her private affairs to be an impertinence on any employer's part."[71] Side by side, these vying complaints reveal that claims to privacy occurred within a context of class and social conflict, not in response to some open invitation to belonging and community.[72] The second and more significant way in which this study counters the notion of an egalitarian economy of privacy is by emphasizing the role of dependence. The autobiographer's public assertion of self-(non)possession depends upon an accepting audience of other self-(non)possessive subjects—a requirement that contradicts the very assertion it ratifies. Williams's portrait of community-building personal narrative seems to overlook this tension. As Ann Fabian points out, if life writing print culture conferred visibility and created social bonds, it also reinscribed hierarchies structured by the power differences between seller and buyer, witness and judge, outsider and insider.[73] The conventions dictating how narratives were presented and received—such as the prefaces written by white male authorities for women's captivity narratives, slave testimonials, and beggar's tales—reveal how fundamentally an autobiographer's claim to independence and equality was conditioned by status and power.

No one was more conscious of the limited and negotiated access to democratic self-(non)possession than the writers whose work I consider here. For even as they were positioned as symbols of privacy values they were also barred from claiming such values. This double bind is vividly illustrated by the case of protofeminist intellectual Margaret Fuller. In her lifetime this famously self-assertive woman was repeatedly portrayed in terms of threatening excess—as in Ralph Waldo Emerson's oft-cited reference to her "rather mountainous me," or in James Russell Lowell's satirical attack upon "Miranda" (one of Fuller's autobiographical pseudonyms):

> Miranda meanwhile has succeeded in driving
> Up into a corner, in spite of their striving,
> A small flock of terrified victims, and there,
> With an I-turn-the-crank-of-the-Universe air
> And a tone which, at least to *my* fancy, appears
> Not so much to be entering as boxing your ears,
> Is unfolding a tale (of herself, I surmise,
> For 'tis dotted as thick as a peacock's with I's).[74]

Fuller's negative press demonstrates that a woman who asserted herself *as* a self in public was guilty of violent disruption. Lowell translates her self-portrayal into an act of physical assault that reduces its audience to a sheepish "flock" (rather than "enlarging" their individuality). A vastly different—yet perhaps no less disabling—interpretation of Fuller emerges from the memoir that appeared after her death in 1850. Emerson, James Freeman Clarke, and William Ellery Channing assembled the text by heavily editing a selection of Fuller's personal writings and framing these with their own recollective and interpretive commentary. Not only do these editors rewrite Fuller—so that one reviewer "heartily wish[es]...she were here to defend and save herself from her friends"—but they also appropriate her as an emblem of their own interiority.[75] Clarke, for example, reports that publishing Fuller's text "is like making a confession to the public of our most interior selves....To print one of her letters, is like giving an extract from our own private journal"; and Channing likens his editorial task to "printing a chapter of autobiography."[76] While Fuller lived, her un-self-effacing autobiographical writing was interpreted as a menacing invasion of the public sphere in order to reinscribe an exclusively male entitlement to public authority. After her death those same texts were appropriated as affirmations of male self-(non)possession. Both meanings were enunciated via the threats of exposure and vulnerability. Both instantiated belonging and barred Fuller from it.

And yet, like any ideological formation, nineteenth-century privacy discourse was susceptible to nonnormative uses. Even Fuller succeeded in diverting its logic toward her own intellectual and political aims, as we shall see in chapter 2. In doing so she, Stowe, Truth, Keckley, and Alcott illuminate the nature and effects of privacy discourse more deeply than would a writer approaching it from a position of untroubled entitlement. Moreover, in their works we find strategies for negotiating publicity that exceed those imagined by the worn critical opposition between privatized silence and disembodied, unmarked public voice. These women reveal that female and nonwhite writers held options beyond textual male impersonation or postcolonial mimicry. In the chapters to follow, I explore the various ways in which the five women instrumentalized their overidentification with privacy. Certainly, the strategy of self-exposure could be disempowering. Shamir illustrates this fact in her astute reading of *The Heroic Slave*, where she finds Frederick Douglass "offering an ironic commentary . . . on the white audience's insatiable desire and assumed privilege to enter the mind and soul of the slave."[77] But speaking from within one's symbolic association with privacy values also afforded forms of authority and leverage. I want to dispute Shamir's conclusion that for Douglass and others, the best option in such cases was to choose silence as a form of "reprieve from social narratives of identity" and "shelter from the eye of power."[78] This reasoning echoes the liberal reduction of freedom to passivity and retreat. It also reifies a notion of presocial selfhood that, in its pretense of unmarked universality, is just as exclusionary and disempowering as its twin of disembodied public selfhood. Finally, silence does not confer privacy. This privilege was gained only by circulating the self and negotiating the delicate economy of self-(non)possession.

To illustrate this difference I offer the example of Sojourner Truth, the ex-slave who became famous as an itinerant preacher and antislavery lecturer. In every cause, spiritual or political, Truth's primary text was her own life story; and as her fame grew this story was widely appropriated and distorted for uses that Truth did not always control. Because she was illiterate, Truth enlisted the aid of various white female ghostwriters, beginning with fellow reformer Olive Gilbert and the 1850 *Narrative of Sojourner Truth*. Other white women published versions of Truth's story on their own initiative and with their own aims—most famously Frances Gage, whose heavily revised account of Truth's speech at an Akron suffrage meeting still remains a sacred text of feminist activism, despite having been discredited by historian Nell Irvin Painter.[79] Combined, these texts make up what Painter calls the Truth Myth, a narrative replete with inaccuracies and inventions that was consumed in varying forms by thousands of readers and spectators over the course of Truth's nearly forty years in the public eye. The changing character of this myth indexes the sorts of racialized privacy values that found public use in midcentury U.S. culture, and in chapter 3 I examine how Truth's story was made to mediate the biracial politics of women's suffrage and sentimental authorship. My point here concerns how Truth participates in and exploits her own mythology, not only adopting the distortions of others but also adding her own. Her canny understanding of privacy discourse is summed up in the phrase she had embossed on her souvenir photographic portraits and used as an epigraph for later editions of the *Narrative*: "I sell the shadow to support the substance."

The first thing to note about this motto is that it instigates and resolves its own privacy crisis. With just eight words, Truth both acknowledges that she risks self-alienation by selling her life narrative and photograph and annuls that risk by asserting an absolute distinction between the textual commodity and the inalienable self it represents. With this double gesture, Truth installs herself within the narrative of inviolable self-(non) possession and its attendant claims to freedom and equality. The maneuver is particularly meaningful from an ex-slave—indeed, the motto might also be said to invalidate the publicly traded Truth and assert exclusive claim to an authentic and publicly unavailable self.[80] However, it would be a mistake to interpret Truth's motto as a retreat into sheltering silence. Rather, the slogan exploits that very dream of reprieve—marketing the ideal of unmarketability—while also commenting ironically upon it. First, Truth subverts the authority of self-(non)possession by pointedly alluding to its material basis; the phrase "support the substance" tropes on the idea of transcendent authenticity but also juxtaposes it with an intensely practical set of priorities—the body her sales will nourish and the house in Battle Creek, Michigan, whose mortgage, Truth frequently reported, she was steadily paying off. These "substantial" conditions of self-possession link her metaphysical claim to the very material foundation that such claims are designed to obscure. Second, Truth's slogan is also legible as a confession of its own recursive action (as if in taunting defiance of the larger privacy discourse within which it operates), blandly spelling out the backward gesture by which the metaphysics of "substance" rely upon the circulation of the "shadowy" public image. Originary selfhood, Truth suggests, exists only as an effect of its public reception.

Like Truth, each of the writers discussed here engages the discourse of imperiled privacy in an effort to access some part of the authority and profit it confers. Like Truth, each must negotiate her own overidentification with privacy values and against self-(non)possession. And like Truth, again, each carries out her negotiation in ways that play upon and trouble the uneasy distinction between property and privacy. Their writing reveals the operation of privacy discourse as it mediates between capitalist and democratic frames of national identification, and collectively they chart its development across the turbulent five decades between 1840 and 1890. The writers featured in the first half of the book engage the discourse of privacy in the context of reform utopianism. Here privacy is closely affiliated with the Romantic ideal of a presocial innocence, and its endangered state signals social ills and political wrongs. Some texts convey resistance to political mediation—the "anti-state nationalism" that Coviello identifies as a prevailing antebellum discourse.[81] Most essentially, antebellum privacy crises reflect the Romantic—and millennialist—opposition between material and ideal domains by imagining a democratic collectivity that is innocent of ownership and above the differences in power, privilege, and status it breeds.

Chapters 2 and 3 analyze two complementary versions of this narrative in works by Margaret Fuller and Harriet Beecher Stowe, exploring how figures of imperiled—and imperiling—privacy shape their respective models of national and postnational reform. Chapter 2 focuses on Fuller's unfinished autobiography (1840) and on the role of autobiographical and biographical strategies in *Summer on the Lakes* (1843) and *Woman in the Nineteenth Century* (1845); chapter 3 investigates the Truth Myth as it appears in Stowe's second antislavery novel, *Dred: A Tale of the Great Dismal Swamp* (1853), and 1863 essay, "Sojourner Truth: The Libyan Sibyl." Both Fuller and Stowe portray the cultivation of self-(non)possession as a moral and spiritual calling. They credit it with the power to perfect not only individuals but also relationships among them, and to open spaces for reciprocal recognition and moral community. Both also depend on tropes of black embodiment to figure the "taint" of material contingency that prevents such progress. For Fuller, black bodies represent that aspect of an implicitly white self that is vulnerable to misappropriation (whether this be appropriation as legal property, into political subjection, or for a symbol of hegemonic cultural meanings) and so obstructs the transcendent equality between selves that she describes as "private relations." For Stowe, black corporeality stands in for how all bodies threaten to defeat efforts toward self-(non)possession by inflicting a state of privation upon subjects who inhabit but cannot master them. Playing upon the fetishized image of Truth's "imposing" physical presence, Stowe imagines freedpeople as a devastating force of surplus embodiment threatening to overwhelm the American political economy. Like Fuller, Stowe simultaneously imagines privacy as a site of universal entitlement and inclusion and identifies that site with immateriality, whiteness, and the eradication of burdensome black bodies.

In chapter 4 I turn to Elizabeth Keckley's *Behind the Scenes: Thirty Years a Slave and Four Years in the White House* (1868), the autobiography of a woman who earned her own freedom from chattel slavery and became seamstress and confidante to First Lady Mary Todd Lincoln. Reading Keckley's text alongside the discourse on racial reconstruction, I trace another narrative in which privacy stands as an imaginary space of individual entitlement and national cohesion that is both threatened by racialized bodies and realized by their elimination. In contrast to the reformist visions of Fuller and Stowe, where "private relations" represent a deferred future of millennial perfection, here privacy stands for the freedom and equality imagined as already in the citizen's (non)possession—the inherent entitlements of democratic individuality. The key in this case, paradoxically enough, is the widespread opinion that rich and prominent Americans have no legitimate claim to their own privacy. In midcentury writing, a desire to protect one's privacy is frequently aligned with aristocratic exclusivity and against democratic egalitarianism. Often the British are invoked for contrast, as in a travel piece that depicts the opulent seclusion of an English railcar, "so arranged, as to give the individual almost the privacy of his easy chair at home," and smugly concludes, "For our talking and equally privileged world, such arrangements would meet with little favor."[82] In commentary about public officials, such declarations increase in number and intensity, voicing a kind of unofficial sunshine law on public personality.[83] "We are not now contented merely to see the senator enveloped in his toga," declares the New York *Mirror* in 1830; "we delight to follow [public men] into the privacy of domestic life, and see how they act.... [I]s there not an advantage in thus denuding public men of all the pomp and mystery of office and situation? ... [T]he ruling men of the time should be known as they really are."[84]

It is crucial to recognize that these arguments focus not on eliminating privacy but on the public's entitlement to it. This distinction is illustrated by the political candidates who preface their campaign biographies by professing modest reluctance that such a text should be published, then gracefully conceding the public's right to access.[85] Their rhetorical two-step does more than allow readers in; it creates a fantasy of inclusion and produces privacy for consumption. Writing about the posthumous privacy of literary figures in 1867, one commentator allies the law of publicly owned privacy with "the best and highest interests of humanity" and asserts that "the only use of which a man can be to his fellow creatures, when once he is no more, is to furnish them with the truth about himself."[86] In this claim, exposure and community ownership are compatible with the identity of privacy. In fact, they sharpen its cogency. The public benefit in question does not derive from exemplary citizenship or moral conduct. Indeed, the information deemed crucial to humanity's "best and highest interests"—an author's "voracious way of eating, his difficulty about early rising"—is remarkably trivial.[87] Its value resides simply in providing the "truth," however banal, of an authentic self whose meaning and value are not determined *by* public consumption, and whom such biographies offer *for* public and national consumption. Here again, privacy completes and fulfills democratic individuality, but now individuality is writ large as national personhood. Self-(non)possession is again mobilized by a danger of misappropriation, but in this context the threat comes from the individual whose life happens to coincide with our prosthetic public privacy.

In chapter 4 I show how this logic operates in the stories of Keckley and Lincoln and their intertwining relationships to the most iconic of national privacies—the First Lady and the First Home. My argument focuses on two interlocking privacy crises. The first of these, known as the "old clothes scandal," concerns Lincoln's disastrous attempt to convert her own iconic stature into personal profit by selling her White House wardrobe. The second arises with publication of *Behind the Scenes* in which, by detailing her role as producer of the executive spectacle, Keckley identifies the origins of national privacy—and the white freedoms it represents—with her own black labor. In public reactions to both Lincoln and Keckley we witness how the threat of misappropriation enables possession of democratic freedom.

As white women and blacks begin to assert their entitlement to political and civil rights in the decades following the Civil War, the narrative of privacy at risk grows more intense and more pointed in its attacks against the putative agents of dispossession. I first address this shift in Stowe's postemancipation portrait of Truth and trace its continuing development in public responses to Keckley and Lincoln. Chapter 5 extends this analysis into the progressive era by examining the role of privacy in two communitarian experiments, beginning with Bronson Alcott's 1843 utopia, Fruitlands, and moving forward to his daughter's fictional commune, Plumfield School, as it appears in her novels *Little Men* (1871) and *Jo's Boys* (1886). In the final decades of the nineteenth century, privacy discourse exhibits little of its former idealism, or even egalitarianism, and openly displays its affiliation with upper-class, male privilege and white supremacy. Visions of inclusive community give place to laissez-faire elitism and social Darwinist celebrations of a competitive U.S. culture in which the strongest prevail and the weakest are culled from the national gene pool. Now populist intolerance for the privacy of the rich is attributed to "the typical socialist, not the typical democrat," and a letter to the home landscaping magazine, *Garden and Forest*, defends upper-class exclusivity:

> Is not the desire for privacy thoroughly healthy and sensible? So long as a man surrounds his property with nothing unsightly, his duty to the public is done. . . . The desire to see into a neighbor's grounds, to enjoy his property without cost, regardless of how much his own use of it may be abridged thereby, is the very opposite of public spirit.[88]

Such displays of class resentment coincide, and often merge, with racist theories of social evolution in which a supposed white racial instinct for privacy is said to demonstrate the superior development of Anglo-Saxons over black and nonwhite immigrant groups.

Chapter 5 reconstructs this transition from idealism to elitism in nineteenth-century privacy discourse by comparing the communitarian theories of Bronson and Louisa May Alcott. Fruitlands marks an extremity of Romantic idealism with Bronson's quixotic attempt to achieve pure self-(non)possession by withdrawing completely from relations of property and exchange. Louisa's commune—the insular world of Plumfield School—delineates a post-Romantic view of privacy. In the 1871 novel *Little Men*, this view is still utopian and both emulates and corrects that of Bronson, most particularly in Louisa's theorization of the interdependent roles of privacy and property in national progress toward racial integration and sexual equality. But this postwar optimism has evaporated when Alcott revisits Plumfield in the 1886 *Jo's Boys*. The later novel reveals her own loss of faith in the nation's democratic promise and her more profound understanding of American privacy's exclusionary action.

Through their various negotiations, Truth, Fuller, Stowe, Keckley, and Alcott illuminate the nineteenth-century discourse on privacy from differing angles. Some juxtapose the ideal of self-(non)possession against the unjust realities of nineteenth-century material relations; some materialize privacy discourse itself, exposing and—in the way of Truth's slogan—exploiting it as a lucrative practice. Although all five are critical of its perceived limits, none of these writers are particularly resistant to the normative operation of privacy discourse. In one way or another, all work affirmatively within its terms to claim its authority toward their own ends. If they revise the gendered and racialized logics of privacy discourse, they also reinscribe them. Moreover, while the writers discussed here challenge and appropriate the authority of privacy discourse, their efforts also expose its power to disable such interventions.

Owning Up does not tell a history of triumphant resistance and subversion. Indeed, the book demonstrates that figures of imperiled privacy continue to circulate in contemporary U.S. culture, shaping notions of democratic individuality and its relation to political and economic life. Throughout the analyses outlined above, I trace connections to recent and ongoing privacy crises, including those relating to identity politics, social recognition, and multiculturalism; welfare reform; Monica Lewinsky and America's "first black president," Bill Clinton; and global economic privatization. Building upon these investigations, I conclude with a brief epilogue that examines the twenty-first-century panic narrative on biotechnology. For many, genetic engineering represents the ultimate invasion—and alienation—of human selfhood. Suddenly our DNA, the life narrative once unpublishable even to ourselves, appears to be at risk of violation and exposure. This closing argument focuses on how such fears play out in the popular imagination by looking at *The Island*, a Hollywood blockbuster clone action film. This choice of text may seem incongruous. Yet, by framing genetic code as the most fundamental site of private identity and the clone as a kind of unauthorized autobiography, *The Island* reprises nineteenth-century privacy discourse—including anxieties about self-disunity, lost origins, and invading marketization—with extraordinary consistency. Moreover, by evoking the notion of bioslavery and including dystopian images of denaturalized reproduction and injured/monstrous white femininity, the film articulates those anxieties through a similar combination of racial and gendered logics. My epilogue explores these echoes and their implications, while also demonstrating how privacy discourse has changed to accommodate a new age of human commodification and globalized market economics. The scope of our anxieties has broadened, as has their power to shape questions about freedom and belonging. For now, it seems, privacy continues to vex us.

CHAPTER TWO

Tarnished Icons, Shining Lives

FULLER'S PUBLICATION OF PRIVACY

She was here, among our anxious citizens... as if sent to refine and polish her countrymen, and announce a better day. She poured a stream of amber over the endless store of private anecdotes, of bosom histories, which her wonderful persuasion drew forth, and transfigured them into fine fables.
—Ralph Waldo Emerson, *Memoirs of Margaret Fuller Ossoli*

In short, I never feel so private as when I know you are here.
—Herman Melville, "Bartleby, the Scrivener"

In her 1843 travel narrative *Summer on the Lakes*, Margaret Fuller sets out to examine frontier life and its significance to the nation's future. It is therefore surprising when, somewhere between Chicago and the Wisconsin territory, she detours suddenly into the biography of a New England schoolgirl named Mariana.[1] The oddness of this digression is perhaps appropriate to its subject. For Mariana is a misfit by nature, "a strange bird" given to "freaks of passion and wit" who often draws attention to herself by dancing like the "spinning dervishes" (118), "[shining] triumphant" in school theatrics (120), and even clothing herself in the guise of heroic statuary: "There was always some sash twisted about her," recalls Fuller, "some drapery, something odd in the arrangement of her hair and dress, so that the methodical preceptress dared not let her go out without a careful scrutiny and remodeling" (119).

Mariana's spectacular nature invites multiple, overlapping interpretations. Fuller portrays it with racial inflection, emphasizing the girl's "Spanish Creole blood," "rich...coloring," and passionate nature (118); but she also invests it with nationalist meanings, giving her heroine a name and dress sense that invoke the French Marianne, symbol of democratic liberty and equality. Finally, there is a direct connection to Fuller's own well-known penchant for self-disclosure: Mariana is an autobiographical creation, based on the writer's experiences as a student at the Prescott School in 1824. Thus the strangest aspect of this episode may well be its opening line, "Mariana, so full of life, was dead" (118). For it seems that Fuller has interrupted her westward journey to announce her own demise.[2] What are we to make of this auto/biographical elegy, with its contradictory gestures of self-display and self-erasure? And what of its awkward interjection here, amid a survey of westward expansion? Answers to both questions emerge as Mariana's story develops into a parable about the dangers of female self-publication and its vital role in national and democratic progress. As I shall argue, Fuller introduces Mariana in order to issue a warning about imperiled privacy. At one level this warning concerns the public misappropriation of private selfhood—a complaint related to that which Samuel Warren and Louis Brandeis would formulate nearly fifty years later. But Fuller is writing for the era of Romantic nationalism and reform. Her concerns focus less on individual autonomy than on a mode of privacy that she imagines as collective and transcendent, vital to the future of American democracy.

Mariana dies not because her privacy is taken from her, but because she cannot find an audience to recognize and receive the private self she offers. As she attempts to fulfill her spectacular nature she suffers a series of harsh punishments that inflict damage on her and others. The pattern begins, as we have already seen, with the "methodical preceptress" who corrects Mariana's heroic fashion sense (119). But it is the girl's schoolmates who draw the first blood. Irritated by her exhibitionist "eccentricities," they decide to teach Mariana a lesson after she begins using her theatrical blush for everyday wear. One evening Mariana arrives at the dining hall to discover the entire school waiting for her, adorned with garish spots of rouge and mocking stares. She returns to her room, convulses, and falls gravely ill. To describe the girl's devastation, Fuller compares her to the abolitionist lecturer Theodore Weld, under attack before a hostile audience:

> When...the Methodist preacher walked through a line of men, each of whom greeted him with a brickbat or a rotten egg, [he] had some preparation for the crisis....Our little girl was quite

> unprepared to find herself in the midst of a world which despised her, and triumphed in her disgrace. She had ruled like a queen, in the midst of her companions; she had shed her animation through their lives.... Now she felt that she had been but a dangerous plaything in the hands of those whose hearts she never had doubted. (121)

The rejection of her spectacular person injures Mariana both emotionally and corporeally. It also severs her connection to community and, perhaps, deters her from some higher calling like Weld's.[3] Significantly, the other girls also suffer, enduring "bitter...penitence" for their cruelty (121). Yet the incident repeats itself with a second public shaming. Mariana again collapses, this time "dashing her head against the hearth." Her teachers and schoolmates are again stricken with remorse. More, this new episode marks the girl with "a black shadow" of resentment (122), a soul "black [and] stained" by anger, and a nearly fatal state of "black despair" (124)—a series of racializing traces that, like the previous reference to Weld, recall Mariana's Creole blood and also, perhaps, the transgressive implications of the rouge that darkens her already "rich coloring" and provokes a kind of minstrel show in parody.

When the story moves from the school to Mariana's marriage, it features more unreceptive audiences. First her husband rebuffs her passionate self-offerings—"his home was his castle. He wanted no scenes too exciting there" (128)—and Mariana becomes dangerously ill. Though she recovers, it is only to find herself spurned by the new friends in whose hearts she has sought "a home such as an orphan asylum may afford": "What she wanted to tell, they did not wish to hear; a little had pleased, so much overpowered, and they preferred the free air of the street, even, to the cinnamon perfume of her palace" (128). With this final blow Mariana dies and the motif of injurious rejection is fully realized: "Such women as Mariana are often lost," Fuller observes, "unless they meet some man of sufficiently great soul to prize them" (131). Mariana herself explains this idea in a posthumously discovered poem that likens her "unprized" state to a blighted landscape:

> A flowerless and fruitless tree,
> A dried up stream, a mateless bird,
> They live, yet never living be,
> They die, their music all unheard. (130)

Mariana's death expresses her unrecognized life.

Yet the biography does not conclude here; and if dying is a symptom of our heroine's plight, it also provides a cure by releasing her from an uncomprehending world. Dying allows Mariana to shed a vulnerable and racialized body, moving from "black despair" (124) into what Fuller imagines as the "white arms of death" where "every shade of doubt [is] removed" (129–30). Death, it turns out, is the necessary condition for recognition and acceptance. Once delivered into its whitening embrace, Mariana is imagined as flourishing under the gaze of the audience she has needed all along—one that can "prize" and "hear" her properly: "When there is such a man for America," writes Fuller, "the thought which urges her on will be expressed" (132). With this vision, Mariana's biography shifts fully into national allegory and her iconic potential as the Marianne is realized at last. Death generates both individual and national becoming.

This chapter investigates the logic of Mariana's apotheosis as it plays out, not only in her story but also in varying forms throughout *Summer* (1843) and in two of Fuller's other works: her unfinished 1840 autobiography and her 1845 manifesto *Woman in the Nineteenth Century*. My argument focuses on how Fuller theorizes the relationship between failed recognition and democratic unity—how, that is, Mariana's tragedy predicates the intimate understanding that occurs between America and her man—and on what this correlation reveals about early U.S. conceptions of privacy. Like other antebellum Americans, Fuller saw the sacred values of individual autonomy and authenticity as synonymous with the projects of national cohesion and association. She placed great priority on the cultivation of what I refer to as self-(non)possession—a state of inviolable, inalienable self-unity—but believed this kind of individual privacy could be achieved only within the utopian setting of community that she describes in *Woman* as "private relations."[4] Here I will demonstrate that Fuller ties the dual realization of individual and collective privacy to the transcendence of historical and material contingency. More, I argue that this transcendence is enunciated by the spectacular sacrifice of embodied selves that, like Mariana's, embed subjects in the phenomenal world through their gendered and racialized vulnerability to appropriation. Fuller theorizes the perfect actualization of U.S. democracy—the full expression of "the thought which urges [America] on" (132)—as a passage from historicity to iconicity, from materiality to ideality, from embodied particularity to transcendent whiteness, from fatal noncomprehension to generative acknowledgment. In this she demonstrates that, even where it purports to serve public reform and majoritarian interests, the discourse on U.S. privacy imagines democratic belonging in terms of historical disengagement and exclusionary acts.

Throughout her brief but intense intellectual life as transcendentalist, feminist, journalist, and reformer, Fuller saw the publication of lives—and of female lives in particular—as a means to promote social reform and millennial transformation.[5] Toward this end she made several attempts to record her own life story. She also integrated biographical sketches throughout her two major works, *Summer on the Lakes* and *Woman in the Nineteenth Century*, the majority of which focus on women, famous and obscure, fictional and historical, national and international. Referring to one of these interpolated life narratives, Fuller explains that "were this biography of no other value, it would be most interesting as showing how the floating belief of nations...is found to grow up anew in a simple, but high-wrought nature" (*Summer* 165). Some individuals, she believed, personify the ineffable ideals of their people, and biography both remanifests these ideals and presents them for others to recognize as their own.[6] Throughout her writing, Fuller equates national progress with the unfolding of a unitary truth and predicts it will be initiated by a spectacular publication of selfhood that irresistibly draws viewers into identity with itself to create an expanding and infinitely inclusive zone of social, national, and ultimately transnational sameness. In 1840 she describes this longed-for condition of homogeneous ideality as "home," and in 1845 as "private relations."[7] Her theory reflects both liberal and republican democratic models, combining a concept of privacy as the location of freedom and self-realization with an emphasis on voluntary association. In Fuller's vision, private relations *are* the democratic public sphere and the circulation of private lives produces it.

At the heart of Fuller's life writing project stands Hegel's concept of recognition, or *anerkennung*. Specifically, she works from his theory that the development of individual consciousness and collective Spirit requires not only the individual's recognition of others—as Kant had posited—but also the experience of being recognized *by* others. The first part of this formulation—that consciousness begins with acknowledging the material world as external to the self while also recognizing it as a fellow manifestation of Spirit—is, of course, a basic tenet of transcendentalism. Other critics have shown that Fuller develops this precept into an exploration of how subjects are formed, and potentially transformed, by acts of reading and rereading their fellows, their epistemological expansion both reflecting and effecting a reconstitution of self.[8] But Fuller was equally interested in Hegel's further propositions—that the self is also constituted and transformed by *being* recognized, and that through the reciprocal action of recognition, individuals gradually manifest God's perfection in themselves and each other and so establish that perfection culture-wide.[9] Fuller encountered Hegel's theories through fellow transcendentalists George Bancroft and Frederick Hedge as well as in her own studies of German idealism. She returns again and again to the idea of self-becoming as activated not only by recognizing the other but also by the recognizing gaze of another, a gaze that simultaneously discerns and bestows upon the individual—and ultimately upon the nation she symbolizes—her higher self. In the course of her career Fuller refers to this ideal selfhood or meaning with different but roughly synonymous transcendentalist terms such as the "law," the "thought," and the "idea." She also frequently imagines its "unfolding" action through the natural metaphors of seeds and buds—as we see in the negative example of the "flowerless and fruitless tree" from Mariana's poem (130).[10] Like Hegel, Fuller approaches the individual's process of intersubjective development as most importantly a mechanism for collective becoming, and makes it the basis for millennial progress—a movement occurring not just within but finally out of history.

Although the concept of recognition was familiar to early Americans—indeed, the very principle of democratic cosovereignty rests upon a premise of mutual acknowledgment among equal, rights-bearing subjects—Fuller is unusual for so heavily weighting the constitutive force of social recognition upon the individual. Her contemporaries embraced Jean Jacques Rousseau's declaration against the "enslaving" constraints of social opinion, and resisted anything that smacked of the old status relations wherein individual identity had derived from inherited class position—a resistance that called, of course, for denying the newer status relations of market capitalism. For this reason, as philosopher Charles Taylor has shown, the impact of recognition upon democratic identity and authority was suppressed within early American political rhetoric and subordinated to themes of self-invention and self-determination.[11] Fuller's emphasis on social recognition also differs starkly from other forms of transcendentalism, Emerson's most clearly. Emerson spent his career exploring what he called "the infinitude of the private man" and, like Fuller, he believed in the transformative power of its publication (1).[12] In his "The American Scholar," for example, the self-reliant life (and text) act as a "pole star" to guide U.S. culture; and his introduction to *Representative Men* declares, "This is the moral of biography . . . in every solitude are those who succor our genius and stimulate us in wonderful manners."[13] For Emerson, as for Fuller, the publication of private truth (of privacy *as* truth) instigates a corresponding self-manifestation in the spectator. And yet, faithful to the dependence-aversive tendencies of U.S. ideology, Emerson refuses to grant a creative role to the action of viewers upon the person viewed. Indeed, he conceives of this influence as degrading and even malevolent. In "Politics," people who desire an audience are "animals" and always limited to that fraction of their selves that can be recognized by a given audience in a given moment (569). In "Self-Reliance" Emerson explains of the self-publisher that "as soon as he has once acted or spoken with éclat, he is a committed person, watched by the sympathy or the hatred of hundreds, whose affections must now enter into his account. There is no Lethe for this. Ah, that he could pass again into his neutrality!" (261).[14] The Emersonian individual must publish his privacy, but it seems he can scarcely tolerate anyone taking notice.

Fuller stands out among her peers, then, for her insistence on the reciprocal structure of recognition and the intersubjective constitution of identity. It is this emphasis that allows her to investigate exactly that which Emerson and democratic mythology elide: the status relations of U.S. capitalism and the links among ascribed difference, institutional inequality, and self-becoming.[15] In *Summer* and *Woman* especially, Fuller's analysis focuses on how her fellow Americans view each other through the distorting logics of possession and domination. It is not by coincidence that the memorial to Mariana's disastrously misrecognized life appears in the context of U.S. expansionism.[16] In this, Fuller might be seen as a predecessor to contemporary philosophers such as Seyla Benhabib and Nancy Fraser, who argue that the principles of Hegelian recognition can be used to generate a model of democratic deliberation rooted in the particularity and embeddedness of political subjects.[17] Such an interpretation of Fuller would fall in step with current critical trends, which find her works increasingly focused on social criticism and institutional analysis—especially after 1842, when she leaves transcendentalist Boston for Manhattan.[18] And yet, as Julie Ellison points out, Fuller's idealism persists alongside her developing analyses of material relations and exerts an organizing logic upon them.[19] In my reading, Fuller's materialist impulses consistently give place to her idealism in a manner that is both analogous and related to what Christopher Newfield describes as the "third step" of Emersonian philosophy—the stage at which apparently irreconcilable tensions between democratic individualism and democratic collectivity resolve in the "submissive center" of liberalism, where the purest form of self-expression becomes surrender to higher law.[20]

The social transformation that Fuller envisions is always shaped by its movement toward the telos of private relations. Her hope is that we may be recognized not *in*, but *in spite of*, our particularity and embeddedness. Fuller's ideal spectator locates, and by locating manifests, the ideal within the fallen spectacle of history. Or, in Ellison's telling choice of terms, Fuller understood recognition as a process of "turning failure into the revelation of essence."[21] Ellison argues that when Fuller calls for "seeing the perfect through the imperfect nay, making it come there," she is seeking an epistemological alternative to the violence of "masculine" critical analysis.[22] Yet, to seek a reflection of one's own true self in the other and "make it come there" is to commit a new form of violence by which the purpose of recognizing others is to eliminate "imperfections" extraneous to transcendent sameness. Thusly interpreted as "imperfection," ascribed difference represents distance from private relations. The democracy born of recognition is driven by sameness rather than plurality, consonance rather than deliberation. Its transformative power acts not within or upon, but as an exit from historical situation and the forms of inequality and unfreedom it constitutes.

Most fundamentally, Fuller's recognition project strives to free privacy relations from property relations, to divide an inviolable and unchanging version of selfhood and community from those versions susceptible to domination and appropriation. And, as this conflict between private and property relations develops in Mariana's story—and in nearly all of the female lives that Fuller deploys—it centers on gendered and racialized embodiment. For Fuller, gender and race mark a body that has been alienated into a form of property—hence the comparison between Mariana's ordeal and Weld's defense of enslaved blacks. Hence, also, the struggle within what Susan Gilmore describes as the "domestic entombment" of Mariana's marriage (191): on her side, Mariana is "so conscious of secret riches within herself, that sometimes it seemed, could she but reveal a glimpse of them to the eye of [her husband]...they could walk hand in hand" (128); he, however, desires the secular riches of "business and the world": as Fuller sadly reports, Mariana "turned out to be only a merchant's [bride]" (127, 129). Her husband's obsession with property relations defeats her attempt to inculcate privacy relations and, ultimately, makes her into property. But gender and race also encode a subject's obstruction of her own self-becoming. Here we might think of Mariana's rouge that both sexualizes and racializes her image and draws attention to herself. Her Creole blood, "rich coloring," and stained soul all similarly suggest a racially encoded excess of embodiment and passion that impede her struggle toward unity with an audience. Fuller mourns the damage done to bodies by property relations; but, in the end, the only remedy for gendered and racialized modes of being owned—by others, or by one's own desires—is disembodiment.

At this stage, gender and race operate differently. Note, for example, that Mariana's final rest in the "white arms of death" removes all traces of darkness (all "shades of doubt") to reveal a purified femininity. To be sure, Fuller laments the loss of "that form, the most rich in energy and coloring of any I had ever seen" (118). But, like a tragic mulatta, Mariana achieves innocence, redemption, and love by sacrificing a racial body. Both gender and race align with the problem of contingency, but only gender endures as an attribute of Hegelian self-other acknowledgment. Perversely, this distinction between durable and nondurable modes of difference is most apparent where Fuller directly addresses historical injustice. In an 1845 column for the *New York Tribune* in which she protests the annexation of Texas as a slave state, Fuller calls for reformation through life narrative. "Much has been achieved in this country since the first Declaration of Independence," she writes,

> but the noble sentiment which she expressed in her early youth is tarnished; she has shown that righteousness is not her chief desire, and her name is no longer a watch word for the highest hopes of the world.... We want shining examples. We want deeply rooted characters.... [I]n private lives, more than in public measures must the salvation of the country lie.[23]

Here, where Fuller prescribes the circulation of privacy as a response to political wrongs, it is clear that her ethic of recognition promotes neither social justice nor democratic deliberation. Fuller's concern focuses not on the enslavement of blacks, nor even on the unwilling complicity of white Northerners that troubled her friends Thoreau and Emerson.[24] Rather, she denounces the nation's diminished authority as an exceptionalist spectacle of democratic principles, its failure to serve as "City upon a Hill" to the global audience. Racial unfreedom signifies only as the "tarnish" of unrighteous "desires" and obscures America's iconic femininity. Moreover, in Fuller's call for the redemption of tainted America through the "shining examples" of "private lives," democratic practice is reduced to passive acts of display. Freedom manifests itself through spectacles of freedom from tarnish.

Here it may be seen that Fuller's model of recognition produces a vision of democracy that is not only empty—of historical context, of historical difference, of deliberative action—but also always in the process of emptying, defining itself by shedding those "imperfections" that require deliberation. Thus, the crisis of contingency (that is, of particularity and inequality) is both inimical and integral to the movement toward freedom and equality. This explains why Mariana's story—not only the biography of a failed life but also the story of a failed biography—can qualify as an instance of transformative life publication. Her fatal imperfection promotes national becoming. For, while displays of tarnished selfhood cause suffering, they also initiate a process of purification.[25] Through the dialectical action of recognition, the publication of tarnished icons and "dangerous playthings" brings readers closer to the shining example.

In what follows, I begin with Fuller's 1840 autobiography to trace her earliest thoughts on how self-publication shapes individual and national progress. Using the example of her own education, she criticizes the hegemonic forms of citizenship and national belonging that require the self-alienation of U.S. subjects. Before her unfinished manuscript breaks off, however, Fuller begins to theorize an alternative model, based on a dynamic of communal privacy that will become her chief preoccupation in later works. In the next section I look at how Fuller thinks through the problem of self-alienation as it intersects with gender and racial difference. Focusing on passages from *Summer* and *Woman in the Nineteenth Century*, I argue that, for Fuller, culturally ascribed difference results from misrecognition and marks distance from the utopian sameness of private relations. Here I begin to examine how Fuller uses racial tropes to represent the problematic of women's gendered difference. The chapter's final section continues to trace this coarticulation and disarticulation of gender and race. Concentrating on *Woman*, I show how Fuller imagines the progression out of history and into "private relations" as a movement toward ideal marriage—a heterocomplementary unity of mutually recognized and recognizing subjects, cleansed of their racialized unfreedom.

AUTOBIOGRAPHY AS ALIENATION IN THE AMERICAN ROME

In a journal entry from 1840, Fuller recalls the moment she awakened to self-consciousness. She describes it in Hegelian terms, as a sudden apprehension of herself as the object of another's gaze: "I had stopped myself one day on the stairs," she remembers, "and asked, how came I here? How is it that I seem to be this Margaret Fuller? What does it mean? What shall I do about it?"[26] Like the German idealists, Fuller understands this event as the first step of self-becoming. But she also represents it as a moment of crisis. Her uncanny object-self only "seems" to exist; it withholds its meaning; and yet it also demands some response on her part. The episode is as much an experience of self-estrangement as of self-discovery, and Fuller plays up that tension with her use of the proper name "Margaret Fuller." As Philippe Lejeune has argued, the autobiographical proper name marks an identity produced by the recursive ontological affirmation of public acknowledgment. This is a self whose identity is always fundamentally alienated, a function of unstable and externally determined meaning and, as Michel Foucault points out, a potential target for punishment.[27] In her short life Fuller would express much anguish and paranoia concerning this vulnerable public double. Mariana's rouge episode offers an apt image of this anxiety—her public self as "a dangerous plaything," cruelly misappropriated by unkind others, dispersed and wielded against her.

In the journal, Fuller resolves this predicament with a second revelation: "I saw that there was no self; that selfishness was all folly, and the result of circumstance; that it was only because I thought self real that I suffered; that I had only to live in the idea of the ALL, and all was mine" (11). Here Fuller severs her uneasy relation to the publicly (mis)mediated self and retreats to a place of inviolability. Playing on the trope of self-possession, Fuller trades possession of "Margaret Fuller"—a claim she can never fully establish—for a state of self-(non)possession in which it is possible to say "all [is] mine." This latter she identifies, predictably enough, as "Home": writing to a friend a month later, she promises, "When we meet you will find me at home.... I cannot be driven from it more. I am now so at home, I know not how again to wander and grope, seeking my place in another Soul. I need to be recognized" (13). Fuller's imagined withdrawal from a self-alienating social economy—a conceit that mimics the domestic fantasy of withdrawal from the market economy—seems at first glance to suggest an Emersonian selfhood that seeks no approval or value beyond itself. But, even as she declares private self-unity, Fuller acknowledges the necessity of social recognition. Indeed, this "home" is what will enable an experience of recognition as nonalienating relation to another.

Fuller returns to the problem of self-alienation in the autobiographical fragment she wrote later that same year—a logical preoccupation, given the nature of such projects as an objectification of selfhood for public affirmation. But, in contrast to the intensely personal analysis of her journal, Fuller's autobiography focuses less on herself than on the nature of U.S. citizenship. Posing herself as a representative American subject, she examines the process of self-becoming as it is mediated by political and economic cultures. Perhaps due to this guise of representative selfhood, the autobiography does not address the differences of identity, power, and privilege among U.S. subjects that concern Fuller in later works. Gender figures prominently in her anatomization of the citizen, but not as the basis of inequality. Instead, Fuller looks at how all Americans are alienated into artificial modes of nationalist identification.

Early American autobiography conventionally opens with a lineage narrative, often going back several generations to establish a genetic heritage of American virtue and patriotism. Fuller plays on that convention when she introduces the source materials of her own representative character through her parents, presenting them not as bloodlines but as the origins of two complementary patterns of American selfhood. Her father, she begins, was raised only to "work for distinction in the community":

> The result was a character, in its social aspect, of quite the common sort. A good son and brother, a kind neighbor, an active man of business—in all of these outward relations he was but one of a class.... His love for my mother was the green spot on which he

> stood apart from the common-places of a mere bread-winning, bread-bestowing existence. She was one of those fair and flower-like natures, which sometimes spring up even beside the most dusty highways of life—a creature not to be shaped into a merely useful instrument, but bound by one law with the blue sky, the dew, and the frolic birds. Of all persons whom I have known, she had in her most of the angelic,—of that spontaneous love for every living thing, for man, and beast, and tree, which restores the golden age.[28]

Here the father exemplifies an alienated public self defined entirely by "outward relations." In contrast, the mother lives at one with nature's higher "law" and beyond the contingencies of industry and production. She represents spatial and temporal displacement from the father's public world, a "green spot... apart from the common-places" and a millennialist "golden age." The word *common* is important in the autobiography and always resonates in multiple registers. Used twice in this passage, it suggests the conformity of her father's character while also punning upon the logic of separate spheres, wherein wife and home serve to secure middle-class male individuality against a public of commoners. The term also evokes the political common, the scene of democratic cosovereignty, and juxtaposes it with a feminine privacy that is the site of higher law.

The story of Fuller's education tracks this gendered division as it occurs within her own representative person and investigates the costs. She begins with her famous "masculine" training at the hands of her father who "had been a high scholar at college" and still enjoyed "the associated memories of success and good repute" (26). "My father was a man of business even in literature," writes Fuller. "He hoped to make me heir of all he knew, and of as much more as the income of his profession enabled him to give me means of acquiring" (26). Theorizing education as transferable capital, she gratefully acknowledges her own lessons as a form of privileged primogeniture. But Fuller also implies that her father has treated her as an investment, literally sinking capital into her "acquisition" of learning that will bring increased returns of "success and good repute" to them both. In this scheme, the value of both learning and learner are determined from without, and measure status rather than knowledge. As she describes the content of her education, Fuller elaborates on this theme of alienated meaning: "He demanded accuracy and clearness in everything: you must not speak, unless you can make your meaning perfectly intelligible to the person addressed; must not express a thought, unless you can give a reason" (28). Here again meaning is a function of use value—the "reason" for each thought determining its worth. More, expression is governed by audience and by the rationalized outward demands of intelligibility and accuracy. Fuller's father began training her in English and Latin grammar and the "artificial methods" of rhetorical argument before she was six. He required her to occupy (in "fetters") an official domain of public discourse that she refers to as both "common sense" and the "common prose world," reprising that key term to denote the leveling, banalizing surrender of individuality that has come to pass for discursive authority.

As the account of her education proceeds, Fuller begins to explore the nature of this "common" and "outward" public selfhood through the metaphor of Rome. Both the subject of her studies and a favorite symbol of U.S. republicanism, Rome comes to stand for all the problems of outward relations. Fuller describes herself during lessons as stranded "amid the Roman pikes...the hum of the forum, the mailed clang of Roman speech," dramatizing her training in forms of selfhood and expression that are artificial, constraining, aggressive, and even martial (30). It is easy to read this feature of Fuller's education as subjection to phallic law. However, more significant to my argument are the ways that her portrayal of Roman America actually turns the gendered logic of masculine democratic identity back on itself. The principles of self-determining democratic citizenship and market agency were incessantly contrasted against the dependence relations that had preceded the political and market revolutions. As scholars like Carole Pateman have shown, these masculinist ideals were also defined against the dependence relations of marriage in which women were privatized by their subjection to patriarchal rule.[29] In her autobiography, Fuller complicates this dependence/autonomy opposition:

> Everything turns your attention to what a man can become...not by letting nature play freely through him, but by a single thought, an earnest purpose, an indomitable will, by hardihood, self-command, and force of expression. These men...did not grow,—they built themselves up, or were built up by the fate of Rome, as a temple for Jupitor Stator. (29)

This extended tribute to Roman character plays on the familiar theme of an "indomitable will" that masters nature and asserts itself in "forceful" language. And yet Fuller characterizes such will and expression as always already Roman—that is, as modes of subjection to Rome and the story of Rome. She portrays the hero of democratic individualism as an effect of disciplinary state grammar, a being produced from utter conformity with the common prose world of common sense: "The names which end in 'us,' seem to speak with lyric cadence. That measured cadence,—that tramp and march" (29). Like the uncanny semiotic alienation of "this Margaret

Fuller," the Roman name represents identity that comes from without, unrooted, "built" not "grown."

Fuller's portrait of the American Roman illustrates the corrupt ethic of recognition that Rousseau identifies in his characterization of social man as "born free, but everywhere...in chains," enslaved by his desire for public approval and divorced from his natural moral sense.[30] Fuller reads Rousseauian dependence into the economic and political terms of possessive individualism, posing a false economy of self-alienation against that plenitude of self-(non)possession she has imagined in her journal. She reflects upon her youthful admiration for Roman history: "I did not then know that such men impoverish the treasury to build the palace. I kept their statues as belonging to the hall of my ancestors, and loved to conquer obstacles, and fed my youth and strength for their sake" (31). Read one way, this passage describes Fuller as a developing citizen who nourishes her youth and strength for public action. Reading differently, with transitive action in the verb *fed*, it is the child's own youth and strength that nourish the American Rome. She becomes the impoverished "treasury" in a cannibalistic political economy that commodifies and consumes its subjects, dividing the national self from the natural self to the detriment of each.

Fuller also extends Rousseau's critique by showing that men betray not just themselves but also each other in succumbing to artificial outward norms. For her, the Roman is not only personally harmed in being misrecognized; he also deprives those who misrecognize him. In this it becomes apparent that Fuller's sense of crisis reflects not just a liberal concern for individual entitlements but also, paradoxically, the republican priority of common good and civic responsibility. Imagining Roman literature as autobiographical spectacle, Fuller writes, "a man rises, he tells who he is, and what he has done; he speaks of his country and her brave men....One wants no universal truths from him, no philosophy, no creation, but only his life, his Roman life felt in every pulse, realized in every gesture" (30). As in the portrait of her father, this Roman's achievements are couched in their own negation: Roman biography is noted for what it does not supply, for its inability to express anything beyond a historical manifestation of self. Its heroic image reveals no higher truth or law. Fuller bluntly asserts her judgment of such self-publications as a diminished and diminishing model for national becoming: "The Eagle should never have been used as a symbol by any other nation: it belonged to Rome" (29).

To examine the individual and collective injury inflicted by the Roman American's self-alienation, Fuller employs a theme of traumatized embodiment. Excessive study, she reports, "made me a 'youthful prodigy' by day, and by night a victim of spectral illusions, nightmare, and somnambulism, which at the time prevented the harmonious development of my bodily powers and checked my growth... and will bring me... to a premature grave" (27). To the critics and friends who obsessively repeated it, this account confirmed the biological truth of sex difference. After her death especially, Fuller is posed as proof of women's physical incapacity for masculine education and citizenship. Curiously, this logic persists in current scholarship, including that which celebrates Fuller's prescient disruption of the sex-gender system in *Woman*.[31] But while the traumatized sacrificial body of Fuller's autobiography—another figure for the Mariana typology—is feminized, it is not female. To be sure, she creates a gendered opposition between her father's Roman lessons and the education she associates with her mother. Fuller writes sadly of "the teaching of the little garden":

> I loved to gaze on the roses, the violets, the lilies, the pinks; my mother's hand had planted them, and they bloomed for me.... [A]n ambition swelled in my heart to be as beautiful, as perfect as they.... Yet, forgive, ye wild asters.... Living and blooming in your unchecked law, ye know nothing of the blights, the distortions, which beset the human being; and which at such hours it would seem that no glories of free agency could ever repay. (32)

Here, where the law of Roman subjection—the precondition of "free agency"—requires breaking faith with the "unchecked laws" of nature and mother, the injured body seems to align with the lost and feminized garden. Yet, interestingly, Fuller never makes that connection overt. In fact, she attributes the negative consequences of her training to youth, not sex. More, she describes her own tragedy as the result of an "all too common practice," again using that important term *common* and presenting herself as a typical case. Hence, to the extent that her text does align the body with a feminized sacrifice of self-in-nature, it indicates a sacrifice made by men as well as women, required of all national selves. This is not quite to say that Fuller finds no difference between men and women in regard to this issue, as we shall see. But the Romantic body-in-nature is not for her normatively the domain of women, and her story of stunted growth and mourned flowers critiques citizenship rather than crying gender victim. In the passage above, what Fuller laments is an act of self-betrayal.[32]

This brings us to the autobiography's analysis of national development and of the collective injury that occurs with a citizen's alienation from embodied self-unity. Fuller vividly portrays this problem of national deprivation with the story of a childhood nightmare provoked by her training in Roman selfhood. In her uneasy sleep, Fuller dreams "as she had just read in her Virgil, of being among trees that dripped with blood, where she walked and walked and could not get out, while the blood became a pool and plashed over her feet, and rose higher and higher, till soon she dreamed it would reach her lips" (27). The dream references two scenes: one acknowledged here, from book III of *The Aeneid*; and another from canto XIII of *The Inferno*—a text mentioned a few pages on—in which Dante overtly builds upon Virgil's themes. Both passages dramatize the costs of national progress. The first depicts Aeneas receiving a grievously bad omen during his quest for a new Troy and the founding of Rome. Having stopped on the island of Thrace to perform sacrifices, he is gathering wood for the ritual when he discovers a tree that bleeds when cut. The tree speaks, and Aeneas recognizes the voice of his countryman Polydorus, who had been sent as an ambassador from Troy and murdered by the Thracians. As Aeneas's initial intentions for the tree make clear, Polydorus is the very embodiment of national sacrifice:

> I am no foreigner; old Troy
> Gave birth to me; this blood drips from no tree...
> An iron hedge of spears covered my body,
> Pinned down here, and the pointed shafts took root.[33]

Any educated midcentury reader would have recognized Fuller's allusion to Virgil's origin myth, where political betrayal and tragic death are integral to the design of national progress. The image of Polydorus's corpse pinned to the earth by "pointed shafts" recalls both Fuller's image of herself imprisoned behind "Roman pikes" and her characterization of Roman biography as nature "pierced" by the Roman will. Here is another bodily sacrifice to the inexorable emergence of Rome, but also a moment of ominous portent—another obstacle that will delay national rebirth.

In his gloss on Virgil, Dante places the bleeding tree at the second ring of the seventh circle of hell, where the sin of suicide is punished: "When the fierce soul has quit the fleshly case/ It tore itself from, Minos sends it down/...to this wooded place" (XIII, 88–90). The wood, a community of souls who have squandered their own lives, provides Fuller with another metaphor for threatened national doom. Dante's images of lifeless growth—"The leaves not green, earth-hued;/ The boughs not smooth, knotted and crooked-forked;/ No fruit, but poisoned thorns" (XIII, 3–5)[34]—echo Fuller's own repeating motif of nationhood uprooted from nature's law: her portrayals of Romans who "did not grow [but] built themselves up" (29); her self-portrait as one for whom "much of life was devoured in the bud" (37); and her epitaph for Mariana as "a flowerless and fruitless tree" (*Summer* 130). Dante also extends this motif of injured bodies. As final punishment, these suicides will never regain the bodies they abandoned. At the second coming, when all other souls are united with their lost flesh, the empty skins of these will be draped over their branches: a horrific illustration of self-alienation as the plight of remaining joined to a lost self without access to its redemptive power.

Through most of her autobiography, Fuller uses her own development to examine the misformation of national subjects and attributes this to an alienating ethic of "outward relations." She establishes the need for a model that will reconnect citizen to body, nation to nature, masculine to feminine, word to meaning, and also self to other. Near the conclusion of the text, Fuller begins to envision such a model with the story of her "first friend," Ellen Kilshaw:

> Should the first love be blighted, they say, the mind loses its sense of eternity. All forms of existence seem fragile, the prison of time real, for a god is dead.... I thank Heaven that this first feeling was permitted its free flow. The years that lay between the woman and the girl only brought her beauty into perspective, and enabled me to see her as I did the mountains from my window, and made her presence to me a gate of Paradise. (38–39)

In this passage, the transcendent economy of self-(non)possession described in Fuller's 1836 journal—the "home" of self-possession without alienation—expands and becomes the creative force for utopian community. Recognition of the other provides not just an image of but access to a higher plane of existence: the vision of her friend is a gate to Paradise. In contrast, to be without such recognition is to be held captive in "the prison of time," fully subjected to a secular idiom like the Roman who is nothing that is not Rome. The two friends move beyond history into a space of synchronic being and communication—hence the emphasis on the visual (and corporeal) image that displaces the diachronic forms of Roman grammar: "She spoke in her whole being," writes Fuller, "rather than by chosen words. Indeed, her proper speech was dance or song" (39); and again: "I had seen her,—I should see her,—and my mind lay steeped in the visions that flowed from this source" (38).

As in the journal where she discovers "I had only to live in the idea of ALL, and all was mine" (11), Fuller describes this later scene in terms of ownership:

> That which she was, that which she brought, that which she might have brought, were mine, and over a whole region of new life I ruled proprietor of the soil in my own right.... All who saw admired her in their way; but she would lightly turn her head from their hard or oppressive looks, and fix a glance of full-eyed sweetness on the child. (39)

Troping on the dynamics of possession and political dominion that structure identity in antebellum public culture, Fuller distinguishes these from the new mode of self-becoming that takes place within a private economy of mutual recognition. The reciprocal, "full-eyed" gaze between these two friends is distinct from the "hard or oppressive looks" in that, rather than attempting to possess the other, it promotes mutual and interdependent self-(non)possession: each acquires new dominion over "regions" within.[35]

As though to formally announce this new normative model for recognition, Fuller glosses the first friend episode with a multitiered theory of association. Human relationships, she asserts, come in different degrees of intimacy. First comes "an outer circle, whose existence we perceive but with whom we stand in no real relation" (40). These relationships occur in the zone of civil society where people appear to each other as functional objects: "They tell us the news, they act on us in the offices of society.... [W]e are nothing to them, nor they to us, except as a part of the world's furniture." In contrast, the innermost circle comprises "a nearer group" for whom

> there is no separation; the same thought is given at the same moment to both,—indeed, it is born of the meeting, and would not otherwise have been called into existence at all! These not only know themselves more, but *are* more for having met, and regions of their being, which would else have laid sealed in cold obstruction, burst into leaf and bloom and song. Both seem to rise at a glance into that part of the heavens where the word can be spoken, by which they are revealed to one another and themselves. (40–41)

Here again, communication via "a glance" engenders a boundless and unifying possession of selves. And, as the reappearance of her fertility motif suggests, Fuller codes this zone of perfect mutual recognition as a national space. Her rule over this fertile "soil" stands thematically opposed to the inorganic regime of American Rome; it is, Fuller explains, "the really New World": "On the promised coasts [the new friend] had found only cities, careful men and women, the aims and habits of ordinary life.... But in the mind of the child she found the fresh prairie, the untrodden forests for which she had longed" (39). This is Fuller's vision of democratic association, a mode of collectivity that is free, equal, and also generative ("these not only know themselves more, but *are* more")—thus guaranteeing its own perpetuation. For, as Hegel has it, to recognize is also to create a higher condition in the other and in oneself.

In this space, where "the word can be spoken," language is likewise restored to wholeness and so is the project of autobiography. Here we might recall Fuller's nightmare of the bloody wood where she stands sole witness to the casualties of national progress. Like both Aeneas and Dante, she is burdened with an untellable narrative. Aeneas, offering the story of Polydorus to Dido's court, interrupts himself even as he begins: "Should I tell this/ Or hold my peace?" (III, 54–55). Dante is urged by the bleeding tree, "Please comfort my memory" (XIII, 71–72), but he has known from the outset that the wood contains "things which in words would be incredible" (19). Fuller's dream sequence reiterates these themes of sacrifice and silencing. In her nightmare, the tree's blood "rose higher and higher, till soon she dreamed it would reach her lips" (27), and when she awakens and tries to explain her terror, "her father sharply bid[s] her 'leave off thinking of such nonsense, or she would be crazy.'" For Fuller, stories like those of Polydorus or Mariana are agonizing burdens in a public that requires its subjects to speak in alienated language and determines meaning by a standard of profitable outward forms. In the works that follow her autobiography, she seeks a new approach for publishing private lives and cultivating recognition. In *Summer*, for example, Fuller explains, tantalizingly, that she won't retell "piquant anecdotes and tales drawn from private life," lest the "frank kindness" of their tellers be

> ill-requited by its becoming the means of fixing many spy-glasses, even though the scrutiny might be one of admiring interest, upon their private homes.
>
> For many of these, too, I was indebted to a friend, whose property they more lawfully are.... May [they] profit others as [they] did me in the region where [they were] born. (109)

Fuller refuses to sacrifice her friend's "property" to the capitalist literary market. Instead, she wants to establish a nonalienating economy of recognition where the circulation of private lives will truly "profit" listeners and "requite" the teller.

In the following section, I examine how Fuller pursues this new ethic of recognition in *Woman in the Nineteenth Century*. There she deploys the "shining examples... of private lives"—as she proposes in her piece for the *New York Tribune*—and tries to promote a new way of reading them. To do this, Fuller significantly revises her approach to corporeality. Although she still associates the body with the damage of misrecognition, she no longer mourns it as a symbol of lost self-unity. Rather than appearing as the vulnerable locus of higher being, bodies now figure chiefly as sites of socially imposed difference, obstructing recognition between self and other. In *Woman*, bodies represent that which must be shed in the struggle for transcendence. Fuller writes in her preface to that work, "From men I ask a noble and earnest attention... such as I have met from many with whom I stand in private relations" (5–6). This request for an intimate audience with men is quite startling, given the risk that Fuller took by addressing topics like prostitution and marital sexuality as an unmarried woman writer.[36] Yet, by naming that tension, she challenges her reader to move past it, to distinguish the sexualized and possessive scene of privatized relations from the private relations that occur beyond possessable bodies. In *Woman*, Fuller positions the shining life in a space beyond history and the diachronic limits of official discourse, a space of absolute freedom, equality, self-unity, and unalienated communication, where truths can be recognized in the synchronic force of an image. Her project will be to deploy that image and widen its scope. But, as we shall see, in Fuller's vision the space of privacy is both infinitely capacious and rigorously exclusive.

MISRECOGNIZING EURYDICE

The first of *Woman*'s shining lives is Eurydice's—taken, appropriately, from Roman mythology. Fuller chooses Eurydice in response to Bronson Alcott's recently published "Orphic Sayings," a series of philosophical aphorisms in which Orpheus symbolizes the ideal horizon of American Manhood.[37] Riffing on her friend's allegory, Fuller presents Orpheus's feminine counterpart as a "far-shining view" of American womanhood (12). However, she also points out that Eurydice has been abandoned to the underworld: "The idea of Man, however imperfectly brought out, has been far more so than that of Woman, she, the other half of the same thought, the other chamber of the heart of life, needs now to take her turn in the full pulsation." Like Eurydice, Fuller declares, women have never had "their fair chance" and now they must take the lead. Through their own development they will "bring out" the "idea" and "thought" of humankind to "aid in the reformation of the sons of this age."

With this vignette, Fuller introduces her central strategy: the publication of iconic Womanhood as a mechanism for inculcating the new ethic of recognition she has referred to a few pages earlier as "private relations" (6). However, like the tarnished "America" from the *Tribune*, Eurydice is not yet ready to serve. She has been "imperfectly brought out," denied her "fair chance" at self-becoming. This focus on Eurydice's unreadiness marks a shift from the 1840 autobiography, where Fuller was concerned with the gendered structure of dispossession within individual citizens and had not yet begun to investigate the politics of gender among such individuals. In *Woman* she will prove deeply attuned to how the violence of self-alienation maps across social geographies, causing the masculine and feminine dimensions of selfhood, Woman and Man, to be misrecognized as historical women and men and divided by unjust differences in power. With this new angle of critique, Fuller offers an important revision of Emersonian transcendentalism, one that potentially requires his idealism to grapple with social politics. Emerson writes often—in a tone that ranges from exaltation in the penultimate section of *Nature* to despair in "Experience"—about the world's "lubricity" that prevents him from apprehending it with immediacy (473). In several places he extends this idea to assert that we never truly register the existence of other individuals.[38] By Fuller's reasoning, this limitation is not inherent to the human condition as Emerson supposes, but a reflection and reconstitution of unjust power. In particular, she is concerned with how, viewed through frames of capitalism, patriarchy, and nationalism, women are misrecognized as prepolitical subjects and the property of masculine possessive individuals. The unreadiness of Eurydice—of American Womanhood—obtains in her subjection to Orpheus's grasping backward gaze that subjects her to the material relations of market capitalism. Privatized as a form of property, she can neither access nor actuate the transcendence of privacy.

However, it is a mistake to read *Woman*—widely considered a founding text of U.S. feminism—as a treatise on women's equality. Fuller demands equality, but only because its absence impedes progress. In fact, she sees the struggle for rights as equally problematic where it reflects an attachment to historical status. Fuller has no identity politics, no use for the recognition of women as women. For her, "women" inhabit a mode of difference that derives from historical contingency, a difference that marks distance from the truth of fundamental likeness—that innermost circle of private relations. Difference, in this sense, is the by-product of a fallen political economy through which we misread the other as property and, because difference manifests itself as a system of interdependent unfreedoms, a perpetuation thereof.[39] This paradigm generates a powerful material analysis of culturally ascribed identity. *Summer* details the injuries inflicted by European misreadings of American Indians, and *Woman* brilliantly analyzes the political, economic, and cultural forms of misrecognition imposed upon women and blacks. Finally, however, Fuller's model of recognition begins and ends with sameness. In this, her project corroborates the theory of recognition advanced by Charles Taylor, who argues that when contemporary activists and theorists call for the equal recognition of marginalized identity groups, they contradict the very philosophical principles they invoke. Recognition, according to Taylor, is always predicated upon an assumption of universal human qualities; the thing acknowledged is not particularity but sameness. Thus, recognition is fundamentally at odds with the goal of equal approbation for cultural differences.[40] In Fuller's hands, recognition not only operates in tension with cultural difference but displays outright intolerance for it. She makes recognition a force *of* sameness—"no separation; the same thought is given at the same moment to both" (*Autobiography* 40)—that expands to reform and unite all of society. Thus, ascribed difference ultimately becomes that which must be stripped away by the struggle for recognition, and nonwhiteness in particular becomes an expression of nontranscendence.

Until recently, most scholars have either overlooked the question of race in Fuller's work or celebrated her cross-racial sympathy toward Native Americans in *Summer*; to date there is still no focused analysis of how racial logic functions in *Woman*.[41] Yet, as Fuller explores the production of women's difference throughout her major works of social criticism, she relies heavily upon tropes of racial difference and racial unfreedom. In *Summer*, where she aligns the possessive gaze with Manifest Destiny, Fuller uses Native Americans to examine the cultural oppression of women. In *Woman*, thinking through women's lack of self-right, she compares it repeatedly to the enslavement of African Americans. This racialization of Woman's unreadiness recalls both Mariana, whose "black stains" and creolized genealogy align with her misrecognized plight, and the allegorical "America" who fails to publish the truth of democratic freedom because she is "tarnished" by slavery. Persistently, Fuller reduces racial difference and racial injustice to signs for the constraints of gender. She chooses her metaphor aptly, then, when she complains that Woman has not had her "fair" chance.

Throughout *Woman*, Fuller literalizes the notion of misrecognition by focusing on the different ways that women (mis)function as public spectacle. This survey includes misogynist representations—at one point Fuller worries (in the voice of Miranda, another of her pseudonymous self-representations) that there exists such a "rooted skepticism" about women in the hearts of men that nothing less than an "age of miracles" would shift it (22). Yet the sort of misrecognition that most concerns Fuller is not denigration, but idealization. "How has a little wit, a little genius, been celebrated in a woman!" she exclaims:

> Sappho! Eloisa! The names are of threadbare celebrity. Indeed they were not . . . suitably met in their own time. . . . [T]heir great impulses did not find due scope. But with time enough, space enough, their kindred appear on the scene. Across the ages, forms lean, trying to touch the hem of their retreating robes. The youth here by my side cannot be weary of the fragments from the life of Sappho. He will not believe they are not addressed to himself. . . . A recluse of high powers devotes himself to . . . Eloisa. . . . He would have been to her a friend, such as Abelard never could. . . . His sorrow is truly pathetic. (26)

Fuller first laments that Sappho and Eloisa were underrecognized, or denied "due scope," during their lifetimes. Yet, when she considers the posthumous admiration accorded these women, her tone is still not quite approving. The satirical touches of "threadbare celebrity" and "truly pathetic" devotion suggest a kind of regard that is both excessive and impotent. The youth's insistence that Sappho's verses are "addressed to himself" reveal an undercurrent of self-interest and possessiveness.[42] Here again Fuller reads power relations into transcendentalist philosophy—specifically, into the concept of idolatry that Emerson and Theodore Parker first developed during the 1830s miracles debate to argue that the dogma of Christ's divinity was a form of self-limiting, world-limiting worship.[43] Like them, Fuller understands idolatry as a constraint upon the idolator; where Emerson and Parker argue that Christianity is deadened by its worship of Christ, she (alluding to their argument via the "forms" who grasp at Sappho and Eloisa's robes) characterizes the idolizing of women as another mode of the American's alienation from his own divinity. The idolater kills part of himself by rejecting the idol's relation to himself: the youth and the recluse are imprisoned by their devotion to dead women. But Fuller also emphasizes that the object of idolatry is constrained. After all, if Orpheus's excessive love costs him Eurydice's company, it sentences her to hell; and idolatry has a similarly lethal effect upon nonmythical women: "Whenever she has herself arisen in national or private history, and nobly shone forth in any form of excellence, men have received her, not only willingly, but with triumph. Their encomiums indeed, are always, in some sense, mortifying" (23). Although this passage appears to acknowledge women's public recognition, its key term is "mortifying," signifying death, immobility, and embarrassing overexposure in the false light of the possessive, misrecognizing gaze.

With this critique, and the shining-lives strategy it advances, Fuller engages the iconographic tradition that Lauren Berlant refers to as "national femininity." Mariana, Eurydice, tarnished America, and now Sappho and Eloisa stand in the trajectory of allegorical figures that scholars have traced from the French Marianne to Britannia, Colombia, and the Statue of Liberty—spectacles of white womanhood used to symbolize democratic values and offer them for possession by national subjects.[44] But Fuller also performs an immanent critique upon national femininity, by arguing that its function is impaired by the possessive gaze. In this, she resembles other women activists of her time who, as Pamela Haag has shown, subverted the patriarchal ownership and control of white women by invoking the ideological precept of Woman's unownability, her "unique character" as a being incapable of being possessed by herself or anyone else (18). Haag examines this strategy in the arguments of the antebellum female reformers who set out to criminalize seduction by framing it as an assault upon the inalienable, nonfungible value of women's chastity and upon the civic resource of "public purity" that depends upon her. These "protofeminist" activists sought to shift the meaning of seduction so that it would no longer be viewed as a crime against a father or husband's property rights, nor even against the woman herself, but instead against the public's (non)ownership of women's virtuous inviolability. Fuller echoes their theorization of seduction when she treats idolatry as misappropriation of something beyond ownership, and links it to profound collective national loss. Like them, she wields the principle of private femininity against its compromised applications in U.S. culture.

But, unlike Haag's reformers, who used Woman's inalienability as the most expedient leverage against male privilege and soon turned their eyes to the prize of female self-right, Fuller is equally condemning of women's self-possession. She interprets women's attachment to themselves as women as just more subjection of Woman to dispossessing misrecognition. This new problem looks in some places like vanity—as in Fuller's criticism of Germaine de Stael who, although among "the shining names of famous women [who] have cast light upon the path," was "tainted" by the fact that "she could not forget the woman in the thought; while she was instructing you as a mind, she wished to be admired as a woman" (55). More often, however, women's self-misrecognition is linked to self-interested desire. Self-interest, even self-advocacy, traps women in the phenomenal world, and in the self-ishness that we see Fuller striving to overcome in her 1840 journal. In a different discussion of idolatry in Fuller's work, Jeffrey Steele argues correctly that she shifts that concept out of a psychospiritual frame and into the context of the "social structures" and "material conditions that fixated human relationships in unequal forms."[45] But this move is less a materialist theorization than a diagnosis of psychospiritual malaise. For Fuller, the trouble is not that injustice takes place within historical and material relations, but that this injustice distracts women from looking beyond those relations. Hence, where she prefaces *Woman* by asking men to read the text in the manner of private relations, she also asks women readers to "ascertain what is for them the liberty of law" rather than a mere extension of "partial privileges" (5). She asks them, that is, to seek freedom from self over possession of self. The women's task parallels the men's, for by inhabiting "private relations" men will also achieve the true "liberty of the law"—the "one law" associated with her mother in the autobiography rather than the father's secular law. Misrecognition—whether misogynist or idolatrous, whether inflicted by male desire or female self-interest—is the primary obstacle to the freedom that Fuller envisions. It makes women property rather than activating Woman as relay to self-(non)possession.

Embodiment is key to Fuller's understanding in *Summer* and *Woman* of how misrecognition—or the imposition of ascribed gender difference—prevents women from revealing Woman. Embodiment is also the place where Fuller uses racial meanings to represent this problem. In the 1840 autobiography, as we have seen, bodies signify a Romantic unity with nature and spirit that, although feminized, belongs to men as well as women. And yet, after 1840 Fuller frequently represents her own body as the locus of a female-sexed identity that she inhabits with deep ambivalence. It is a burden, a limit, and a vulnerability: in her journal she laments, "A man's ambition with a woman's heart is an evil lot," and wonders elsewhere if "as a woman" she is "bound by a physical law, which prevents the soul from manifesting itself."[46] Throughout Fuller's writings the body names a site of injury and loss, but after 1840 this no longer implies the alienated self-in-nature. Rather, it corresponds to the prison of misrecognized femininity.[47] Fuller attributes this plight, first, to the gendered dualism that reduces Woman *to* embodiment: "It is in vain," she writes in *Woman*, "that the truth has been recognized, that woman is not only a part of man, bone of his bone, and flesh of his flesh, born that men might not be lonely, but that women are in themselves possessors of and possessed by immortal souls" (32). The American Roman not only alienates himself from the body; he compounds that mistake by deflecting embodiment onto woman. His privatizing gaze misrecognizes women as the incarnation of his own alienated values, and renders these in hypostatized form as an object to be yearned for, dominated, and possessed—an outcome that Fuller poses in this passage as antagonistic to women's own self-(non)possession.

It is in the context of this problem of embodiment that Woman's unreadiness repeatedly takes on a racial dimension. In *Woman* Fuller argues that, because the Romans believed that "the *body* was inherited from the mother, the *soul* from the father," they also "permitted a man to lend his wife to a friend, as if she were a chattel" (30). Reduced to corporeality, women become property, and even commodities to be exchanged among male agents.[48] Here Fuller draws on the rhetoric of marriage reform, where comparing the one-flesh rule of marital coverture to chattel slavery was already established practice. But she pushes this logic a step further by aligning all female embodiment with slavery. A few pages on Fuller asserts that there are two conditions wherein sexual equality is possible—absolute thrall and absolute freedom: "In slavery, acknowledged slavery, women are on a par with men. Each is a work-tool, and article of property, no more! In perfect freedom ... each is a purified intelligence, an enfranchised soul,—no less!" (36). As enslaved property, one is nothing but a body, the contingency of flesh and "no more!" There (Fuller wrongly supposes) men and women are equal in the utter alienation of self within U.S. capitalism, equally unfree. In "perfect freedom," Man and Woman exist equally again in the disembodied unity of "purified intelligence." Here Fuller might as well have repeated her first flourish "no more!" instead of replacing it with "no less," for she is describing an absence—mind and soul without the burden of possessable and contingent embodiment.

As the trope of enslaving corporeality develops in *Woman*, not only slavery but nonwhiteness itself aligns with the thrall of corporeality. For the association between blackness and embodiment is overdetermined in an analysis like Fuller's, that also addresses the sexualization of female bodies and pathologizes women's self-interest: body as wounded target of desires, body as seat of desires. Thus Fuller instructs women to seek relations with men that are "free from slavery in the body" (79) and urges them to "clear your souls from the taint of vanity"—borrowing a term from the racist discourse of miscegenation to describe self-ish desire (83). Elsewhere, she defends women's right to speak in public, but also concedes that there is impropriety in their doing so for reasons of self-interest or self-promotion: "What can pollute and tarnish is to act thus from any motive except that something needs to be said or done" (19). Here the word *tarnish* suggests that by indulging self-interest women render themselves a kind of coinage to be exchanged, implicating themselves in fallen material interests. At once, it echoes the metaphor Fuller uses that same year in her *Tribune* article, where chattel slavery "tarnishes" the female face of U.S. democracy and reveals "that righteousness is not her chief desire" (149). With this circle of overlapping constructs, Fuller maps nonwhiteness, transgressive sexuality, self-interest, and status as property over each other as expressions of the embodied limits imposed on Woman. This illustrates the different difference of race in Fuller's imagination. Racialization is not just another mark of cultural difference produced by misrecognition, equivalent with feminization. It is the fundamental marker of difference from sameness, the difference between women and Woman.[49] Such a conflation of nonwhiteness with racialized, imprisoning embodiment recurs where Fuller needs to think about what women must leave behind to "bring out the idea of Woman."

Fuller's ambivalent treatment of ascribed difference demonstrates that the principles of sacrosanct privacy and recognition work less to promote plurality—as democratic mythology suggests they should—than to eradicate it. In this, her project has interesting implications for twentieth- and twenty-first-century social theory in which Hegelian recognition is taken up as a strategy for social and economic justice. For some contemporary philosophers, recognition theory is a way to focus attention on destructive patterns of cultural representation. Axel Honneth, for example, argues that demeaning cultural stereotypes should be viewed as forms of misrecognition that deprive particular groups of that acknowledgment which Hegel deemed necessary for full self-becoming. Equal social respect, by this reasoning, will address human inequality at its roots. Other recent theorists of recognition, including Charles Taylor, Seyla Benhabib, and Nancy Fraser, find little value in this approach. Fraser criticizes Honneth's model as one that "treats misrecognition as a free-standing cultural harm" and overlooks the role of economic inequality. Its logic, she points out, locates the source of inequality within the damaged psyches of misrecognized individuals—in effect, blaming the victim—without addressing the institutional origins of social stigmatization and inequality.[50] Fraser proposes a different model that focuses on how difference is rooted in institutional exclusion, and defines recognition as those forms of institutional inclusion—equal access to marriage, employment, political office, and so on—that enable full agency in civil society. With this formulation, she argues, recognition promotes transformation of (and not just assimilation into) static, preestablished orders of identity and membership. Its aim is not "affirmation" but "transformation," not "self-realization, but justice" (74).

As we have seen above, Fuller's approach to recognition is diametrically opposed to that outlined by Honneth. For her, cultural difference only impedes the operation of recognition, delaying the discovery and propogation of sameness. Her theory compares more interestingly with Fraser's, in that although it reflects many of the same principles it does not predict the same outcomes. Like Fraser, Fuller attributes difference to institutional exclusion, and sees material inequality and social stigma as intertwined. Yet this attention to formative contexts does not prevent her from also identifying difference as a pathology located within individuals. By her reckoning difference still amounts to injury—and might, from a different angle, look like deviance and criminality. Also like Fraser, Fuller proposes institutional inclusion as a mechanism for transformation rather than assimilation. But, as we shall see below, she conceives of this transformation as occurring not within or upon institutional contexts but as an exit from them. This is because Fuller's model of recognition is driven by a vision of individual and national unity in the Law. The ideal of private relations from which her concept of progress begins, and to which it yearns to return, trumps any structural corrections that might arise from her critique. In Fuller's hands, Hegelian recognition exhibits a teleological bent that Fraser may underestimate when she asks that theory to generate a more capacious, flexible, and diversely populated civil society. Fraser seems to elide the role played by sameness—that is, by an absolute, unitary standard of inclusion (for Fraser this is "justice") that stands outside of the negotiation between self and other (or between institutions and those they exclude) and transforms them into conformity with itself.[51]

This raises a final issue, concerning what happens to difference during the transformations variously imagined. If difference—an outcome of institutional exclusion—is used as a kind of leverage to shift institutional norms into more inclusive shapes, difference itself will logically disappear along with the structures of institutional privilege it transforms. Here, then, although difference stands at the heart of radical transformation, it is valued only as the key to its own eradication.

REPRODUCING DEMOCRACY AND THE "VIRGIN MOTHER OF A NEW RACE"

In their 1998 essay "Sex in Public," Lauren Berlant and Michael Warner draw our attention to an image that exemplifies the public iconography of privacy and its link to American democratic fantasy. The image, which comes from the cover of a special issue of *Time* magazine on immigration, shows a computer-generated portrait for which head shots from a diverse group of U.S. ethnicities have been combined to produce "the new face of America." Berlant and Warner write,

> Naked, smiling, and just off-white, *Time*'s divine Frankenstein aims to organize hegemonic optimism about citizenship and the national future. *Time*'s theory is that by the twenty-first century interracial reproductive sex will have taken place in the United States on such a mass scale that racial difference itself will be finally replaced by a kind of family feeling based on blood relations... hundreds of millions of hybrid faces will erase American racism altogether: the nation will become a happy racial monoculture made up of "one (mixed) blood."[52]

Exactly 150 years before *Time*'s special issue, Fuller offers a strikingly similar portrait of immigration, amalgamation, and manifest destiny in *Summer on the Lakes*. It appears immediately following the tragic auto/biography of Mariana, which ends, as we have seen, with a tableau of heroic recognition between a feminine America and her ideal consort: "When there is such a man for America, the thought which urges her on will be expressed" (132). Having invoked heterosexual reproduction in allegory, Fuller continues to think about it as a matter of particular import for westward expansion. "This is indeed the great problem of the place and time," she remarks:

> The children of the present settler may be leaven enough for the mass constantly increasing by emigration. And how much is this needed where those rude foreigners can so little understand the

> best interests of the land they seek for bread and shelter. It would be happiness to aid in this good work, and interweave the white and golden threads into the fate of Illinois. It would be a work worthy the devotion of any mind. (133)

Like *Time*'s portrait, this passage engages white anxiety about immigration and envisions the absorption of cultural difference through "devoted" efforts at "white and gold" procreation. At one level, Fuller's vision clearly subverts anti-immigration sentiment, which was intensifying in this period with formation of the Know-Nothing Party. Her phrase "rude foreigners" refers as much to New Englanders as to more recent immigrants, and indicates an inability to understand the "best interests of the land" rather than inferior blood or ethnicity. More, she avoids biological arguments by imagining an entirely disembodied version of national reproduction—one that discounts issues of "bread and shelter" and takes place in "any mind."[53] And yet, on the whole, *Summer* works with, not against, the grain of nativism. For Fuller, progress obtains in the purifying reproduction of sameness. Her normative democracy prioritizes a utopian future in which citizenship is recast as the marriage of American to America and national belonging as, in Warner and Berlant's term, "a kind of family feeling." Here, "rude" and "foreign" interests are not negotiated, but rather "leavened" by native interests.

This marital version of private relations appears in Fuller's writing repeatedly as she struggles with the unfreedoms structured by sex and race in antebellum America. In a sense, she is already working it through in the autobiography where her parents' marriage symbolizes the paired aspects of her education. In *Woman*, Fuller portrays democratic political progress as a mystical convergence of male and female principles, reimagining marriage as an ever-widening domain of freedom and equality that absorbs the contingencies of sex, race, and, ultimately, nation at its borders. Her dependence on this strategy suggests a significant nineteenth-century antecedent to the "national heterosexuality" that Warner and Berlant identify in the twentieth and twenty-first. It presents another aspect in which, as Amy Kaplan has shown, the liberatory and imperialist impulses of American democratic exceptionalism are always, inextricably, intertwined.[54] More, it shows how the force of privacy acts within liberalism to reduce democratic ideals to imperialist spectacle, democratic process to a millennialist overturning, and democratic deliberation to consensus and consonance.

As we have begun to see in the previous section, *Woman in the Nineteenth Century* is part social critique and part millennialist tract. It focuses at one moment on the legal and social subordination of women and, at the next, calls readers to move beyond these provisional concerns to the "holy work that is to make earth a part of heaven" (5). Critics have made much of the fact that *Woman* disengages sex and gender, pointing to Fuller's analysis of gendered cultural prescriptions and her famous assertion, "There is no wholly masculine man, no purely feminine woman" (69). This is surely an important feature of Fuller's thought and one that begins to develop well before 1845 with her autobiographical query into the gendered cultivation of national subjects. Yet, if Fuller disrupts the sex-gender system, she reaffirms heteronormativity at every turn and, in *Woman*, invests it with ultimate political and metaphysical authority. While she describes masculinity and femininity as "fluids" that "are perpetually passing into one another," this fluidity remains contained within a complementary logic of unity: the male and female are "two halves of one thought" (5) and "two sides of the great radical dualism" that together give birth to "one creative energy, one incessant revelation" (69). For Fuller, as Ellison points out, "ideality" is "inseparable from symmetry."[55] Only in heterounity is higher law fully recognized and made manifest through the exchange of complementary gazes.

Marriage acts as a dominant motif throughout *Woman in the Nineteenth Century*, always tied to the problem and possibility of recognition. The text opens by presenting its central problematic, mankind's struggle to find and communicate "eternal truth" and "pre-existent harmony." It then immediately turns to Orpheus and Eurydice, who offer themselves to each other as spectacular images in which to discover these meanings (8). He is a "law-giver by theocratic commission" who "told [nature's] secrets in the form of hymns, nature as seen in the mind of God" (11). She is his "far-shining view" (12). But Orpheus loses sight of Eurydice after his excessive, idolatrous love casts them both in thrall: "Again his love must lose through too much love" (12). Further on, Fuller offers a corrective to this failure in the heterocomplementary design of the Greek zodiac:

> I cannot complain of the age and nation, which represents its thought by such a symbol...gods and goddesses, arranged in pairs. The circle breathes the music of a heavenly order. Male and female heads are distinct in expression, but equal in beauty, strength and calmness....[C]ould the thought, thus expressed, be lived out, there would be nothing more to be desired. (31)

Here, as in the heterofantasies of *Time* magazine and *Summer on the Lakes*, Fuller celebrates the transcendence of inequality, the silencing of complaint, the cancellation of desire. Nothing remains but preordained harmony. *Woman* concludes in a similar mode, with another heroic pairing, "Las Exaltadas," by whose match the world "would, at last, be exalted too" (91). Here again marriage is linked to spectacle; but this time the couple offer themselves for Fuller's process of recognition rather than each other's: "I have in my eye a youth and a maiden. . . . To them I look, as, perhaps, the harbingers and leaders of a new era." Marriage, then, publishes and manifests the liberty of law on two levels. Recognition occurs between the two partners, and the transformative force of their union expands by interpellating others.

Of course, Fuller was not the only nineteenth-century American to view marriage as the key to cultural elevation. Midcentury reformers vigorously promoted it as a structure that would contain "private passions." Politicians and industrialists alike urged marriage upon the working class, recognizing its power to channel the disruptive ambitions of capitalist individualism into stable patterns of consumption and labor. In the words of Henry Ward Beecher, marriage and family were considered "the digesting organ of the body politic," mechanisms for neutralizing radical bodies and desires and diverting their energies to a higher national goal.[56] This discourse on marriage was particularly forceful in the years leading up to *Woman*'s publication, due to increased advocacy on behalf of the undigested, heterodox desires of white middle-class women and blacks. Female reformers who sought to obtain the rights of divorce and property ownership for married women were denounced for threatening the very foundation of stable and moral society.[57] Opponents of abolitionism demonized William Lloyd Garrison and other antislavery radicals by suggesting that the inevitable outcome of emancipation—and of women's participation in the movement for it—was racial intermarriage, amalgamation, and the loss of white purity. As Elise Lemire demonstrates, the specter of miscegenation was used deliberately to incite antiabolitionist riots in New York City throughout the 1830s, and pervaded pro- and antislavery rhetoric during the 1840s, while Fuller was writing *Woman*.[58]

Fuller responds to her culture's discourse on marriage in complex ways. Although her own idealization of marriage stems directly from nineteenth-century U.S. attitudes, she is also deeply critical of marriage as a patriarchal legal and economic institution. In *Woman*, actually existing marriage is chief among the forms of privatization that Fuller contrasts to the ideal of private relations. In this she sides with marriage reformers and against their detractors—such as the one she imagines here:

> "Is it not enough," cries the irritated trader, "that you have done all you could to break up the national union, and thus destroy the prosperity of our country, but now you must be trying to break

up family union, to take my wife away from the cradle and the kitchen hearth to vote at polls and preach from a pulpit." (15)

Fuller subverts the argument that marriage reform would disrupt natural and national order by linking that view with a proslavery stance and putting it in the mouth of her "irritated trader" (slave trader pointedly implied). More specifically, she emphasizes the crucial distinction between privacy and privatization. The trader has evoked normative domestic privacy by contrasting the "kitchen hearth" with "polls and... pulpit." But Fuller points out that such a marriage is no sanctified retreat from economic and political life. Rather, it is another institution for male economic interest, where husband and wife are analogous to slaveholder and slave. Citing the laws that denied married women control over their own property, wages, persons, or children, Fuller wryly concludes: "It may well be an Anti-Slavery party that pleads for woman" (17). In marriage as it operates within U.S. capitalism, women and their labor are goods to be traded for the profit of men.

Fuller also denounces the way marriages are brokered. Denied choice, women are utterly controlled by patriarchal authority and interests and subjected to a fallen version of domestic privacy that constrains their self-becoming:

> It has been the tone to keep women ignorant on these subjects, or when they were not, to command that they should seem so. "It is indelicate," says the father or husband, "to inquire into the private character of such an one. It is sufficient that I do not think him unfit to visit you." And so, this man, who would not tolerate these pages in his house, "unfit for family reading," because they speak plainly, introduces there a man whose shame is written on his brow... and, presently, if *respectable* still, and rich enough, gives him his daughter to wife. (90)

Here again, Fuller poses marriage as a capitalist venture with the husband or father as "trader," women as commodities, and privacy (that of the family, that protecting the suitor's character) as a hypocritical convenience serving male privilege. But this reasoning is already familiar to Fuller's audience from marriage reform discourse. Her more pressing argument is that this privatized marriage expressly prohibits women from their own practice of self-freeing, world-freeing recognition. Forbidden to "inquire into [the suitor's] private character," wife and daughter are forced to pretend they cannot decipher the text "written on [his] brow." Fuller queries, "What sort of mental intimacy can we expect here?" As privatization, marriage prevents mutual recognition, the defining feature of true marital unity.

What differentiates Fuller's critique from other marriage reform rhetoric is that she argues not on behalf of women's welfare, but on behalf of marriage. Thus, she interrupts her own argument for the prosecution of abusive husbands, saying she will not, after all, "demand from men a partial redress in some one matter, but go to the root of the whole. If principles could be established... marriage and all other relations would by degrees be harmonized with these" (18). Fuller wants, finally, not to improve historical forms but to replace them with their Platonic forms. And it is in this distinction that her project reveals a dynamic within Hegelian recognition that opposes institutional transformation. At first glance Fuller's critique of nineteenth-century marriage suggests a model of recognition similar to that proposed by Fraser—she, too, focuses on the institutional politics of difference, demands institutional equity (ability to hold property, equal self-right under marriage law), and predicts that such modes of recognition will transform the institutions in question. But, unlike Fraser's, Fuller's arguments see this dialectical process through to its logical conclusion, where women's institutional position simply evaporates and historical reforms culminate in millennial transformation:

> Without attaching importance, in themselves, to the changes demanded by the champions of woman, we hail them as signs of the times.... We would have every path laid open to women as freely as to man. Were this done... we believe the divine energy would pervade nature to a degree unknown in the history of former ages, and that no discordant collision, but a ravishing harmony of the spheres would ensue. (20)

In Fuller's explication of Hegelian recognition, utopia displaces history, Woman supplants women, and iconic marriage trumps the negotiation of historic ones. This reading diverges from the view among many Fuller scholars that one of her characteristic strengths is an ability to investigate cultural ambivalences and contradictions without seeking to resolve them into final, unified truths. Critics including Bell Chevigny, Caroline Sorisio, and especially Christina Zwarg persuasively demonstrate Fuller's dedication to putting traditionally binarized terms into nonteleological "conversation."[59] In my reading, however, Fuller's reliance on the liberal fantasy of privacy overrides her instinct for placing incommensurable perspectives or frameworks in dialectical tension with each other. She wields the ideal of private relations against its corrupted form within capitalist property relations. Indeed, this is the intended function of *Woman* itself, as indicated in the passage referred to earlier, where the matchmaking father refuses to "tolerate these pages [meaning the text of *Woman*] in his house," as "'unfit for family reading.'" This moment of textual self-reference recalls

Fuller's opening request that men read her text in the mode of "private relations"—a request this man fails to honor, and a fundamental requirement for national progress that this marriage fails to uphold. The juxtaposition also suggests that *Woman* is more than a text to be read. It is also a target for recognition that both requires and creates a new kind of private relations among and with its audience. As readers, we participate in a reciprocal evolution that matches the reciprocal evolution of marriage. *Woman* is not just a utopian critique of history but a utopian strategy enacted upon it.

The tendency of Hegelian recognition (as national heterosexuality) to subordinate political engagement in *Woman in the Nineteenth Century* is most clear where Fuller addresses racial injustice, always either aligning it with or making it stand in for the suppression of women's unfolding into Woman. The trope of racial difference is key to Fuller's ability to imagine a movement out of misrecognition and into the "ravishing harmony" of privacy. In *Woman*, the different difference of nonwhiteness represents that which must be overcome—or "digested"—through the purifying gaze of reciprocal recognition. However, in this process historical particularity is not simply extraneous. Even in its intolerance for historical differences, the ideal of private relations requires the "imperfection" of social difference as the grounds for its own continuing self-production. Here Fuller again follows Hegel, for whom difference is necessary to the dialectical unfolding of Spirit toward cultural unity. Only through the "struggle for recognition" described in his famous master-slave dialectic, a struggle against the prison of misrecognized positionality, will higher consciousness emerge.

In her theory of shining lives, Fuller regards lives and texts alike as finite and inadequate glosses on infinite truth. But she concludes that these are, finally, more evocative *of* truth than the thing itself could ever be. The ideal may be read only in its absence. In her oft-noted account of visiting Niagara Falls in *Summer on the Lakes*, Fuller evaluates and rejects various conventions of landscape art, ridiculing any attempt—including her own—to translate this spectacle.[60] Referring to "a 'guide to the falls,' who wears his title labeled on his hat," she remarks ironically, "One might as soon think of asking for a gentleman usher to point out the moon" (75). A few lines on, however, Fuller encounters another national symbol and offers a very different view on the compromises of translation. Describing an eagle that is kept caged at the falls, she recalls that as a child she saw one "chained" in a museum. She then compares these two captives to a third eagle she once watched flying majestically free in the White Mountains: "I know not that I felt more on seeing the bird in all its natural freedom and royalty, than when, imprisoned and insulted, he had filled my early thoughts with the Byronic 'silent rages' of misanthropy. . . . [A]ll the king was visible, though sorrowful and dethroned" (74). In the spectacle of the bird, and in her own outraged response, Fuller experiences the same transcendent recognition she had previously experienced with Ellen Kilshaw in the innermost circle of self-other intimacy. Yet there is a strangely violent edge to this later version, where freedom is made legible by captivity. Such logic is crucial to the role of cultural difference, and of racial difference in particular, as these relate to progress.

Summer is full of caged eagles.[61] The fact that most are Native Americans reconfirms the different way that racial difference makes meaning in Fuller's economy of recognition. As many critics have observed, Fuller aligns the condition of white women and Indians throughout *Summer* to show that both are objects of calculated misrecognition. Both, of course, are associated with nature—specifically, in Fuller's treatment, with the "New World" of North America—and subjected to the domineering, appropriative gaze of settlers who look only for profit and not higher insight.[62] Yet, in Fuller's portrayal, the misrecognition of Indians differs categorically from the misrecognition of women. As Zwarg demonstrates, Fuller self-consciously juxtaposes, and so exposes as contingent, the differing interpretive frames that Europeans brought to their encounters with natives. However, as Zwarg also notes, this exploration frees the white spectator from her own epistemological limits while leaving intact the spectacle of the misrecognized Indian.[63] In a sense, the Indian is a symbol of misrecognition rather than its victim in his own right. He helps the spectator perceive her own place in that violent epistemological system and pass beyond it. And, in this, his injury opens the way to national progress. Writes Fuller,

> I feel that I have learnt a great deal of the Indians, from observing them even in this broken and degraded condition. There is a language of eye and motion which cannot be put into words.... I feel acquainted with the soul of this race; I read its nobler thoughts in their defaced figures. There *was* a greatness, unique and precious, which he who does not feel will never duly appreciate the majesty of nature in this American continent. (221–22)

Referring to this passage, Sorisio aptly describes Fuller's Indians as "victims of their own bodies"—doomed and unable to change (171). But, like the eagle, the noble savage who is caged within his broken and tragic body is freighted with useful meaning—a meaning indivisible from its caged condition and necessary for entering the New World. There is a narrative of futurity and continental expansion at hand in this proposal that is inextricable from the narrative of manifest destiny.

Representations of African American slavery in *Woman* hold similarly ambivalent value. Slavery "tarnishes" the shining image of America, but also provides benefits like those of the caged eagle and battered Indian by provoking a discourse on freedom that serves women and portends national change. The "champions of the enslaved African," Fuller argues, best express the true desire for liberty; "and this band . . . makes, just now, the warmest appeal in behalf of women" (15). Further on she adds: "It is with women as with the slave, 'Tremble not before the free man, but before the slave who has chains to break'" (36). In this aphorism, which Fuller borrows from Schiller, it is the chains that create the power—not as an argument against but as an image of unfreedom. Like the caged eagle, the chained slave provides the conditions for imagining perfect liberty.

Such racial logic underwrites Fuller's heteromillennialist thinking from the very beginning of *Woman*, first emerging in her discussion of Orpheus, Eurydice, and the lack of "fair chances" that prevent their true union. After announcing Eurydice's unreadiness, Fuller abruptly shifts to the topic of the French Revolution and asserts that the "species of equality" it awarded to women was too limited to an "idea of happiness [that] did not rise beyond outward enjoyment, unobstructed by the tyranny of others" (12). She argues, in other words, that political freedom—freedom from privatization—falls short of the freedom of privacy. Characteristically, Fuller also links this example of female self-interest to sexual impropriety: "The Goddess of Liberty," she declares, "was impure" (13).

On the heels of the impure Goddess comes a second abrupt turn, as Fuller again recasts the obstruction (and advancement) of Eurydice, now in the form of racial injustice:

> Every thing has been done that inherited depravity could do, to hinder the promise of heaven from its fulfilment. . . . But I need not speak of what has been done toward the red man, the black man. Those deeds are the scoff of the world. . . . Here, as elsewhere, the gain of creation consists always . . . in the continual development of that thought, the thought of human destiny, which is given to eternity adequately to express, and which ages of failure only seemingly impede. Only seemingly, and whatever seems to the contrary, this country is as surely destined to elucidate a great law . . . though freedom and equality have been proclaimed only to leave room for a monstrous display of slave-dealing and slave-keeping. . . . [S]till it is not in vain, that the verbal statement has been made, "All men are born free and equal." . . . That which has once been clearly conceived in the intelligence cannot fail sooner or later to be acted out. . . . This law cannot fail of universal recognition. (13–14)

In this long passage, the injustice done to Native and African Americans substitutes for the cultural unfreedoms of women.[64] More directly (and significantly) it substitutes for women's self-imprisoning desire *for* freedom, as though slavery appears only as a gloss on the Goddess's impurity—again as a form of tarnish. At first glance, Fuller seems to be drawing parallel trajectories: just as the lifting of restraints from Eurydice will free her to manifest Woman, justice for slaves and Native Americans will enable America to live out her exceptionalist destiny and reveal the "one law" of democracy. And yet, while women's interests are subordinated to transcendence, they are nevertheless recognized as a necessary and "not unimportant" step in the movement toward national democratic fantasy (13). Racial justice, conversely, is never ventured at all. In fact the disenfranchisement of nonwhites appears already under erasure: "I need not speak of it," prefaces Fuller. In the manner of caged eagles, imperialist violence exists to publish the ideal; the city upon a hill of democratic freedom actually requires genocide and slavery "to be acted out" for "universal recognition."[65] Notice the spectacular unfolding of law is impeded "only seemingly"—the phrase repeats for emphasis—by the "failures" of U.S. race relations. Furthermore, the red and black man do not give birth to their own Platonic forms of African and Indian in the way that women and men engender Woman and Man. Instead, here and with nearly every mention of slavery or removal, racial unfreedom occurs to advance an abstract law into which racial otherness disappears.

In this pattern *Woman* becomes legible as another amalgamation narrative such as the two from *Time* and *Summer*: like them it portrays iconic pairings that absorb difference into a heterocomplementary union identified with freedom and equality. Fuller inverts the racialist prophesies deployed by antiabolitionists. In her scheme, the racial other does not dilute white blood, but is subsumed and erased by it; rather than endangering white marriage, emancipation permits it to grow more encompassing. Fuller offers this reassurance as she advises women to become abolitionists, suggesting that if sympathy with blacks provides outward motivation for such work, the deeper compulsion comes from "the tendency of Woman to favor measures which promise to bring the world more thoroughly into harmony with her nature" (67). Just as the "monstrous display of slave-dealing and slave-keeping" makes it possible to "elucidate a great law" in the previous passage, here racial bodies evaporate into an image of freedom they "elucidate" (14). The joining of women to the antislavery cause is a political marriage that will produce no unwhite progeny; according to Fuller it will reproduce only the ideal of Woman.

Amalgamation logic continues to structure Fuller's argument through the final portion of her text, which features a taxonomy of marriage illustrated by a transnational, transhistorical range of examples. Like the circles of increasing intimacy from Fuller's autobiography, this catalog begins with the most embodied and embedded forms of alliance, and culminates in the incorporeality of private relations. The progression brings all the threads of *Woman* together, tracing human advancement as a process of mutual purification that is effected through the reciprocal recognition of sameness and the erasure of racially coded unfreedom. The first category of marriage types consists of those based on a cheerful division of labor; the second features mutual idolatry—marriage as a prison in rather than liberation through each other; and the third focuses on intellectual companionship (42). The fourth state of marriage, a "pilgrimage toward a common shrine," comprises unions that are generally celibate and brief, ending in sublime death, as though Fuller must completely remove the tarnish of bodies to guarantee freedom from possessive misrecognition.[66] Here is her ideal of citizenship and association. Here, also, is her vision of national reproduction, as we see when she introduces the imaginary couple she names "Las Exaltadas": "I have in my eye," writes Fuller, "a youth and a maiden whom I look to as the nucleus of such a class. From them would issue a virtue by which [the world] would, at last, be exalted too... for never yet have I known minds so truly virgin, without narrowness or ignorance" (91). This pair represents an ethic of disembodied progeneration by "imagining"—a term that Fuller often uses to describe the creative dimension of recognition. Themselves the offspring of Fuller's "eye," they will produce in turn a new class through the intercourse of their virgin minds that is bodiless and desireless. In the closing sections of *Woman*, Fuller repeatedly returns to this theme of extracorporeal reproduction—and to its racialist logic, as when she writes, "I have many, many times seen the image of a future life, of a destined spouse, painted on the tablets of a virgin heart," then begs her women readers to seek a marriage "free from slavery in the body" (79–80). Fuller's vision of national futurity exhibits what Alys Weinbaum refers to as "the race/reproduction bind"—meaning the "inextricability of the connection between race and reproduction... within transatlantic modernity's central intellectual and political formations."[67] Specifically, Fuller's argument belongs within the class of texts that Weinbaum describes as engaging the race/reproduction bind "tacitly"—and perhaps unconsciously—"in their production of rhetorical and conceptual coherence" (7). Identifying freedom with a condition of privacy that must be enacted and reenacted—produced and reproduced—as a movement out of contingency, Fuller gives that process cogency in a story of heterosexual racial reproduction where freedom-as-whiteness is generated from and against embodied limits. As in *Summer*, where Fuller's narrator longs to counteract the dissenting interests of "rude foreigners" by helping to "interweave the white and golden threads into the fate of Illinois," the narrator of *Woman* exhorts her reader to become the new Eve in whose "pure child, or influence, shall the new Adam, the redemption, arise. Innocence is to be replaced by virtue, dependence by a willing submission, in the heart of the Virgin Mother of the new race" (60).

In many ways, the racialist narrative of Fuller's heteromillennium predicts the racism that would shape women's rights activism in the decades to come, where upper-class women promised—if enfranchised—to deploy their ameliorative whiteness against the effects of black citizenship. In the next chapter, I explore this dynamic further in representations of Sojourner Truth by white female suffragists and reformers including Olive Gilbert, Frances Gage, and Harriet Beecher Stowe. I want to conclude my discussion of Fuller, however, by returning to how the racist implications of her racialist hierarchy—the implicit whiteness of the family feeling she seeks—reflect her notion of true citizenship as triumph over history. Ultimately, the heteromillennial narrative of *Woman in the Nineteenth Century* restructures democracy itself as both the project and product of overcoming historical difference, first on a national and then on a global scale. Fuller rewrites the origin and future of American nationhood as a series of transnational love stories. She first credits the marriage of Isabella and Ferdinand with uniting Spain and thereby enabling the financial partnership of Isabella and Columbus that "brought [the New World] into alliance with the civilized world" (38). Zwarg sees Fuller here as acknowledging women's complicity in nation building through conquest.[68] And yet, if Fuller criticizes Woman's role in national violence, she nevertheless posits it as Her natural function in the continuing procreative "unfolding" of New World freedom that is America's exceptionalist destiny. The world is waiting, Fuller declares—echoing her earlier discussion of Orpheus and Eurydice, now within a transnational imaginary—for the full becoming of Woman to emerge from the United States: "Here is a less encumbered field and freer air than any where else. And it ought to be so; we ought to pay for Isabella's jewels" (64).

Unmistakably, this series of transnational marriages suggests a cosmopolitan vision of the future and prioritizes a role for Woman *and* women in it. Yet Fuller also casts membership in the millennial world order as a familial structure in which citizenship derives from kinship rather than participation, and cosmopolitanism resides in biospiritual universalism. Her genealogy performs a kind of international heterosexuality whereby, as Warner and Berlant put it, "a historical relation to futurity is restricted to generational narrative and reproduction."[69] With this, the very principles that Fuller invokes on behalf of disenfranchised peoples become mechanisms of exclusion. Freedom and equality become

> a mirage...from which citizens are thought to come into political discourse and to which they are expected to return in the (always imaginary) future after political conflict...a promised haven that distracts citizens from the unequal conditions of their political and economic lives, consoles them for the damaged humanity of mass society, and shames them for any divergence between their lives and the intimate sphere that is alleged to be simple personhood.[70]

Fuller's heteromillennium confirms the exclusionary logic of "simple personhood"—the "mirage" that, like her shining lives, draws cultural subjects into identity with itself and includes both everything and nothing. More, her vision demonstrates the power of this mirage to preempt the modes of public-political action by which such exclusions are challenged—both in the erasure of nonwhiteness that describes national progress in *Woman* and *Summer* and, perhaps even more powerfully, in the death of her autobiographical double, Mariana. For the democracy of private relations is, finally, a space in which Fuller cannot imagine a place even for herself.

CHAPTER THREE

Stowe's Truths

PRIVACY, PRIVATION, AND THE MOB

> I edit myself....I hold myself tightly and never spill into the world that hates brown spills. I'm afraid that everything I am will pour out onto the ground and be absorbed without a word. I may disappear. So I hold onto myself because I still have much left to say....One day I will give birth to myself, lonely but possessed.
>
> —Patricia Williams, *The Alchemy of Race and Rights*

> There is always something awful in the voice of the multitude.
>
> —Harriet Beecher Stowe, *Dred*

The preceding chapter on Margaret Fuller's millennialist vision of reform demonstrates one way that conceptions of embodiment, difference, and property came together during the nineteenth century to produce a narrative of imperiled national privacy. This chapter focuses on how those same terms could also combine to generate a different kind of privacy crisis, one that simultaneously inverts and complements the first. In the discourse of surplus embodiment, we again find a logic of racialized bodily excess that threatens white democratic freedom. But where Fuller imagines embodiment as that which subjects the self to being possessed, the problem of surplus bodies focuses on a failure at self-possession. Rather than a private self that suffers invasion, it describes one that refuses to stay within its bounds. A version of this latter emergency appears in an essay by Harriet Beecher Stowe, published in the *Atlantic Monthly* in 1863 and titled "Sojourner Truth: The Libyan Sibyl." In the essay, Stowe recalls her first meeting with the famous ex-slave

Figure 3.1. *The Libyan Sibyl* (1860), William Wetmore Story. The Metropolitan Museum of Art, Gift of Erving Wolf Foundation, 1879 (1979.266). Image © The Metropolitan Museum of Art.

and itinerant lecturer—an event that had taken place a decade earlier. She opens with Truth's arrival, unexpected and uninvited, at Stowe's Andover home. Already entertaining guests, Stowe goes to the door "prepared to make the interview short."[1] But this intention is soon forgotten in the face of two formidable forces: one is Truth's body—a "tall, spare form" that suggests to Stowe "a full-blooded African" and "a physical development which in early youth must have been [a] fine...specimen of the torrid zone"; the other is Truth's desire to talk—"An audience was what she wanted.... [S]he had things to say, and was ready to say them at all times, and to any one" (118). Stowe summons her other guests and, without warning, Truth launches into her life story. The telling occupies most of the essay. Her listeners pose questions at

Figure 3.2. *Cleopatra* (1858), William Wetmore Story. The Metropolitan Museum of Art, Gift of John Taylor Johnston, 1888 (88.5a–d). Image © The Metropolitan Museum of Art.

long intervals, but Truth holds the floor and their interruptions only enhance the conceit that Stowe and her friends are the captive audience of this black woman's dominating person. Like Fuller's Mariana episode, Stowe's essay concerns the perils of female self-publication. But here the threat is posed *from* the autobiographer. It is Truth's uncontained selfhood that disrupts and constrains. Also in contrast to Fuller, who uses autobiographical fiction to recount her own plight, Stowe writes a fictional autobiography: she invents Truth's disruptive self-publication and, with it, a crisis of surplus embodiment through which to refashion her own public persona.

Stowe's portrait of embodied excess presents a classic example of what historian Nell Painter terms the Truth Myth, a set of conventions established over Truth's forty years in public life, some based in fact, many not. The Truth Myth was created with Truth's participation. But, because she was illiterate and published her autobiographies with assistance from amanuenses, all of its meanings were refracted through white women writers and reformers.[2] For the most part, Stowe's essay adheres to the usual pattern. She breaks with convention, however, when she concludes by shifting, abruptly, to the subject of two recent works by the celebrated American sculptor William Wetmore Story: his 1858 *Cleopatra* and 1860 *Libyan Sibyl.* Stowe admits she has not seen the statues herself; they have been produced in Rome and exhibited in London since her last trip abroad (see figures 3.1 and 3.2). But she transcribes a lengthy description of both from the *London Atheneum*, and then closes with a single remark: "We hope to see the day when copies both of the Cleopatra and the Libyan Sibyl shall adorn the Capitol at Washington" (133).

In most respects, this closing digression seems unmotivated and non sequitur. Although Stowe associates the sibyl with Truth, and even claims to have personally inspired the piece by telling Story about the famous ex-slave during a breakfast in Rome, the artist never corroborated any connection between his statue and either Truth or Stowe.[3] Moreover, the image described in the *Atheneum* contradicts the vocal and physical exuberance that the essay has depicted up to that point. According to Stowe's source, the sibyl is "a secret-looking dame" who leans forward and looks away rather than meeting the viewer's gaze, resting "her shut mouth upon one closed palm, as if holding the African mystery deep in the brooding brain that looks out through mournful, warning eyes" (132). To be sure, the British journalist fetishizes the sibyl's body much as Stowe does Truth's. He describes her "full-bloom proportions of ripe womanhood" and notes that she is "bare to her hips," in direct contrast to Cleopatra, who is "covered to the bosom." But where Truth radiates physical power and purpose, the sibyl withdraws into herself and signals vulnerability in her half-naked state. Meanwhile, the second statue also performs a revision. A popular artistic subject in Stowe's time, Cleopatra appeared widely as a misogynist symbol of women's hypersexualized, hyperembodied, self-interested, and power-hungry nature. Stowe, however, has chosen an account in which Cleopatra leans back "in meditative ease" and smiles "as though some firm, wilful purpose filled her brain." Rather than representing illegitimate power, she wears in her headdress the "twining basilisk of sovereignty"—even, in Stowe's final words, at the very seat of democratic governance (132). How might this Cleopatra's uncharacteristic self-possession concern the sibyl's nakedness? How does her air of focused purpose relate to the other's withdrawn silence? Why, finally, does Stowe invite us to envision both figures exhibited side by side in the nation's capitol?

In 1863, U.S. culture was no less than now what critical race theorist and legal scholar Patricia Williams vividly describes as a "world that hates brown spills."[4] It was also a world that required and incessantly portrayed brown spills. With images like Stowe's overpotent and hyperembodied Truth, white Americans confirmed to themselves the excessive nature of black subjectivity and generated fantasies of containment that grew more violent and punitive as they became increasingly vital to the national imaginary. These representations constitute a dystopian strain of U.S. privacy discourse, a recurring narrative in which the racialized threat of privation—a condition of radical subjection to embodiment without recourse to self-transcending self-mastery—demands action on behalf of white democratic freedom. As Toni Morrison and others have demonstrated, images of embodied black unfreedom circulated constantly in early American culture as a backdrop against which to project the fantasy of white disembodiment.[5] In Stowe's pairing of the sibyl with Queen Cleopatra, we can see the figure of black privation deployed in precisely that function, helping the writer to negotiate her own burdensome construct of feminine corporeality. In the white cultural imaginary, similar images operated within a broader frame of meaning to depict the reversal of possessive individualism and moral self-government. Here, the brown spill became a way to represent and displace a nationwide plight of surplus embodiment—the realities of homelessness, unemployment, economic depression, and unjust labor relations that betrayed the promises of freedom through self-right and market capitalism. In the ethnographic theory of the African's "natural" incapacity for self-government, in the specter of slave insurrection, in the characterization of freedpeople as a "vast hegira" of invading dependency, white Americans—North and South—found distance from their own failures at self-mastery and self-sufficiency.[6] More, they found ways to imagine redemption. For, as the ironic-wistful conclusion of the Williams epigraph suggests, the public menace of unrestrained, racialized privation also reaffirmed the promise that true self-possession could, finally, cancel the body altogether. In the process by which Stowe's essay silences Truth and places her alongside a gloriously liberated Cleopatra in the halls of Congress, we can trace a dream of restored white freedom that shifts blame to and enacts revenge upon the black surplus body. We can locate that punished surplus body literally at the center of an imagined new national sphere.

This chapter investigates narratives of surplus embodiment and black privation in the periods immediately before and after the Civil War, focusing on Stowe's 1856 novel, *Dred: A Tale of the Great Dismal Swamp*, and

1863 essay, “Sojourner Truth: The Libyan Sibyl.” In doing so, it reveals a new aspect of Stowe’s relationship to nineteenth-century U.S. privacy discourse. Previous criticism has focused heavily on *Uncle Tom’s Cabin* and its celebration of domestic privacy. There, critics have shown, Stowe imagines a haven from the market forces that commodify bodies, alienate individuality, and generate moral chaos.[7] We see this in the example of Senator Bird. In his public role he supports the Fugitive Slave Law and protects white ownership of blacks. Within the domestic circle, however, the senator learns to identify sympathetically with a fugitive slave, Eliza Harris, and aids in her escape. Echoing this logic of idealized privacy is the novel itself, a space presided over by Stowe’s mother-narrator where readers are guided toward their own experiences of affective moral knowledge and sympathetic immediacy with abject black subjects. However, focusing on Stowe’s antislavery writing after *Uncle Tom*, I find that she all but abandons this utopian mode of privacy discourse. With *Dred* she begins to develop a perspective wherein privacy—as privation—endangers democratic freedoms rather than ensuring their perfect realization. Where she had previously shown political conflict and market alienation invading the sacred spaces of privacy and violating the individual’s self-entitlement, she now reverses this dynamic. In *Dred* and “The Libyan Sibyl,” and in the national discourse within which they operate, disaster stems from a failure of self-possession that begins with the individual and releases a flood of prepolitical passions, appetites, and idiosyncracies into the democratic public sphere. The boundary between public and private evaporates to create those conditions that political philosopher Hannah Arendt identifies with the silencing of public reason, the disabling of self-transcendence, and the loss of political freedom. As with Fuller, sameness plays a key role in this panic narrative. But where Fuller envisions a utopian sameness beyond bodies, Stowe (with Arendt) focuses on the sameness of bodies—sameness without distinctions, sameness without self.[8]

The concept of privation comes from classical republican ideology, where political virtue and freedom are associated with rising above private selfhood. Here, privacy is the domain of irrational, inexorable corporeality. It energizes the political sphere but represents, in itself, a state of privation—or deprivation—where individual choice, will, and creativity are sacrificed to the body’s mundane demands. Images of privation pervade midcentury privacy discourse, even in contexts where privacy is also represented as the location of liberal democratic freedoms. Tocqueville, for instance, celebrates the liberal possessive individual whose enlightened self-interest fuels democratic process. But he also warns against the “wild fire” of unmediated interest and worries that universal suffrage will place government in the thrall of mass “propensities” for immoderation and immediate gratification.[9] In the complementary operation of privacy and privation, it becomes evident that republicanism and liberalism are best approached not as successive regimes, but as what Bruce Burgett describes as "two antithetical and inseparable possibilities inscribed within the larger idea of democratic self-government."[10]

Preceding chapters have shown that the notion of an inviolable relation to self—a relation I refer to as self-(non)possession—simultaneously underwrites and resists the logic of self-possession by positing a condition that precedes it, a selfhood prior to property relations. In U.S. discourse, self-(non)possession promises separation from the institutions of political and market activity. Yet it also names a form of service to those institutions, an obligation of self-governing self-containment that is required for the preservation of civic freedoms. In both aspects, self-(non)possession is defined against materiality, imagined as selfhood free from embodiment and historical contingency. As Chris Castiglia shows, antebellum reformers who instructed on the duty of self-governance deliberately elided material concerns. They revised self-right from a legal and economic entitlement to a moral responsibility, and cast self-sufficiency as the result of virtuous democratic will rather than material privilege.[11] Bodies were both extraneous and central to this ideal of moral self-government. At its core stood the fantasy of having no body at all, an annulment of desires and needs. Yet bodies and the affective interiority that they so often represent were also the ground upon which self-(non)possessive normativity performed its moral action. The nineteenth-century discourse of moral self-government focused on a privative embodiment that resisted but ultimately succumbed to political will. Through such publications, democratic subjects could experience that cancellation for themselves, over and again, reaffirming their own place in a privacy defined by freedom from other bodies and from their own. Thus, privation and privacy worked hand in hand in a collaboration that became increasingly important as the material constraints upon self-possession became increasingly apparent.

In the next section, I explore the conception of freedom as cancelled embodiment as it centers on the trope of black privation in *Dred*. Like *Uncle Tom*, *Dred* portrays a U.S. political economy corrupted by slavery. But rather than offering her novel as an intimate space in which readers may resist market commodification by developing sympathetic bonds with blacks, Stowe now discourages cross-racial identification and presents the novel as an instrument for containing black privation. Although still opposed to the commercial circulation of black bodies, Stowe proposes in *Dred* an alternative mode of circulation that is based on moral rather than material interests and produces the freedom of white incorporeality.

In the two sections that follow, I continue to investigate how the discourse of black privation functions in the U.S. national imaginary by examining how Stowe uses it in *Dred* and "The Libyan Sibyl" to redefine her own female authorship. As Elizabeth Young and Naomi Sofer have shown, Stowe was an important transitional figure for nineteenth-century American women writers, standing between an early generation whose authorship was legitimated by its moral function and a later generation whose writing could address political questions and aspire to elite, aesthetic achievement.[12] Stowe, that is, helped redraw the gendered boundaries of literary endeavor. For her this meant not simply appropriating features of masculine authority but renegotiating relationships among female authorship, embodiment, privacy, and publicity. Working at the intersection of political and literary cultures, Stowe challenged the gender norms that defined white womanhood in opposition to public-political authority. In this, she risked association with the very problem of antidemocratic privation she aims to resolve in *Dred*. Female authorship was easily interpreted as another manifestation of ill-contained corporeality that would overpower moral self-governance and disable public life. Like blacks, white women were considered incapable of self-possession and deficient in the political will required to abstract oneself from the body. Thus, a woman's attempts to go public could be interpreted as violently incompatible with democratic association. The mere idea of female suffrage provoked what Margaret Fuller describes with asperity as "ludicrous pictures of ladies in hysterics at the polls, and senate chambers filled with cradles"[13]—scenes that pathologized women's political aspirations by placing them in a body that spills over its own nonboundaries upon leaving its private setting. This antisuffrage strategy was reproduced (so to speak) in response to efforts by women like Stowe in the literary sphere: Hawthorne's infamous "dam'd mob" may stand accused of antidemocratic tendencies in ways that have as yet gone unexamined. In *Dred* and "The Libyan Sibyl," Stowe negotiates the burden of her own surplus embodiment by dramatizing the disruptive influence of black privation upon various democratic publics, and presenting her own authorial function as the key to its containment. Against charges that female writers eroded the barrier between privation and public freedom, she aligns her authorship with those aspects of normative white femininity that—like the republican mother who produced citizens from individuals, or the True Woman who converted sons and husbands into capitalist agents—entailed mediating the passage of private bodies into the body politic.[14] In this role, Stowe could distance herself from privation and gain access, or at least proximity, to a kind of public-political identity. Against the backdrop of the national emergency of surplus bodies, she could take an entirely new form.

Stowe's use of black privation to remodel her own identity and envision a reformed democratic political economy is vividly illustrated in her writings about Sojourner Truth. Therefore, I end the second section below with a discussion of Milly, a character from *Dred* whom Stowe openly based upon Truth; and in the section following I return to "The Libyan Sibyl." The practice of associating Truth with black privation is not exclusive to Stowe, nor did it originate with her. It runs throughout the Truth Myth, beginning with Olive Gilbert's 1850 *Narrative of Sojourner Truth* and passing forward via Stowe into writing by Frances Gage, Elizabeth Cady Stanton, and others. Truth's privation is most immediately evident—and most commonly noted—in its benign aspect. Many critics have pointed to the tendency of white women writers to depict her as docile, accommodating, and even, in Painter's words, as a kind of "pet" who supported their causes without making demands of her own.[15] In such cases, Truth becomes prepolitical; she claims nothing for herself and seems, in her childlike simplicity, incapable of doing so. She is less a "being" than what Hortense Spillers describes in reference to representations of slaves as a "being for"—a distinction emblematized in the fact that she was widely referred to by the possessive trope of "Stowe's Libyan Sibyl" after the 1863 essay.[16]

Yet the full meaning of Truth's prepolitical benignity is legible only in the context of how she is also insistently associated with threatening surplus embodiment. As Christina Accomando shows, Truth was habitually rendered as a thing rather than a person. Described as a "creature," compared to a palm tree, or drawn exclusively in images of huge and ambiguously gendered embodiment, the ex-slave was reduced to a physical presence without self-awareness.[17] While such representations reinforced the "pet" motif, they could also generate a sense of danger. In Gilbert's *Narrative*, for instance, Truth's body appears both heroic and overwhelming. Indeed, surplus embodiment figured centrally in Gilbert's very first impression of Truth when they met at the communitarian Northhampton Association. Shocked at the other woman's worn appearance from years of hard labor, she worried that Truth expected long-term support from the already disintegrating commune.[18] Quite literally, Gilbert saw a body produced by the corrupt U.S. market economy but without a place within any of its institutions. It seems significant, therefore, that she opens the *Narrative* with a protracted account of how Truth's parents were turned off their owner's land (i.e., "emancipated") when too old and enfeebled for work. Here Truth's parents make powerful images of racialized privation; they acquire self-right but lack the ability to wield it over their cumbersome corporeality, dramatizing the terrifying unfreedom of embodiment in a way that Karen Sánchez-Eppler has shown to be typical of white women's antislavery writing.[19] As Truth's father drags himself from farm to farm, seeking sanctuary for the "burthen" of his "decrepit" flesh, Gilbert writes for Truth a genealogy of black subjectivity immured in black embodiment.[20]

For Truth herself, the Truth Myth pictures a body that is not merely burdensome but also excessive in a way that threatens to foist its unfreedom onto others—hence the insistent association of Truth with situations on the verge of mob violence, where her own imposing physical presence confronts but also mirrors a mass of frightening bodies. In writings by white women, Truth faces down rioting revivalists, calms rowdy prayer meetings in the New York slums, and soothes hostile crowds at numerous political gatherings. The best known instance comes from Frances Gage's revisionist recollection of the 1851 Akron Women's Rights Convention, which invents a mob of antisuffragists whom only Truth can quell. Although Truth eventually wins the day for white female suffrage, the suffragists view her as another invader up to the deciding moment: they "tremble" upon "seeing her march deliberately into the church" and "gasp" in horror as she advances to the pulpit.[21] Gage casts the event as a confluence of transgressive public bodies: the "mobbish spirit" of the throng; the "Amazon form" that appropriates the stage; the "deep wonderful tones" of her famous (and fictitious) mantra "Ar'n't I a woman?"; and the fainting white suffragists "staggering under the weight of disapprobation" (166–68). Painter has established that this account is largely fabrication: the actual audience consisted of sympathetic abolitionists and supporters, and Truth was probably a familiar guest to the convention organizers. Why, then, does Gage conjure that antidemocratic mob and align Truth with it? One answer lies in how this revision positions Truth as a site of shifting identification, placed at the intersection of gender, race, and surplus embodiment. She is of the mob as well as the means of subduing it, both aggressor and savior.[22] More, she is aligned with and against the white women on whose behalf she speaks, making the invented query—"Ar'n't I a woman?"—seem more than rhetorical. This twinned liminality permits writers to identify both with and against Truth in a crucial double movement of appropriation that, as Sánchez-Eppler demonstrates, enabled female "suffrage-abolitionists" to deploy black unfreedom as both a symbol of their own disenfranchisement and an image of absolute otherness against which to reaffirm white womanhood.

Crucially, the Truth Myth does not produce Truth as the abject target of sympathy most typical of antislavery writing. A closer likeness is to the figure of "unruly blackness" that Elizabeth Young identifies with the murderous Cassy and mischievous Topsy of *Uncle Tom's Cabin.* Stowe, Young argues, uses disorderly black female characters—who not only violate the rules of white female civility but also disrupt national order—to register her own frustrated desire and political rage. At once, unruly blackness allows her to displace those impulses away from herself, and so stands in the novel as "both utopian fantasy and demonized grotesque."[23] As I will show, portrayals of Truth reveal a similar double movement of identification with and against the power of black surplus embodiment. But they also exhibit a third movement, beyond identification, where this preliminary ambivalence resolves into a display of mastery over both female and black embodiment.

Coming between Gage and Gilbert, Stowe was a key producer of the Truth Myth and, specifically, of its narrative on privation and containment. After their 1851 meeting, Stowe wrote four versions of Truth. Two are fictional: the slave Milly from *Dred* and a black servant named Candace from *The Minister's Wooing* (1859). Stowe's first (ostensibly) nonfictional account of Truth, published in 1860, describes a confrontation in which Truth interrupts Frederick Douglass as he calls for militant action, rising to bellow "Frederick, Is God Dead?" Scholars question the story's veracity, but it became a staple of the Truth Myth and even followed Truth to her grave: the phrase "Is God Dead?" appears on her tomb.[24] The fourth and last of Stowe's Truths appears in "The Libyan Sibyl." All four versions feature the singular and massive body and powerful voice that overwhelm those nearby. In Stowe's imagination these aspects of Truth's person, combined with Truth's growing celebrity as a lecturer and autobiographer, seem to resonate with her own questions about female authorship. Milly's significance in *Dred* centers on her acts of storytelling; and authorship is overtly at stake in "The Libyan Sibyl"—the term *sibyl* being a common label for women writers in the nineteenth century. Indeed, Truth's first words to Stowe in the latter—"So this is *you*. . . . I jes' thought I'd like to come an' have a look at ye. You's heerd o' me, I reckon?"—create a deliberately uncomfortable mirroring effect, as though Truth might transfer her own hyperembodiment onto Stowe by conflating Stowe's literary persona with her embodied person (117). Stowe also uses both Milly and the sibyl to invoke the problematic of black privation, tapping into the fear of slave insurrection and postemancipation resentment toward freedpeople. As we shall see, the pre- and post–Civil War portraits differ significantly, and this difference reveals how the logic of black surplus embodiment intensifies and calls for increasingly punitive responses in postbellum U.S. culture.

SURPLUS BODIES AND STOWE'S PLANTATION UPON A HILL

Although regarded as Stowe's second antislavery novel, *Dred* is more centrally a novel about surplus bodies, a problem that was just coming into focus in the national consciousness during the 1850s and concerned those bodies not sustained, and thus not contained, by the self-possessive will of democratic subjectivity. Responding to proslavery attacks on the inadequacies of the Northern free labor system, Stowe turns that critique back on the South and focuses, in particular, on the failure of slavery to contain black privation. She depicts the disastrous effects of black bodies that, when circulated as economic commodities, spread their privative nature to whites and destroy democratic freedom. Her solution is to insulate black bodies from the reach of white economic interest so they may serve white moral interests, instead.

Dred's focus on the problem of surplus bodies and moral self-containment was largely provoked by Southern attacks on *Uncle Tom*. With a barrage of essays, articles, and novels, anti-Tom writers defended their plantation economy by exposing the ruse of "free" labor. Self-possession, they argued, did not guarantee self-sufficiency and, lacking that, the Northern laborer was far less free than his Southern counterpart. The critique had merit. Conditions in Northern cities belied the great promise that democratic socialization and the market economy's invisible hand would together end poverty and other aberrations from self-sufficient individuality. Decades of overrapid industrialization and urbanization, the influx of nearly five million impoverished immigrants, the 1837 financial collapse and ensuing depression—all of these had resulted in widespread homelessness, escalating class tensions, and early anxieties about the prospect of a permanent dependent population and welfare state.

Anti-Tommers focused heavily on the surplus embodiment of Northern workers, deploying representations of abject and grotesque corporeality that echoed the lurid imagery of abolitionist discourse. "Let the inhabitant of the North turn his eyes towards home and look into the actual conditions of the white slaves at the North," writes one editor:

> Let him investigate the factory system, where the groans of childhood mingle with the crash of machinery. Let the well fed citizen...pause and hear the wail of a famishing family, the cries of a brood of starved children....[The laborer] knows if he becomes incapacitated to work that gaunt penury stares him in the face; he starves in a garret and rots alone and neglected![25]

Among the more accomplished anti-Tom novelists, Caroline Lee Hentz was particularly adept at resignifying antislavery imagery by transposing it to "the free and happy" North:

> Poverty, with a scourge of iron and a scorpion lash, stands behind them and urges on the life-consuming task.... If this is freedom, give us bondage instead.... Do songs ever gush from those bloodless, pallid lips? Do those weary feet ever spring in the light and joyous dance? Alas! no! The breath of life comes struggling from the weak and wasting lungs, and every step is impeded by the dull, heavy lead weight of despair.[26]

Putting the whip in the hand of the Northern industrialist and replacing the slave's suffering with that of the factory worker, writers like Hentz turned the abolitionist's own images against him.

Proslavery had an important advantage in this volley of abject bodies. For, unlike Northern claims to free and equal self-possessive individuality, the Southern narrative of happy dependence relations never relied on a tacit denial of bodies and their relentless demands. "Now, Mrs. Stowe," writes one editorialist, "be good enough to show me... where the old are taken care of and fed and lodged when sick or unable to work, as are our slaves?"[27] Critics of free labor forced the abstraction of moral self-possession to confront its fleshly double; they rematerialized self-right by dramatizing the burden of embodiment and by emphasizing the economic prerequisites of freedom. "I don't see freedom what it's cracked up to be," remarks a slave in Hentz's novel *The Planter's Northern Bride*. "It does mighty well for rich folks: but poor, working folks can't be free any way."[28] Elsewhere in the same work, a New England servant receives a ten-dollar gold piece and "gaz[es] fondly through her tears at the golden eagle, almost believing it an optical illusion."[29] Freedom, proslavery writers suggested, was an expensive proposition.

The point of these attacks was to champion slavery as a system that did liberate laborers from their bodies' demands; and this point drew its force from the widely accepted idea that Africans, in their putative incapacity for democratic self-sovereignty or capitalist self-possession, epitomized un-self-sustaining embodiment. When Russell Moreland, the hero of *Northern Bride*, asserts that "freedom would be [the African's] direst curse," he imagines freedom as literally an inhospitable climate for their differing constitution: "The air of freedom, which gives luxuriant growth to his vices, does not foster his peculiar virtues. His social character degenerates."[30] Hentz illustrates this claim with the case of Crissy, a slave who is persuaded by seducer-abolitionists to escape, but soon returns to Moreland, for "glorious freedom... had proved to her the only slavery she had ever known."[31] This ethnographic argument reassured and justified slaveholders, but it could also be used to arouse fear. Southern editors pointed to the mass of unfree freedmen already mixing in with the "Irish, Germans, Swiss, Alsacians . . . turned loose in our large cities by ship-loads," and queried, "If the abolitionists cannot take care of those already free, what would they do if three millions in addition were suddenly thrown broadcase upon their heads?"[32] Other proslavery advocates painted a frightening picture of the postemancipation West Indies in chaotic disorder under the deficient ownership of emancipated blacks: "They are a miserable, wretched set of people, and the sooner these beautiful possessions are taken from them the better it will be for them and the world. . . . Let the Abolitionists take warning by the state of these islands, virtually destroyed by emancipation."[33] Hentz and others took this paranoia to its logical conclusion with stories about insurrectionary slaves that again illustrate the "fact" of black incapacity for self-right. In *Northern Bride*, for example, a group of slaves are taught by a satantic antislavery "fanatic" to resent enslavement, only to fall under his evil sway. Animated by his malice (rather than their own will), their susceptible bodies nearly destroy Moreland and his bride.

Writing *Dred* in the wake of the anti-Tom assault, Stowe engages the crisis narrative about surplus bodies and their power to spread unfreedom, and strategically locates the origins of that crisis in Southern slavery. In stark contrast to slavery's self-portrait of luxury, leisure, and abundance, Stowe presents a failing Southern economy with plantations on the verge of bankruptcy—most significant among these is Canema, the family home of siblings Nina and Tom Gordon, who are the novel's heroine and villain, respectively. A prominent subplot features Miss Sue, a white woman descended from "one of the most celebrated families in Virginia," but now dying, homeless, and unable to care for her illegitimate offspring.[34] Sue, we learn, was raised on a "worn out and broken-down old plantation, where everything had run down, through many years of mismanagement and waste." Worse, she has been seduced by a dissolute young man whose family had likewise gone to ruin, having "been so unfortunate as to obtain possession of a few negroes" and developed a disdain for labor (89). Here is Stowe's entropic South, a system without the virtuous momentum of free labor, populated by bodies it can neither support nor contain.

Black intermingles with white in Stowe's theory of surplus embodiment. For, although she rejects the Southern stereotype of slothful, helpless Africans, she accepts—indeed requires—the construct of radically uncontained black bodies. Stowe counters the proslavery narrative by writing blacks as extremely able economic agents whose labors rescue feckless white families. Nina and Tom Gordon are saved by Harry—their accountant, overseer, slave, and half-brother—who delays buying freedom for himself and his wife in order to keep Canema solvent. Homeless Sue and her children are sheltered and nursed by their faithful slave, Old Tiff, the one remnant of Sue's Virginian genealogy. Critic Lori Merish, noting a similar pattern of black economic agency in *Uncle Tom*, argues that Stowe uses it to demonstrate black self-sufficiency and self-possession.[35] And yet Stowe disconnects self-possession from the black productivity she emphasizes in *Dred*. In spite of their impressive industry and initiative, blacks are persistently coded as workers but not agents, able producers but incapable of possessing their own productive force. Here Stowe follows the theory of Alexander Kinmont, the antebellum ethnographer and abolitionist she had known in Cincinnati, who pronounced blacks natural Christians but found they lacked the faculties of self-determination and aggression exhibited by Anglo-Saxons and required for self-sovereignty.[36] Both sides of Stowe's equation are important in *Dred*'s logic: the novel repeatedly celebrates the beauty, power, passion, and productivity of black characters; and just as consistently it asserts that their political faculty is underdeveloped—and even potentially absent.

Stowe's theory on the limits of black political subjectivity appears in *Dred* under the auspices of her hero, lawyer and slaveholder Edward Clayton, whose life ambition is to educate his slaves and "demonstrate the capabilities of... this Ethiopian race" (23). Clayton aims to cultivate a form of possessive individualism in his slaves: "There is to be a graduated system of work and wages introduced—a system that shall teach the nature and rights of property, and train to habits of industry and frugality, by making every man's acquirements equal to his industry and good conduct" (24). But, although this scheme seems to move toward assimilation and racial cosovereignty, such hopes are given as uncertain at best. First, Clayton must transfer his slaves to Canada to see his plan through—a development reflecting Stowe's belief that the U.S. political economy would never accommodate black self-right. Second, although Clayton's plan for teaching possessive individualism to blacks is presented at the story's outset, its realization is postponed until the final pages of the final chapter. Intervening is a very long novel that dwells upon the disturbing manifestations of non-self-possessive and ill-contained black bodies within U.S. borders. The delay invites skepticism about whether the training that Clayton has in mind will ever be possible—whether black non-self-possession is ontological or developmental. In fact, midway through the narrative Clayton revises his earlier vision:

> "The Ethiopian race is a slow growing plant, like the aloe... but I hope, some of these days, they'll come into flower; and I think, if they ever do, the blossoming will be gorgeous.... There is no

use in trying to make the negroes into Anglo-Saxons, any more than making a grape-vine into a pear-tree. I train the grape-vine." (328)

This second account of Clayton's plan qualifies the first, making it clear that he expects the development of different races to follow distinct trajectories toward distinct and—given the tendency of vines to cling—intertwined and differentially empowered destinies.

That long postponement of Clayton's racial garden feeds a sense of mounting pressure from the black bodies in question. Stowe develops this mood with an episode in which whites are unnerved by the unleashed passions of a revival meeting where blacks "scream, dance, and shout, and fall in trances" in accord with their "tropical lineage and blood" (245). But the central focus of threatening black privation is a plot line concerning a planned slave revolt and its leader, the novel's title character, Dred. Here Stowe again likens blacks to plant life. This time, however, the metaphor's vehicle is a swamp—literally the place where Dred and his band of escaped slaves hide out and organize, figuratively an image for their multiplying numbers and burgeoning rage. Stowe's title, *Dred; a Tale of the Great Dismal Swamp*, performs the conflation before we even open the book, and a key passage develops it further:

> There is no principle so awful through all nature as the principle of growth. It is a mysterious and dread condition of existence, which, place it under what impediment or disadvantage you will, is constantly forcing on; and when unnatural pressure hinders it, develops in forms portentous and astonishing. The wild, dreary belt of swamp-land which girds in those states scathed by the fires of despotism is an apt emblem, in its rampant and we might say delirious exuberance of vegetation, of that darkly struggling, wildly vegetating swamp of human souls, cut off, like it, from the usages and improvements of cultivated life.
>
> Beneath that fearful pressure, souls whose energy, well-directed, might have blessed mankind, start out in preternatural and fearful developments, whose strength is only a portent of dread. (496)

Without proper training, the vine grows and reproduces itself beyond control, its "delirious exuberance" recalling the alarming fervor of the black revivalists. Critic Maria Karafilis reads the swamp as a symbol of resistance, arguing that because its fluid and unchartable terrain allows it to remain "unclaimed as private property" it "offers the men and women settling it a nurturing space of freedom."[37] Yet, while the swamp does suggest utopian possibilities in its externality to market capitalism, it is precisely in its resistance to possession that it also echoes the novel's most terrifying vision of national futurity—the cancerous spread of ungovernable bodies, the "awful...principle of growth." The swamp's dystopian aspect is reinforced by its association with insurrection. Dred (the double entendre of his name pointedly spelled out at the start and end of the passage above) is identified in the novel as the son of the real insurrectionist Denmark Vesey and explicitly based on Nat Turner. He frequently spouts bloody visions of the race war he hopes to lead.[38] Unsurprisingly, Stowe kills Dred off before he can take his revolutionaries into action. But she also daringly endows him with tragic heroism and demands that readers recognize the justice of his rage. It is important, as we shall see, that Dred is among the characters in *Dred* drawn from the example of Sojourner Truth. In his life and death we may find a family resemblance of dangerous power and reassuring containment.

Like Hentz, then, Stowe deploys black characters as images of surplus embodiment. In *Dred*, however, the chief danger posed by black bodies is not their potential to generate insurrection (which makes her treatment of that potential all the more radical). Rather, it is their wanton availability to white economic and political interests. Unable to possess themselves, black bodies act like rocket fuel to the possessive interest of whites—that self-serving Anglo-Saxon aggression identified by Kinmont. In this, they enable a pattern of destruction and violence that stands in the novel as symbolically equal to a race massacre and, in terms of narrative weight, as more than equal—a virus of white greed that feeds upon black bodies and disrupts the liberal balance between private property interests and regulatory civil society. Anti-Tommers frequently complained that Stowe's first novel defied the reality of human self-interest by depicting whites who murdered and abused their own property; they argued that man's economic reason prevented such atrocities. In *Dred*, Stowe counters such logic by characterizing slavery interests as rapacious, unrestrained, irrational, and ultimately self-destructive. In doing so, she also reflected prevalent attitudes about the specific impact of black bodies as property. For many, the slave commodity was a contaminant within the democratic economic and political spheres, communicating its essential uncontainability that defied black and white self-government alike. From the synergistic combination of irrational slave interests and uncontainable black embodiment came the erosion of mediating political structures and the direct intrusion of private desires into democratic publics.

The relation Stowe poses between black bodies and white interests—part exploitation, part contamination, part conflation—echoes rhetoric from the sectionalist conflict that was at its highest pitch as she wrote *Dred*. Northern politicians had long ago conflated the growing number and distribution of slaves with the expanding influence of Southern interests that threatened the common good, the national union, and the democratic process. Even as early as the Federal Convention, black bodies were treated as carriers of white Southern interests in the dispute that produced the three-fifths rule—a compromise by which blacks were reduced to a fragment of a human being in order to achieve balance between Northern and Southern congressional representation and cement national union. From the very origins of national U.S. political culture, black bodies stood in the national imaginary as the origin and substance, rather than result, of antidemocratic action.

This was never more true than in the period leading up to the Civil War when, in the statehood of Texas, the 1850 compromise, and the 1854 Kansas-Nebraska Bill, Northerners equated the growth of Southern political power with the flood of enslaved blacks into new states. In his famous speech against the last of these legislative acts, Abraham Lincoln demonstrates and exploits that association:

> Missouri adjoins these territories, by her entire western boundary, and slavery is already within every one of her western counties. I have even heard it said that there are more slaves, in proportion to whites, in the north western county of Missouri, than within any county of the State. Slavery pressed entirely up to the old western boundary of the State, and when, rather recently, a part of that boundary, at the north-west, was moved out a little farther west, slavery followed on quite up to the new line. Now, when the restriction is removed, what is to prevent it from going still further?[39]

The open-ended, seemingly unanswerable question that concludes this passage (and echoes throughout the speech) is a brilliant device. Supporters of the bill like Stephen Douglas had already, and repeatedly, provided their answer: popular sovereignty. They argued that the democratic constituencies of each state should be free to determine their own relationship to the slave economy. But Lincoln—whose own answer was federal regulation—poses that central question again and again, rhetorically mimicking the insistent pressure of interests that would erode those structures upon which Douglas relies. His repeated return to that nagging problem, as though Douglas's answer counts as no answer, dramatizes the insufficiency of popular political will against the creeping force of slaveholding power—power imaged in the form of enslaved bodies that have, in just four years, invaded all of Missouri's counties, outnumbered her white population, and begun to "press" at her northern boundaries.[40]

Like Lincoln's speech, *Dred* often seems less concerned with the actual enslavement of black people than with the impact of slavery as an institution on white legal and economic structures of democratic mediation. The novel's dramatic development obtains chiefly in the process by which slaveholding interests invade the political and juridical spheres, preventing rational public action toward the common good. At the heart of this progression is a court case involving one particularly imposing black body and its relation to the balance of white moral and economic interests. One of the central events of the novel, the case involves Milly, a beloved slave whose character Stowe bases on the life of Sojourner Truth. In yet another attempt by a slave to save the failing Gordon plantation, Milly has hired herself to a neighboring farmer who then injures her in a drunken rage. The result is a lawsuit on Milly's behalf argued by none other than Stowe's lawyer-slaveholder, Edward Clayton. Clayton initially wins the case with an impassioned speech on the white man's moral duty to his black dependents; but the decision is later overturned, and Clayton decides to leave his profession. Strikingly, his decision does not rest upon a categorical condemnation of slavery, nor does it lead to freeing his own slaves. Rather, Clayton specifies that slavery and, subsequently, the law have been corrupted by self-interested whites who make both institutions serve themselves rather than justice and morality.

Stowe develops this argument in ensuing chapters on antiabolitionist mob violence, titled "Lynch Law" and "Lynch Law Again." These chapters literalize the convergence of law with slavery interests. More, they suggest that all laws under a slavery government are extensions of mob rule: "Our house is the state, and our house is on fire by mob law," declares Clayton (491). Later, when neighboring slaveholders (including a judge) threaten to use the mob to stop him from educating slaves or receiving abolitionist newspapers, Clayton asks, "Is this hydra-headed monster, the mob, to be our governor?"

> "O, it is only upon this subject," said all three of the gentlemen, at once; "this subject is exceptional."
>
> "And do you think," said Clayton, "that
>
> '*—you can set the land on fire,*
>
> *To burn just so high, and no higher*'?
>
> You may depend upon it you will find that you cannot. The mob that you smile upon and encourage when it does work that suits you, will one day prove itself your master in a manner that you will not like." (533)

Clayton predicts that unmediated interests, rooted in the unfreedom of black bodies, will ultimately enslave whites as well. Describing the mob of slaveholders first as "governor" and then as "master" over other whites, he insinuates that slavery's unfreedom will transfer to the slaver's fellow citizens like a racial taint.[41] Clayton's cynical friend, Frank Russel, puts it baldly: "These men are our masters; they are yours; they are mine; they are masters of everybody in these United States. They can crack their whips over the head of any statesman or clergyman, from Maine to New Orleans, that disputes their will" (465).

Dred's eruption of privative energies resembles the emergence of what Hannah Arendt describes in her critique of modernity and mass culture as "the social"—a formation that occurs when the privative modes of embodiment, appetite, and brute passion escape their proper confinement in the household. With the growth of the social, both privacy and democratic publicity are lost; political discourse among distinct individual subjects is displaced by a mob of subjected bodies and unthinking sameness. Although developed in the wake of World War II, Arendt's theory sheds light on the horror that Stowe invests in the supposed black incapacity for self-possession and transcendence, and on her use of black bodies to symbolize unregulated, unreflecting mass interest. When Clayton describes slaveholding interests as growing like "a parasitic weed" that had "struck its roots through the whole growth of society, and was sucking thence its moisture and nourishment" (391), his metaphor evokes not just slavery but also the privative bodies it produces, unmistakably referring back to that central image of the Great Dismal Swamp and the band of fugitives identified with it.[42] For Stowe, as for Lincoln, the kudzulike invasion of unmediated white property interests aligns with "the awful...principle of growth" and the "fearful pressure" of the uncontained black body (496). She makes a radical move by aligning the terror of slave insurrection with marauding white capitalists. In doing so, however, she also imagines black embodiment as an overfertile ground that nurtures the uncontrolled growth of white economic interest. Her construction echoes the trope of black hypersexuality and hyperreproductivity in which the white rapist's violent lack of self-government was displaced onto black women's bodies. Here the theft of black self-right is similarly displaced. The two figures converge, of course, in that rape was a deliberate tactic for increasing slave property, while the myth of black hyperreproductivity drew blame for the problem of surplus embodiment. Here, then, is a version of the familiar idea that slavery corrupted the enslavers. Certainly Stowe identifies absolute power as one agent of that corruption, as Clayton's court case demonstrates. But she also locates corruption and contamination in the black body and consequently makes it the locus of her solution.

As with all the crisis narratives discussed in this book, portrayals of racialized, dystopian privacy served specific needs. Most obviously, they pathologized black political desire and "proved" it unconvertible to democratic virtue. At once, they addressed a more encompassing problem of democratic and capitalist identification. For, through the figure of black privation, it was possible to represent the surplus bodies of liberal capitalism as both ontologically other—specifically, nonwhite—and resolvable. Displaced onto the African race, uncontainable embodiment became finite and manageable. For Southerners like Hentz, such management meant the dependence relations of slavery. For free-labor ideologue Stowe, the solution *should* have involved that training in self-right which Clayton proposes in her first chapter, by which blacks would "learn" to contain their own corporeality and restore the boundary between private and public-political modalities. But Stowe ultimately finds black self-possession unworkable in *Dred*. This is indicated in part by the references to black racial undevelopment that persist nearly to the novel's end—for instance, where Clayton, having been rescued from a lynch mob by Dred and his followers, lies observing the well-organized swamp community and reflects "with a sigh" (and no trace of authorial irony) on Dred's wasted potential: "How much might have been accomplished by a soul so ardent and a frame so energetic, had they been enlightened and guided" (510). More telling, perhaps, is that Dred, Harry, and every other candidate for black self-determination places himself or herself outside of the American polis. The swamp itself is a sign for this separation. It operates in the novel as a space beyond U.S. jurisdiction—not only as a topographical substitute for Africa, but also as what Karafilis identifies as a kind of Eden. Stowe also signals black externality in more official ways. Giving background on Dred's father, Denmark Vesey, the narrator laments that he naively set about "the hopeless project of imitating the example set by the American race, and achieving independence for the blacks" (204). Where Stowe attributes the "hopelessness" here is disturbingly ambiguous and, as Gregg Crane points out, her "reference to the 'example set by the American race' implies that natural right theory is a cultural artifact and a possession of the white race, not a set of universal truths."[43] This theory of democratic freedom as differential property is further developed with Vesey's "son." In a significant revision of a device borrowed from William Wells Brown's novel *Clotel*, Dred and his band read the Declaration of Independence aloud together. But where Brown's character identifies with that document's argument, Stowe's group read satirically to reaffirm their alienation from the U.S. political contract (451). All of these scenes clearly fault U.S. political ideology for its hypocrisy, but not—as in *Clotel* or Frederick Douglass's famous Fourth of July speech—with the aim of holding it to its word.[44]

Similarly to *Uncle Tom*, where Stowe notoriously kills or expatriates all freed blacks without broaching the idea of racial cosovereignty, *Dred* finds moral closure by removing black bodies from the U.S. political economy that so disastrously animates them with white self-interest. Clayton emigrates to Canada with his slaves and most of the fugitives (leaderless after Dred's abrupt death), where he realizes his dream of schooling them in property management: the closing pages of the novel offer a short catalog of black characters who have acquired and are working their own farms. Yet, Clayton's colony is not quite a biracial free labor system. One glaring discrepancy is that, in spite of the tacit emancipation that occurs with entering Canada, Clayton never explicitly frees his property. In fact, the novel ignores the legal significance of the national border: describing Clayton's new home, the narrator states, "To this place he removed his slaves" (543). Another complicating factor is that the Canadian colony stands on Clayton's land. Thus—with the exception of Harry, who is "rapidly acquiring property and consideration in the new community"—the emigrated blacks continue to stand in ambiguous relation to ownership, including ownership in themselves. Clayton's colony functions as a quasi-dependence/obligation system that uncannily anticipates the postbellum black codes, whereby black bodies would be neutralized by the pseudo-contract relations of racial reconstruction.

And yet, in one regard Stowe does envision the Canadian colony as fundamentally distinct from the U.S. political economy that is polluted, South and North, by slavery. Through Clayton's project she pictures an economy based upon investments of moral interests and poses it as a corrective to the one that serves capitalist material interests. Only through this substitution is it possible to realize Clayton's life ambition as set out in that key introductory scene:

> There isn't a sublimer power on earth than God has given to us masters.... A plantation such as a plantation might be would be a "light to lighten the gentiles." ... The raising of cotton is to be the least of the thing. I regard my plantation as a sphere for raising *men and women*, and demonstrating the capabilities of a race. (23–24)

With the second diaspora of blacks to Canada, Clayton has his "plantation such as a plantation might be" at last. There he can occupy a new kind of possessive relation to his slaves. Unlike material possession, moral possession creates a safe container for black physicality: for instance, it redirects the energy of an enormous slave called Hannibal, who now "instead of slaying men, is great in felling trees and clearing forests" (544).

Most significant, the Canadian plantation allows whites to coexist with blacks without being infected by their potent privation. Instead of contaminating Clayton with uncontrolled, unpossessed embodiment, moral propriety frees him of materiality altogether. It effects, in Clayton's own term, white sublimation, converting him to a higher ethereal state. This outcome is predicted earlier when Clayton's friend Russel responds to the sublime plantation scheme by asking how it will support itself—"Are you going to live for them, or they for you?"—and Clayton replies, "The strong ought to live for the weak—the cultivated for the ignorant" (25). This principle is, as Russel points out, "cursedly expensive to keep" and untenable within a U.S. political economy driven by the necessity of individual "success." Russel's observation forecasts the delay of Clayton's project and names the novel's central problematic—how the body exceeds the control of moral self-government. But Clayton's next response—that moral paternalism is just as much "a *necessary* of life" as food and shelter—predicts Stowe's conclusion, where moral exigency will simply trump material exigency. In Canada, Clayton's sublimity is demonstrated when "he buil[ds] for himself a beautiful residence, where he and his sister live happily together, finding their enjoyment in the improvement of those by whom they are surrounded" (543). There is a strangely loud silence on how Clayton "built for himself" that home. The line appears amid accounts of the industry of Clayton's "slaves" and "tenants"—what bodies did his building, and support that happy life? For Stowe, Canada seems to represent a kind of zero-gravity zone. There are no laws to either enslave or, apparently, emancipate slaves; their relation to Clayton is mediated only by moral paternalism. More fundamentally, there is no pull of material necessity to constrain Clayton or make him susceptible to immoral interests. Without his own body, he can live morally with—and free from—black ones. In this sense, Stowe suggests that Clayton's plan to demonstrate "the capabilities of a race" applies more pressingly to whites than to blacks.[45]

In this point, *Dred*'s ideal moral possession differs importantly from the proprietary relations that many critics find encoded in the cross-racial dynamics of antislavery sympathy. In their respective theories of "sentimental possession," both Gillian Brown and Lori Merish emphasize that this construct corrects and suppresses its alliance with the corrupting influence of capitalist possession by thematizing resistance to alienation. Sentimental property is not a commodity; it does not circulate and become subject to the chaotic and proliferating meanings of market value. Moral possession in *Dred* works toward similar principles in that Clayton places moral welfare above material welfare and values the human potential of blacks over their potential as economic producers. But the commodification and circulation of those developing black subjects predicate such efforts. In the passage quoted above, Clayton imagines his dream plantation as a place for raising not just cotton but also the byproduct of "*men and women*" who will illustrate his success (24). Indeed, as this example suggests, while the moral commodity circulates apart from its material counterpart, it does so both in imitation of and in close proximity to—even symbiotic relationship with—capitalist market relations: "What a lot of ivory," remarks Russel when Clayton's well-cultivated slaves have assembled for inspection (326).

Clayton's originary vision also indicates the purpose of this circulation where he cites the founding text of American exceptionalism in hopes that his plantation will become a righteous example, or "a 'light to lighten the gentiles'" (23). In her preface, Stowe prefigures this logic:

> The issues presented by the great conflict between liberty and slavery do not grow less important from year to year. On the contrary, their interest increases with every step in the development of the national career. Never has there been a crisis in the history of this nation so momentous as the present. If ever a nation was raised up by Divine Providence, and led forth upon a conspicuous stage, as if for the express purpose of solving a great moral problem in the sight of all mankind, it is this nation. (3)

Again, this is curiously not a call for abolition, but a call for a new investment and economy of "interest." In advance, it frames Clayton's plantation upon a hill as the place where black "tenants" provide the hill or "conspicuous stage" upon which moral governance can take root and produce not a swamp, but a vineyard.[46] With this, alarming fecundity is turned to a new productive purpose in which racial difference is preserved and racial potential developed on both sides. Blacks still figure as raw material from which goods are produced for white use—sublimity, moral self-governance, and political virtue.[47] In Canada, this moral economy operates "conspicuously" in view of the as yet unreformable U.S. economy—simultaneously protected and made possible by the national border, legible as a kind of moral extensionalism that, as though attempting to balance the Kansas-Nebraska Bill, annexes a bit of Canadian territory. Stowe's plantation on a hill simultaneously rejects, corrects, and extends U.S. polity, just as Winthrop's city does for English Protestantism.[48]

DISCIPLINING THE "DAMN'D MOB"

There is a second way in which to view Clayton's Canadian plantation upon a hill, and that is within the context of Stowe's early attempts to reframe her own relation to black bodies as an antislavery author. For Stowe, writing *Dred* as a woman—and particularly as a sentimental authoress—constituted a privacy crisis all her own. For she risked enacting the very problem of uncontainment that the novel addresses. Thus, as she works out a new ethic of moral possession and white sublimity, Stowe also revises her own role. Rather than drawing readers into the utopian privacy of the domestic novel and cultivating cross-racial sympathy, she now defends the public/private divide and promotes cross-racial disidentification. It is in this context that Sojourner Truth emerges as a vital presence in *Dred*, for Stowe uses Milly both to demonstrate and to stand in for her newly defined authorial function. Milly signals the beginning of Stowe's identification with and against Truth as a strategy for managing her own relation to the potentially disruptive public embodiment of female authorship.

Anti-Tom critics vilified Stowe's first novel as a destructive invasion of U.S. public culture. For Southerners, the book not only incited "the bursting out of a slave insurrection"; it was an insurrectionary outburst in itself, a "festering...malignant virus," "written in that florid and inflammable style which suits the minds of...fanatics."[49] When favorable critics cited the book's unprecedented sales as evidence of its value, Stowe's opponents interpreted the same numbers as proof of irrational proliferation comparable to "the tongues of Babel," and characterized it as a kind of promiscuity.[50] That this effect was seen to implicate Stowe's own person is spelled out in the letter of one "Southern lady" to her sister in the North, "reprinted" in a Southern newspaper. Writes the lady, "I do not like this Harriet, for she has proved herself false to her womanly mission—a stirrer up of strife, rather than a 'peace maker,' deficient in the delicacy and purity of a woman, inasmuch as she has painted from her own libidinous imagination scenes which no modest woman could conceive of."[51] The remarks attack not the book but the author and, more specifically, her body that wantonly fails to stay within bounds. "The woman has unsexed herself," asserts the writer. Another finds it "difficult to conceive of how a woman could...so completely unfrock herself" and condemns the North for producing "such monstrosities, such men-women, such moral hermaphrodites" as Stowe.[52] As Diane Roberts and Elizabeth Young have shown, in anti-Tom criticism Stowe's body becomes frighteningly fluid—across reviews it morphs from woman to man to monster to devil.[53] If normative white womanhood obtained in utter cancellation of the body and its desires, Stowe's display of "libidinous"—or political—rage risked cancellation of womanhood itself.

In what might be taken as a response to these indictments, Stowe uses *Dred* to conduct her own critique of both sentimental writing and sympathy. To be sure, *Dred* performs many sentimental verifications of character and knowledge. Nina and Edward, for example, prove themselves worthy of each other by grieving Sue's tragic death (110). But the novel repeatedly questions the wider efficacy of sentimental communication. *Uncle Tom* models and instantiates a sentimental economy in which the circulation of black bodies propagates the sameness of embodied moral knowledge, the unifying ability to "feel right," as an antidote to divisive political abstraction. Senator Bird acts in sympathy with Eliza, moved by the spectacle of her injured body—"the magic of the real presence of distress—the imploring human eye, the frail, trembling human hand" (*Uncle Tom* 86). Yet this strategy fails to reform the political sphere and only temporarily displaces its function—the senator's vote, after all, has already been cast in support of the Fugitive Slave Law. By the time Stowe gets to *Dred*, she is ready to examine the limits of sympathy in the public-political sphere. Thus, when Clayton plans to exhort a group of clergy on the abuses of slavery, his father warns, "They will have great patience with you—they will even have sympathy with you—so long as you confine yourself merely to the expression of feeling; but the moment your efforts produce the slightest movement in the community, then, my son, you will see human nature in a new aspect" (395). In terms of political consequences, Stowe suggests, the power of sympathy is superficial and ephemeral.[54] More, the sentimental author who deploys it is not to be trusted. In the love plot between Nina Gordon and Edward Clayton, for instance, Stowe discredits an early suitor who is of "your sentimental sort—writes the most romantic notes on pink paper, and all that sort of thing" (9) by contrasting him to Edward, whose letters are "so manly and sincere...so removed either from adulation or sentimentalism" (41). It is not uncommon, of course, for sentimental novels to criticize sentimentality and oppose it to authentic sentiment. But something more specific occurs with this epistolary rivalry. Edward's courting is almost exclusively textual to allow Nina space for a reasoned decision. He also invites her to write back: "Do it in the freest way....You shall say what you please, do what you please, write when you please, and not write when you please, and have as many or as few letters as you like. There can be no true love without liberty" (131). In this passage, Stowe goes beyond the standard defenses of sentimental writers against charges of mawkishness; she aligns sentimentalism with antidemocratic coercion and disembodied text with autonomy, consent, and freedom.[55] Here, the ideal love letter functions as political contract rather than embodied heart to heart. Stowe further associates sentimental authorship with coercion by linking it with slavery. In a particularly interesting moment of metanarrative, Nina reports that she has "made a sentimental story" to convince an old Frenchwoman to sell her a slave named Lisette: " 'French people always have a taste for the sentimental. The old thing was really quite affected—wiped her little black eyes, pulled her hooked nose as a tribute to my eloquence...and gave me a little lecture on the tender passion, which I am going to lay up for future use'" (151). Here Nina's sentimental tactics appear cynical, manipulative—even plagiarizing. They act coercively upon the Frenchwoman's body to produce a sympathetic response that Nina then satirizes. At once, Nina's tale acts coercively upon Lisette's body, literally taking it into possession. Nina's motives are pure: she makes the purchase to protect Lisette from becoming Tom's concubine. But the scene suggests that Stowe herself had recognized a problem that critics have since identified in her first novel: a disturbing parallel between sympathetic and legal possession of human beings. The Frenchwoman's body circulates as an object of derision for Nina's audience even as Lisette's body circulates within the slave economy—a startling acknowledgment of sentimental commodification and power relations. Completing the link between sympathy and slavery is the fact that, when Nina later dies, Lisette becomes Tom's slave by inheritance. The sentimental strategy is finally not just ineffectual against, or similar to, the system it opposes: when Nina's sentimental possession becomes Tom's capitalist property, we understand that the two economies are fully interdependent.

Stowe saves her strongest condemnation, however, for the excesses of sentimentality, where affective narrative produces swamplike results within the democratic public sphere. This is illustrated when Edward wins his case in favor of Milly's right to legal protection against an abusive master, only to have his father overturn the verdict. Judge Clayton reasons that regardless of the moral view of the situation—which he admits to sharing—the law simply cannot tolerate a verdict on behalf of a slave's human rights. Stowe bases this entire sequence of events upon a well-known historical case, with Judge Clayton's speech closely following that delivered in 1829 by Judge Thomas Ruffin of the North Carolina Supreme Court. "The power of the master must be absolute," Ruffin had explained, "to render the submission of the slave perfect."[56] Many critics regard Ruffin's separation of moral and legal judgment as one of *Dred*'s chief objects of critique, and interpret Judge Clayton's defense of amoral law as a demonstration of corrupt logic. And yet Stowe relays his argument without irony or censure and echoes its logic elsewhere in the novel.[57] Ultimately, Stowe honors the position taken by Judges Clayton and Ruffin, however reluctantly, because she also understands moral and juridical interests to be incommensurable at that juncture of U.S. political development—hence the separatist arrangement of Canada.

Specifically, Stowe sees an evil greater than slavery in an invasion of the political-legal spheres by privatized modes of action. Like Arendt, she seems to identify a quality in embodied knowledges like desire, sympathy, or pain that prevents them from entering political discourse without losing authenticity and acquiring false power.[58] When Judge Clayton says,

"I don't pretend to justify it. But Edward has great power of exciting the feelings, and under the influence of his eloquence ... humanity [may] triumph at the expense of law" (301), it is impossible not to hear an ironic resignification of Ruffin's decision—surely humanity *should* triumph over law? And yet Stowe also affirms Ruffin's point and shares his recognition of a tragic impasse. Important here is that Judge Clayton does not prioritize law over "humanity" or morality, but only insists they are incompatible standards. More, he likens their combined impact to that of a manipulative sentimental narrative: Edward's "eloquence" that has "great power of exciting feelings." Like Nina's appeal to the Frenchwoman, Edward's victory is morally correct. But its reversal does not vilify his father or the law; it articulates a disjunction that Stowe likewise values—or at least adheres to in an effort to negotiate what critic Gregg Crane has termed "the unresolved tension between expiatory sympathy and revolutionary wrath" in her vision of moral reform and law.[59] Edward's power to excite feelings contra legal principle resonates too closely with the actions of Tom Gordon, who raises lynch mobs through exhortation and free liquor, and with the methods of Dred himself, whose power to stimulate affect nearly produces a massacre. Scholars often remark on Stowe's new militancy in *Dred*, measuring it in the vast difference between Uncle Tom and Dred. Yet the more significant change may well be Stowe's new insistence upon a distinction between private and public domains of knowledge and action—a distinction that permits Dred's radical desires and compelling arguments by keeping them utterly segregated from contact with the white body politic—and her concomitant anxiety about the sentimental publication of bodies. If black property overpowers white moral self-government, the circulation of black bodies in affective narration seems to provoke a "fanatical" response that similarly overwhelms moral reason and cannot be tolerated, even if it produces "moral" results like Milly's victory—or black self-right.

What, then, is a sentimental authoress to do? Stowe's solution is to mark a sharp distinction between her own literary productions and the acts of narration faulted in *Dred* for blending private and public modalities. Theorizing her own authorship, Stowe describes a process of transforming slavery into an aesthetic object far removed from the reader's world.[60] She initiates this strategic remodeling in her preface:

> The writer of this book has chosen, once more, a subject from the scenes and incidents of the slaveholding states.
>
> The reason for such a choice is two-fold. First, in a merely artistic point of view, there is no ground, ancient or modern, whose vivid lights, gloomy shadows, and grotesque groupings, afford to

> the novelist so wide a scope for the exercise of his powers . . . that evolve every possible combination of romance.
>
> Hence, if the writer's only object had been the production of a work of art, she would have felt justified in not turning aside from that mine whose inexhaustible stores have but begun to be developed.
>
> But this object, however legitimate, was not the only nor the highest one. It is the moral bearings of the subject involved which have had the chief influence in its selection. (3)

In this self-conscious defense Stowe responds to those who characterized her writing as wanton, promiscuous, and dangerously exciting to readers, and to the many others who accused her of exhibiting enslaved bodies for monetary gain.[61] She carefully deflects these criticisms by claiming masculinized artistic license and aesthetic motivation that remove her female embodiment from the scene of literary production *and* remove the literary production from real-world consequences. More important, Stowe theorizes her writing as an economy of conversion. Her black characters will not rise unaltered from life in the style that invites sympathetic immediacy. They are to be "mined" and "developed" to "produce" a work of art. With phrases like "an exercise of his powers" and verbs like "evolve," Stowe emphasizes her own artistic intervention between enslaved subjects and the "production" offered to readers.

At the end of the passage, Stowe promises that this authorial industry will manufacture a commodity with "moral bearings." If this sounds like Clayton's sublime colony, it should; Stowe clearly signals the parallel. This passage directly precedes the one quoted earlier in which she predicts that the increasing moral "interest" of slavery will make the nation a "conspicuous stage" on which to "solv[e] the great moral problem in the sight of all mankind" (3); and this call for an exceptionalist publication of democratic justice and freedom overtly forecasts Clayton's plantation upon a hill. Thus, Stowe's discussion of authorship inaugurates a series of parallel normative models for moral racial relations: slavery is first the "ground"—or "mine"—that produces moral art, then the holy city of moral American government (3–4); the model then reappears with Clayton's plan for making slavery the medium of white sublimity, and again with the plan's realization in Canada. Stowe poses literature—and specifically this novel—as a space that, like the Canadian plantation, can function apart from, but supplementarily to, the U.S. political economy. Clayton's colony provides an image of what the novel itself achieves. Both insulate the uncontainable, incommensurable black body from U.S. capitalism and establish it as a disjunct but fertile ground—an "inexhaustible store"—for moral production (3).

Stowe's authorial self-refashioning anticipates a shift that Naomi Sofer finds occurring in her later novels, where Stowe leaves behind the feminized project of reform and moral didacticism and aligns herself with the elite, antiutilitarian, and masculinized pursuit of artistic achievement. Rather than providing moral lessons in service to social reform, the new model offers aesthetic beauty as a kind of moral meaning unto itself and a focus of cultural nationalism. This new aesthetic defines itself against material, embodied, contexts—as Sofer notes, James Russell Lowell describes the desired shift as "the struggle to transform the U.S. from a nation of 'toil' to a nation of 'art.'"[62] In *Dred*, Stowe is not yet willing entirely to abandon moral productivity, as her metaphor of the "mine" suggests. But she begins to separate literary productivity from materiality, imagining that the novel, like the zero-gravity zone of Canada, provides a "demonstration" of moral property in which readers may invest moral interests and gain increased white racial capacity for incorporeal moral self-government.[63]

As Robert Levine reminds us, Stowe made an effort with *Dred* to remedy the omission of black perspectives that in *Uncle Tom* had provoked criticism from many abolitionists. Her second novel draws deeply from personal acquaintance with and writings by Truth, Douglass, Martin Delany, William Wells Brown, William Nell, and others—including, even, insurrectionists Denmark Vesey and Nat Turner, who receive extraordinarily approbatory treatment. Levine rightly objects to the assumption that white nineteenth-century writers must inevitably appropriate black narratives to racist ends, in part for the way this assumption poses blacks as helpless victims. Levine's argument usefully underscores not only the greater range and complexity of black characters in *Dred* but also the novel's astute analyses of racial relations—including white paternalism—that complicate the structures of racialist moral closure I have traced above.[64] And yet, when Stowe imports the examples and words of recognizably "real" African Americans, these materials are not exempt from her authorial intervention. Just as Dred's radicalism is isolated in the swamp, black narratives are framed in ways that deflect their impact upon readers. It is significant, for instance, that Dred's apocalyptic sermonizing repeatedly proves incomprehensible to white listeners. Stowe clearly means to include black perspectives when she gathers her insurrectionists in the swamp to recite, in turn, brief accounts of enslavement. But their autobiographies are directed to each other as rites of alliance, functioning not as antislavery arguments but as pledges of black alienation from white America (456–57).[65] Also,

Stowe repeatedly compares black characters to visual and literary art in a way that discourages a too-intimate, too-identified reading. A striking example here concerns Milly, who, while telling Nina the story of her son's murder by a white overseer, becomes overwrought in the "violence of her emotion." As Nina "shudders" in fear, the narrator swiftly intervenes to describe Milly as "a black marble Nemesis in a trance of wrath" (181). As though restrained by this prophylactic aestheticization, Milly instantly quiets and apologizes to Nina.

In Stowe's ambivalent use of black life narrative, Sojourner Truth stands out as an especially prominent case. Unmistakably, Stowe recognized and admired the power of Truth's physical presence and oratory. Just as unmistakably, however, she rewrites these materials to accommodate them to her own racialist perspective, to the limited possibilities of resolution recognizable from this perspective, and to the project of managing her own public persona. Though it is important to heed Levine's question—"Did Stowe's encounters with African-American writings and people during the 1850s serve the ends of knowledge or appropriation?"—it also behooves us to resist the false binary he constructs: Does knowledge ever exclude some aspect of appropriation?[66] When Stowe wrote *Dred*, Truth was already famous for her dramatic and quirky style on the religious and reformist lecture circuit, and for preferring, as Stowe would point out in "The Libyan Sibyl," to use her own life as her basic text (119). She was also known for the printed account of this story, the *Narrative of Sojourner Truth*, which she had produced in collaboration with Olive Gilbert and sold energetically at every venue. Writing Milly, Stowe borrows that trait of powerful, autobiographical oratory. She also draws on the *Narrative* itself to reproduce Gilbert's conflation of blackness with prepolitical unfreedom.

Lifting pieces of Truth's physical description, life history, and dialogue directly from the *Narrative*, Stowe makes Milly a figure for black privation and its containment. Introducing the character, she focuses on Milly's body and renders it fantastically other, a spectacle and commodity cataloged right down to its "splendid and perfect teeth" and compared repeatedly to palm trees and other African signifiers:

> She was a fine specimen of one of those warlike and splendid races.... Placed among the gorgeous surroundings of African landscape and scenery, it might be doubted whether any one's taste could have desired, as a completion to her appearance, to have blanched the glossy skin whose depth of coloring harmonizes so well with the intense and fiery glories of a tropical landscape. (50)

Describing Milly first in ethnographic terms as a "specimen" of Africa, Stowe then shifts to create a scene that is part *tableau vivant*, part auction block, part repatriation argument by "placing" Milly's body against its proper African setting. The image is explicitly offered as an object of consumption to satisfy viewers' "tastes" rather than elicit their sympathy (and metadiscursively signals Stowe's role as artist—later Milly will be described as made of "black velvet"; 49). The portrait also calls us to recognize that this body belongs outside of U.S. contexts. Indeed, the very first mention of Milly introduces her as "a character so marked that we cannot refrain from giving her a separate place in our picture of her surroundings," and this logic persists (49). "Why," observes her owner Nina Gordon, "I really think, if Milly had been educated as we are, she would have made a most splendid woman—been a perfect Candace queen of Ethiopia" (15). In one gesture, Stowe creates Milly's "splendid" presence and displaces it utterly from U.S. geography, culture, and politics.

This appropriation of Truth for a narrative of surplus and containment, insurrection and mastery almost certainly reflects a fearful and admiring response to that woman's actual successes for herself and for black civil rights and advancement. Truth was highly self-assertive—particularly, as Accomando has shown, in the area of law. She pursued and won three lawsuits against white defendants—one in 1827 to prevent the unlawful sale of her son, another in 1835 to dispute libelous claims, yet another in 1865 to prosecute a white trolley driver for assaulting her person and barring her access to public space. She bought two houses on the sales of her autobiographical texts and supported several children and grandchildren. After the war, Truth developed numerous plans for moving freedpeople out of economic dependency in the South, working with the Freedman's Bureau to establish farming jobs in upstate New York and, later, an all-black settlement in Kansas. These accomplishments enter Stowe's narrative in paradoxical ways. Some survive in the character of the black leader, Dred. But with Milly, Stowe inverts the self-possessive, self-assertive facts of Truth's life to create a portrait of elaborately surrendered self-right. Stowe appropriates Truth's litigious history and rewrites it to cleanse Milly of political or legal agency.[67] Where Truth successfully sued a powerful white woman for selling her son out of New York State, Milly forgives an old mistress for selling *nine* of her own and then tells the story to others as a religious lesson in self-denial.[68] In Gilbert's account, Truth confronts her opponent, asserting "in tones of deep determination—'*I'll have my child again*'" (31). Milly, however, admonishes her husband, "This child isn't ours" (176). As we have seen, Stowe does take one of Milly's grievances to court in the case against an abusive white employer; but she nearly erases Milly from the event, making it Clayton who brings suit and even overturning his victory. This is the incident that teaches Clayton to hate the law (for protecting white self-interest in blacks instead of promoting white paternalism toward them), but it teaches us Milly's perfect separation from self-possessive, rights-bearing citizenship.

Key here is that Milly repeatedly chooses to offer up her rights and body to serve her white family: she has been hired out to the abusive man by her own initiative and against Nina's objections—an act of Christian surrender that clearly indicates her lineage with Uncle Tom. Even when deciding to escape along with the rest, Milly does it for her grandson, not herself. The narrator intones:

> As far as her own rights were concerned, she would have made a willing surrender of them, remaining patiently in the condition wherein she was called, and bearing injustice and oppression as a means of spiritual improvement. . . . Every individual has an undoubted right, if he chooses, thus to resign the rights and privileges of his earthly birthright. (521)

In her practice of self-disenfranchisement, Milly resembles what Chris Castiglia describes as the subject of "sympathetic discipline"—the ex-slave narrator who must perform self-mastery by tailoring his story, "conceal[ing] extremes or anomalies, or translat[ing] them into scenarios with which the abolitionist audience will be familiar" so as to present a palatable object for sympathetic consumption.[69] In Milly's case, it is not affective but juridical and economic character that gets tailored: she performs voluntary privation—making herself a prepolitical reservoir of physical and spiritual energy to fuel a white moral economy. Like the black narrator in Castiglia's analysis, Milly demonstrates self-mastery within a scheme of "differential power" that "naturalizes social hierarchy without necessitating government involvement" (37).

In her performance of self-discipline that disavows self-right, Milly plays out within her own person the drama of mastering black embodiment. But Milly also externalizes that drama, repeatedly extending her ethic of self-disenfranchisement to other bodies: "Dere's no use talking about *rights*, honey," says Milly to her fellow slave, Harry. "We must all do jest what we *ken*. Don't make much odds whether our rights is one way or t'other" (141). Here Milly stands in for Stowe's authorial function, especially in that her instrument of conversion—like Truth's—is her own story. Milly's life narrative appears in *Dred* three times, once related by the narrator, twice by Milly. She tells the story of her children to Nina as a lesson on self-denial. She tells it again to Dred's insurrectionists, stopping them on the brink of a murderous rampage (and counteracting their autobiographical compact). Here, the relationship between Dred and Milly is critical. Their shared lineage from Truth is evident in their similar physical descriptions and Africanization, but they divide Truth's combination of self-denial and self-advocacy between them—Milly surrenders self-right while he, within the safe margins of the swamp, demands it. At crucial points they compete through performative speech to recruit other blacks to their ways of thinking. The culminating instance occurs when Dred has assembled the revolutionary mob with his passionate exhortation, a "wild jargon of hebraistic phrases, names, and allusions" (509). As Dred preaches destruction and revolt, Milly approaches through the swamp, singing a hymn. The fugitives stop hearing Dred and actually begin reciting along with her. Milly's alter ego also recognizes her power: "When Dred saw her, he gave a kind of groan, and said, putting his hand out before his face: 'woman, thy prayers withstand me!' " (461). Milly promptly delivers a thumbnail version of her life story and the process is complete: "A dead silence followed this appeal. The key-note of another harmony had been struck" (462). The event—drawn from both the Truth-Douglass confrontation and an episode in the *Narrative* where Truth calms a riotous revival meeting by singing hymns—indicates that Truth's performative voice and life story have caught Stowe's imagination. In a manner, Milly's presence in the novel reduces to that voice and story: for all her resemblance to Uncle Tom, Milly differs in that where he converts by self-example, she converts by self-narrative. Milly *is* Stowe's new ethic of benign literary production that, in direct opposition to narratives that "incite" or "enflame," subdues listeners and averts revolution. Her storytelling acts upon bodies in a manner antithetical to Nina's sentimental influence: where Nina's story delivers Lisette into Tom's slavery plantation and fuels white property interest, Milly's story delivers the insurrectionists into Clayton's plantation of sublime white morality.

Stowe renovates the novel to insulate black privation *from* while also supplying it *to* the white U.S. political economy, converting it into a kind of meaning-commodity that she and Clayton circulate before white audiences. Where sentimental circulation collapses publicity into privacy, *Dred* becomes a space for displaying privation as remote and disjunct. This new relation differs from sympathy—even where sympathetic relations feature theatrical spectacularity and install power difference—in that it requires a boundary between private and public modalities. The literary display of privation produces not sympathy but sublimity. Ultimately, what Milly's presence stands for and engenders is an economy with no surplus—in classic literary closure all bodies are accounted for, bounded, and poised for productivity. It seems crucial here, in light of the proslavery attacks on free labor, that Milly does not go to Canada with the rest. Instead, she stops off in New York City to spend the rest of her days training street orphans for domestic service.[70]

In *Dred* Stowe takes up the problem of privation to envision a paternalistic moral economy that can recommodify the dangerous surplus of enslaved black bodies to better serve the white democracy. At the same time, she uses it to negotiate her own surplus embodiment, and Sojourner Truth plays a key—and benevolent—role in both operations. As Stowe continues her struggle on both of these fronts in "The Libyan Sibyl," Truth figures even more centrally, but in a very different guise. In 1863, Stowe's Truth invades white culture and makes herself its focus. Instead of serving, submitting to, or symbolizing Stowe's authorial power, she challenges it. Instead of converting black embodiment to produce white sublimity and a moral public made free by its own paternalistic suspension of material interests, she imposes her embodied self upon white listeners and threatens to embody Stowe. In "The Libyan Sibyl," Stowe revises Truth yet again, in order to manage the changing aspect of surplus embodiment within the national political and literary economy.

SIBYLS AND QUEENS

With the end of chattel slavery, the weight of surplus embodiment upon the U.S. political economy grew heavier. As Stowe's proslavery critics had predicted, emancipation revealed more starkly than ever that free labor could not guarantee democratic liberty and equality. By 1863 homelessness and poverty were already rampant among the white working class, and labor and relief organizations were lobbying hard for reforms. The dependence relations of Old World feudalism, it was argued, prevailed again under New World industrialism. Rather than working to alleviate these conditions, legislatures set about criminalizing them with the first antivagrancy and antibegging laws. Literally outlawing indigence, the new codes interpreted poverty as a choice and so upheld imaginary oppositions between free labor and dependence, consent and coercion. Even charity organizations that tried to publicize the desperate conditions of urban poverty also touted the "natural law" of the labor contract in the very same reports.[71] On both sides, the situation was vividly interpreted as a problem of burdensome and proliferating bodies. Prolabor rhetoric like the poem that read, "My useless arms have failed to win/ A crust, a place to stay./ Earth has no work; no room for me!" offered the abject body of the unemployed as an object for sympathy.[72] Yet this tactic surely backfired in at least some contexts, for it confirmed and echoed antivagrancy invective against the "proverbial plague" of unwashed urban homeless that "seemed to spread everywhere."[73]

Emancipation fed into the growing mood of intolerance by drastically increasing the numbers of potential dependents and necessitating a clearer distinction between unfreedom and freedom. That is, after 1863 it became more urgent than ever to identify a condition of unfreedom that was categorically separate from that visited upon whites. The public discourse on freedpeople soon answered that need. Since the beginning of the war, the large gatherings of contrabands at military camps and border cities had become objects of both sympathy and hostility in the public eye. With emancipation, the problem of surplus bodies reached full pitch—both geographically, as state after state refused asylum to dislocated blacks, and economically, as white labor organizations throughout the North refused to integrate. As Saidiya Hartman has shown, the freedman became an icon of "burdened individuality"—an image like Gilbert's account of Truth's "freed" parents, "emphasiz[ing] hardship, travails, and a burdened and encumbered existence."[74] The absence of material support from the federal government combined with Southern black codes made it extremely difficult for freedpeople to develop economic independence. For many whites, this confirmed the African's racial incapacity for free self-possession and was used, Hartman suggests, "to engender resentment toward and justify the punishment of those who fell below 'the threshold of responsibility' or failed to achieve the requisite degree of self-control."[75] Like proslavery Southerners from before the war, Northern whites now criticized each other for extending sympathy and benevolence to freedpeople when so many whites were in need. Here again, as Susan M. Ryan shows in an analysis of reconstruction lithographs, the image of the obtrusive black body that crowds out a "far thinner white counterpart" stood in for the problem of limited resources.[76] In this way the failures of racial reconstruction centered blacks as emblems of unsustainable and, as Hartman puts it, "blameworthy" freedom.

Stowe herself would later recall the fearsome aspect of "this emancipated mass" by comparing its effect to the "untold horrors" of the French Revolution (613, 605).[77] She actually intends the comparison as flattery: writing in 1879 about freedpeople's education and industry, she praises the appetite for learning and free labor agency that set blacks above "all other liberated masses" in history and averted a disaster like the one in France. Nevertheless, to make this point she must reprise the fearful expectations from fifteen years earlier, repeatedly conjuring the old specter of unleashed terror. Stowe describes the nation's abrupt shift to a biracial body politic as "shooting Niagara"—a metaphor suggesting absolute surrender to some great, destructive, undifferentiated torrent: "Our ship of state," writes Stowe, "has been through those mighty rapids and plunged down that awful gulf" (605). If in 1879 Stowe looks back on this passage with relief and celebration, in 1863 she imagines herself and her nation poised at the very top of Niagara Falls and this informs her new portrayal of Truth.

As Stowe returns to the problem of surplus black bodies, she again makes it a place for managing her own public embodiment, which had become more cumbersome than ever. During the postbellum era, U.S. women fought for mastery over their bodies: suffragists demanded the disembodied voice of the vote; activists for women's property and wage reform rejected the dependence relations of coverture and the antebellum construct of inviolable, unpossessable corporeality.[78] Predictably, opponents represented both movements as modes of transgressive and promiscuous embodiment. More immediately of concern to Stowe were developments within postbellum print culture toward a new class- and gender-inflected hierarchy of genres and markets. Publishers and journals had begun cultivating distinct readerships corresponding to new distinctions in literary style and value. At the top of this hierarchy would emerge the group of mostly male writers who published in *The Atlantic*. Somewhere below this pinnacle stood the popular writers, primarily women, of sentimental and sensational genres. In 1863, however, this hierarchy was still forming and Stowe's position within it was particularly indeterminate.[79] *Uncle Tom's Cabin* had placed her, however tenuously, among the literary luminaries of her day, and admitted her to an international cultural elite that included, for example, William Wetmore Story. Just a month before publishing "The Libyan Sibyl," Stowe had received a standing ovation at an emancipation celebration. Yet she had also gone many years without a notable literary success and was feeling the strain in both financial and public status. It is suggestive that Stowe writes her essay about Truth at this moment—a decade after the meeting it describes, and just months following formal emancipation, as though using the opportunity to reinvigorate and retool her former authority.

In "The Libyan Sibyl," however, it is Cleopatra who most directly represents the problematic—both political and literary—of Stowe's female embodiment. Displayed alongside the sibyl at the 1862 London Exposition, the statue had caused an international stir. This was due in part to Nathaniel Hawthorne, who had described it in his 1859 novel, *The Marble Faun*.[80] But Cleopatra was already a resonant and widely circulated symbol in nineteenth-century U.S. culture. Nearly always depicted in a state of despair or on the verge of her famous suicide by asp, the Egyptian queen provided an object lesson on the dangers of female sensuality, ambition, and self-display. This tradition extends back to the Roman emperor Augustus who, having captured the queen and spurned her sexual advances, promised to parade her in the streets of Rome as his slave. When Cleopatra escaped this fate by killing herself, Augustus had her likeness cast in stone and exhibited that instead. Thus, at the very foundation of Augustan rule (which he dated from Cleopatra's capture) was the display of a female body encoded with mismanaged passion, shamed sexuality, corrupting self-interest, and their always already defeat.[81] The new Rome of American democracy would follow suit in its own political iconography. Some antisuffragists, for instance, used Cleopatra to symbolize the illegitimacy of feminine governance, her lush embodiment illustrating the irrationality and selfishness of heterodox womanhood, her catastrophic fate proving her incompatibility with public-political life.[82] The nineteenth-century Cleo is also often nonwhite—critics referred to the "African" features of Story's version, and Hawthorne describes her as both "Egyptian" and "Nubian"—exemplifying the intersecting logics of race and gender that structure the U.S. figure of surplus embodiment (98).

Capturing Cleopatra at the moment between rejection and suicide, Story faithfully reinscribes the narrative of defeated female political desire—as does Hawthorne, who wrote her into his novel after a series of visits to the artist's Rome studio. Hawthorne goes a step beyond Story, however, by also linking Cleopatra to a narrative of gendered artistic triumph and failure. His novel features the statue in a scene between its fictionalized creator, Kenyon, and a female painter, Miriam, who has come to visit the sculptor's studio: " 'I will not offer you my hand,' said he;—'it is grimy with Cleopatra's clay.' " Miriam responds, "I have come to try whether there is any calm and coolness among your marbles. My own art is too nervous, too passionate, too full of agitation" (91). In Kenyon, Hawthorne represents the possibility of pure, disembodied artistry. His sculptures appear as though "wrought with a word" and promise to "calm and cool" their audience. The idea of marble sculpture as an antidote to passion came to Hawthorne from the culture of Roman studios and galleries. As art historian Mary Hamer explains, "the marble itself was supposed to offer a guarantee of moral value. Discourses of purity, chastity, aloofness and white silence which circulated about white marble statues claimed for them an unspoken language of disinterest and truth."[83] To be sure, Hawthorne satirizes this ideal; in reference to the fact that sculptors modeled works in clay and hired workers to chisel marble copies, his narrator dryly remarks: "His creative power has wrought it with a word. In no other art, surely does genius find such effective instruments, and so happily relieve itself of the drudgery of actual performance" (90). Yet this irony in no way alters the gendered binary that informs Miriam's visit. She, inevitably, represents the reverse of Kenyon's disembodied powers. Like Cleopatra, whose sovereignty pollutes and is polluted by the "grime" of her female body, Miriam's artistry pollutes and is polluted by hers: her art as she describes it above is so embodied that it seems to suffer a nervous disorder; and later her paintings and beauty taint the purity of the virginal painter Hilda and drive an innocent man to murder. Also like Cleo, Miriam is ultimately humiliated and eliminated while Kenyon and his marbles pass on to success. In this way, Hawthorne maps a narrative of gendered artistic authority over the history of Cleopatra and Augustus. Two regimes, political and artistic, are founded in the display of a silenced, denigrated, ambiguously racialized, female body. By invoking Cleopatra in her own essay—and in the pages of the *Atlantic Monthly*—Stowe attempts to reappropriate that inaugural display of despised feminine privation. She places her queen in revised form at the center of a new moral democratic regime, and in the process resignifies her own white, feminine authorial identity. Both achievements follow from the pairing of her Cleopatra with the Libyan Sibyl. That is, they require posing herself in relation to a new version of Truth—one that recalls the "Niagara" of emancipated slaves and imagines stemming its flow.

In "The Libyan Sibyl," Stowe uses the conceit of invasion and domination to lend a comedic tone and emphasize Truth's awesome presence. Yet this conceit also resonates strongly with public images of invading, ontologically unfree freedpeople. Stowe begins, "Many years ago the few readers of radical Abolitionist papers must often have seen the singular name of Sojourner Truth, announced as a frequent speaker at Anti-Slavery meetings, and as travelling on a sort of self-appointed agency through the country" (116). Referring in her very first sentence to Truth's itinerant lifestyle and "self-appointed agency," Stowe names three of the most prevalent charges against freedpeople: their failure to seek stable employment, their excessive and random mobility, and their presumption of equality with whites.[84] She also lampoons Truth's pretensions as a public figure by minimalizing her audience and reputation and labeling these "radical." All of these implications are reinforced immediately as we see Truth arrive, uninvited, to confront Stowe as a peer. Interestingly, Stowe describes Truth as "perfectly self-possessed and at her ease" at this juncture—the only place the essay acknowledges emancipation, even obliquely. But she proceeds to subvert this compliment by observing an "unconscious superiority . . . in the manner in which [Truth] looked down on me" (117). Here is that comedic tone, but also a note of censure at the visitor's effrontery: Truth's next words are, "So this is *you*. . . . I jes' thought I'd like to come an' have a look at ye. You's heerd o' me, I reckon?" (117). Near her conclusion, Stowe again links Truth to fears concerning freedpeople by likening her to Rachel Felix, an actress famous for scenes from the French Revolution:

> It is said that Rachel was wont to chant the "Marseillaise" in a manner that made her seem, for the time, the very spirit and impersonation of the gaunt, wild, hungry, avenging mob which rose against aristocratic oppression; and in like manner, Sojourner... seemed to impersonate the fervor of Ethiopia, wild, savage, hunted of all nations. (124)

Linked to yet another mob, Truth becomes here the voice of black mass interests, the converse of the Marianne's transcendent white femininity and freedom. In the panic narrative about freedpeople, black self-representation and self-advocacy were prominent concerns. As Ann Fabian argues, antebellum slave narratives had always been contested by Southerners and Northerners alike, often on the grounds that blacks were incapable of honesty.[85] These attitudes persisted in responses to the atrocity tales that ex-slaves and veterans told about Confederacy barbarism. Initially a focus of great public interest in the North and used to feed wartime fervor, this testimony soon fell into disfavor for its sensational assault upon the public sensibility and, eventually, its presumed unreliability. Among war-sick postbellum audiences, the public story of black suffering came to be received much in the way that Stowe's antislavery novels had been by the antebellum South. This context lends significance to Truth's unsolicited act of self-narrative, and to her overwhelming and embodied presence. More important, it focuses attention on how Stowe links the two. Before she is silenced into stone, Truth dominates the essay as a force in which verbal and physical power are fused. In the "undescribable" eloquence of its posture and the "speaking gestures" of its great arm, it is her body that generates meaning.

This "speaking body" stands at the very heart of the Truth Myth and its story of black privation, signifying physicality so overwhelming that it makes meanings only to swallow them into its own "singularity," and thereby eclipses all potential public authority. Writes Gilbert in 1850,

> The impressions made by Isabella on her auditors, when moved by lofty or deep feeling, can never be transmitted to paper, till by some Daguerrian act, we are enabled to transfer the look, the gesture, the tones of voice, in connection with the quaint expressions and spirit-stirring animation that pervades all she says. (31)

For Gilbert, Truth's body is the medium of communication; meaning derives from the look, the gesture, the animation: "her manner and tone spoke louder than words" (90). And, because it is fixed in her body, that meaning refuses to abstract into public textuality. Indeed, the only way Truth's voice could be made audible would be through film—which Gilbert prophetically imagines as evolving from the daguerreotype, and uses to represent the absence of mediation. When Frances Gage writes her version of Truth's Akron appearance, she picks up and extends Gilbert's motif. Her Truth likewise features "great speaking eyes" (166) and a resistance to translation:

> I have given but a faint sketch of her speech. I have never in my life seen anything like the magical influence that subdued the mobbish spirit of the day.... I might multiply anecdotes (and some of the best cannot be told) till your pages would not contain them, and yet the fund not be exhausted.[86]

Like Gilbert, Gage casts Truth's speech as idiosyncratic and ineffable; in an interesting echo of Stowe's preface to *Dred* where slavery is an "inexhaustible store" of meaning (3), Gage refers to Truth as an inexhaustible "fund." The speaking body is a central image in sentimental reform writing, where scenes of corporeal distress are incessantly offered as communicative forms. According to the precepts of "sympathy," one body could impress itself upon another through the channel of the sentimental text to impart moral lessons. The body was, or should be, more morally acute than the mind—hence William Lloyd Garrison's decree that readers must respond to *The Narrative of the Life of Frederick Douglass* with "a tearful eye, a heaving breast, an afflicted spirit," or prove themselves possessed of "a flinty heart."[87] Arguably, the recurring images of Truth's evocative corporeality participate in this tradition. Yet they are repeatedly linked to an insistence on *lack* of communication, as when Gilbert regrets that although Truth's prayers are "perfectly original and unique, and would be well worth preserving... no adequate idea of them can be written while the tones and manner remain inexpressible" (45). Here is a voice that resists transcendence, refuses to go public. A similar instance appears where Gilbert describes Truth's first whipping: "He whipped her till the flesh was deeply lacerated, and the blood streamed from her wounds—and the scars remain to the present day, to testify to the fact" (15). Initially the scene seems, like its many equivalents in other slave narratives, to instruct a sympathetic readerly response. Yet, instead of directing us to our own embodied echo, Gilbert returns directly to Truth's body. Suspending her own narration, she quotes Truth: "And now, when I hear 'em tell of whipping women on the bare flesh, it makes *my* flesh crawl, and my very hair rise on my head! Oh! My God!" The circuit of sympathetic bodies remains closed, beginning and ending with Truth's speaking and listening flesh. Here, one black female body may speak to another, but only by virtue of common experience. Communication embeds itself in personal history rather than translating into the codes of public sympathy that incorporate, and ultimately dissolve, the privative body and experience within the sentimental body politic. This *is* the speaking body, then, but its voice never goes far. In a manner that anticipates Stowe's sibyl, stifled by her own hand, Gilbert constructs a body that generates meaning but eclipses voice.

This representational strategy serves Gilbert and Gage in obvious ways. Both continually pose within their texts as observers who stand apart from Truth within a literary public that has formed around the black woman's spectacular image. Gilbert dominates her narrative as a rather overbearing I who relates, interprets, and often judges Truth's life. Unnamed and unmarked, her bodiless authority stands remote from the scenes it explains—scenes that Truth inhabits bodily, always represented with direct speech. Truth's incapacity for public voice predicates, even requires, that capacity in Gilbert.[88] Gage also uses privative Truth as a ground upon which to establish white female publicity, but significantly expands the scope of that project. She begins her Akron narrative by referring to Stowe's recently published essay:

> The story of "Sojourner Truth," by Mrs. H.B. Stowe, in the April number of *The Atlantic* will be read by thousands in the East and West with intense interest; and as those who knew this remarkable woman will lay down this periodical, there will be heard in home-circles throughout Ohio, Michigan, Wisconsin, and Illinois many an anecdote of the weird, wonderful creature. (166)

Here Gage envisions a print public taking form through "interest" in Stowe's "weird, wonderful creature," and expanding with additional biographical "anecdotes" to extend from coast to coast. Her scenario resembles the literary public sphere that Jürgen Habermas describes as helping to create the eighteenth-century political public sphere. Gage plots a similar evolution. Her literary public, decorously located in "home-circles," evolves by the essay's conclusion into a political public, still organized around Truth's black alterity. Truth's speaking body carries the white suffragists "safely over the slough of difficulty," and into new public political positionality (168).

Stowe likewise centers the trope of the speaking body and suppresses its voice in service to her own in "The Libyan Sibyl." Like Gage, she juxtaposes a literary (or cultural) public with a political one: predicting the day when Cleopatra and the sibyl would "adorn the Capitol at Washington," Stowe links the two modes of public belonging and authority. But, where Gage wants to collapse the distance between these modalities, Stowe preserves it. This difference perhaps reflects Stowe's unwillingness to completely relinquish the power of her own embodied authorship (as mother-narrator of moral literature) for the disembodied power of suffrage that she sometimes viewed as unwomanly.[89] Certainly, she understood authorship as her most powerful medium of intervention. As in *Dred*, she represents her literary labor as disconnected from but necessary to U.S. political process. Stowe's manipulation of Truth's speaking body begins with her first physical description:

> She was evidently a full-blooded African, as fine a specimen of the torrid zone as Cumberworth's celebrated statuette of the *Negro Woman at the Fountain*. Indeed, she so strongly reminded me of that figure, that, when I recall the events of her life, I imagine her as a living, breathing impersonation of that work of art. (116)

In classic style, Stowe makes embodiment Truth's dominant aspect. Especially interesting, however, is that Stowe immediately likens Truth's body to art. This move references Stowe's authority as a famous cultural producer and aligns her, in the way Sofer describes, with the high-culture aesthetic of the emerging literary elite. It also establishes a shared vocabulary through which Stowe may converse with an imagined community of other cultural consumers—a strategy like Gilbert and Gage's demarcation of a common discursive space shared with readers and based around Truth's alterity. For Stowe the common space is high culture, and established with references to fine art and literature; it is a space that Truth enables but only enters as the object of reference. As Nell Painter puts it, "Stowe and her family appear as people of culture who appreciate Sojourner Truth as a primitive *objet d'art* and source of entertainment."[90] Reinforcing this structure is Stowe's stiff and impersonal prose style that registers in pointed contrast to Truth who, Stowe observes, "seems to derive as much elevation and comfort from bad English as from good" (123).[91]

Stowe surpasses Gilbert, however, by writing a Truth who challenges the authority of the public register. In the passage above, Truth subsumes the public sign of Cumberworth's statue into her own idiosyncratic body, becoming its "living, breathing impersonation." Although the statue is well known, even "celebrated," Truth literally incorporates it in a manner that renders it—in Stowe's insistently repeating terms—"original" and "singular" (116). As the sketch proceeds, the attack on publicity continues. When Truth begins to sing "in a strange, cracked voice, but evidently with all her soul and might," Stowe describes her as "carried away with her own feeling" and singing with "the strong barbaric accent of the native African" in "indescribable upward turns" and "deep gutturals." The description conflates the voice with the body—specifically a body that is othered (Truth would later object that she had never even visited Africa)—and again burdens it with an "indescribable" particularity that disables publication. This is a heroic romanticization and a strategic rendering of nondemocratic discourse: Truth sings with "such an overwhelming energy of *personal appropriation* that the hymn seemed to be fused in the furnace of her feelings and come out recrystallized as a production of *her own*" (124, my italics). Once universal in its familiarity, the hymn becomes inalienable from Truth's person; it is rendered nonreferential, nonexchangeable—no longer a point of collective reference and connection. The hymn becomes intensely private and limits its audience to those nearby—sometimes excluding even them, as when Truth, "swelled" by her own performance, withdraws into reverie (119). Stowe's fancy is obviously meant to underscore the power of Truth's presence. But critics like Levine and Peter Gibian, who read Truth's domination of the narrative as historical evidence for her authority as a public speaker, elide both Stowe's act of constructing that dynamic and the likelihood that white nineteenth-century readers would have viewed displays of forceful, upstaging, black authority with deep ambivalence.[92] I want to suggest that Stowe cultivates that very ambivalence to make postemancipation racial tensions the unnamed focus of her antebellum anecdote.

Ultimately, Stowe's Truth ceases to overwhelm the public domain of high art. Her speaking body is converted into the sibyl, silenced but evocative in a new way that performs Stowe's ability to claim and manage her own embodiment. The writer's identification with her subject is stronger here than in *Dred*. It is evident from the opening moment, in which the two women face off, to the final image of Story's paired statues. In fact, Stowe reports twice substituting for Truth as the model for Story's sibyl, and, according to Painter, the writer was celebrated for her Truth impersonations at social events in Rome.[93] Through the "love and theft" of her identification with and against Truth, Stowe projects the tension within her own public persona onto this agonistic dynamic, a conceit that betrays—and portrays—her ambivalence toward embodiment and sets the stage for its mastery.[94]

Truth's conversion, and the restoration of normative racial power relations, begins as her narrative concludes and Stowe regains the floor. The shift is signaled, for instance, in the scene where Calvin summons Truth to "come and sit among the pictures and ornaments . . . the central object of attention" (5). Suddenly the visitor is docile and decorative; she talks on command and only within Stowe's exposition rather than through direct speech. Gradually, the speaking body is resituated within Stowe's narrative to act, like the enslaved black subject from *Dred*, as a "mine" for the white city on a hill. Fittingly, one of the artifacts to which Stowe compares and reduces Truth in this final phase of the essay is Milton's "Il Penserosa"—his ode to the muse of melancholy who represents humanity as earthbound and tragic, gazing mournfully toward heaven, and repeatedly described as "black." Like Stowe's Truth, the muse inspires but cannot achieve creative release from herself.[95]

But the chief emblem of Truth's new condition is the Libyan Sibyl, whose genesis Stowe describes in terms strikingly similar to those from the preface to *Dred*:

> The history of Sojourner Truth worked in [Story's] mind and led him into the deeper recesses of the African nature, those unexplored depths of being and feeling, mighty and dark as the gigantic depths of tropical forests, mysterious as the hidden rivers and mines of that burning continent whose life-history is yet to be. (131)

If Story did not associate the sibyl with Truth, we can readily see why Stowe did. Sibyls, as imagined by Virgil, Tasso, and Michelangelo, are passive and earthly channels of divine prophesy that pertains specifically to national fate. In many traditions they are chained and tortured by the rigors of prophesy. Virgil's Cumaen Sybil—among the best known examples—refuses to answer Aeneas's questions clearly; her voice is enigmatic, "wrapping truth in darkness" until she reveals the destiny of Rome.[96] The Libyan Sibyl, like the muse of "Il Penserosa," is a degraded source of inspiration. For both Story and Stowe, her image would have come from the Sistine Chapel, where Michelangelo painted five sibyls and placed the Libyan last in the series. Art historians suggest that, unlike the rest, the Libyan Sibyl has not received inspiration or knowledge: Michelangelo captures her as she turns, resignedly, from an open book. We might say here that Stowe has killed Truth into art—and in a sense we would be right, because although the real Sojourner Truth was still alive in 1863, and would remain so for some twenty years, the writer pronounces her dead. "Though Sojourner Truth has passed away from among us," Stowe elegizes, "her memory still lives in one of the loftiest works of modern art, the Libyan Sibyl, by Mr. Story" (131).[97]

By writing the two statues into her essay, Stowe stakes a place alongside Story and Hawthorne among the cultural elite of her day. But she also reappropriates Cleopatra from them by choosing a description that flouts the Augustan tradition and restores confidence, grace, and bodily command to the poster child of disgraced public womanhood. Stowe selects as her source an art review in which the queen's surplus embodiment is displaced onto the sibyl—along with her racial taint: the *Atheneum* reattributes the descriptor "Nubian" from Cleo to the sibyl. But the principal focus of Stowe's self-modeling is her narrative voice. It was a common practice at sculpture exhibits to provide interpretive pamphlets, especially for controversial works. These pamphlets were conventionally written by men and it was encouraged that men read them aloud to female companions at the actual exhibit. In the case of "racial statuary" like Story's sibyl, these pamphlets also addressed questions about racial difference and developmental potential. Such works thereby became "ethnographic portraits," as Hamer explains, so that although Story's art was destined exclusively for the salon, it was "created and viewed in an international context where sculpture was already expected to support a 'scientific' interest in race."[98] Hawthorne's Cleopatra scene from *The Marble Faun* was written and used as an exhibit pamphlet for Story's Paris exhibition.[99] By writing "The Libyan Sibyl," Stowe likewise participates in this custom. First, she offers from the *Atheneum* an interpretation of the figures that differs markedly from Hawthorne's and, in a manner, reads it aloud to her reader companions. Second, her essay acts as another exhibit pamphlet, managing our encounter with the "objet d'art" that is her portrait of Sojourner Truth. The status of salon pamphleteer, one that structures and is structured by gender and racial difference, helps Stowe distance herself from the literary domain of sympathetic identification and embodied intimacy. Through it, she creates a relationship to the textual object that is based upon aesthetic distance, protecting readers from disturbance or contamination. With this new authorial stance Stowe enters the very halls of the Capitol, advising state power as it prepares to negotiate the postbellum problems of black and female bodies.[100]

The image of the sibyl, silenced and contained, allows Stowe to refashion her own public voice and public corporeality. It also serves her as a basis from which to propose a new model of white national belonging. For Stowe's closing maneuvers project not just herself but also her readers into the space of democratic power. Organized around the essay's portrait of black privation, we become an imagined community, asked to imagine itself at the Capitol, apart from but proximate to the political sphere. What is the nature of this new regime? Jean Fagan Yellin writes of Stowe's sibyl that she "possesses knowledge but she cannot act on it; further, because her language cannot readily be understood, no one else can use her knowledge as the basis for effective action."[101] This aptly characterizes the impasse that Stowe deliberately stages in her portrait of Truth, but Yellin overlooks the new mode of knowledge that Stowe makes available with the sibyl. The essay transforms its subject from an invading presence that consumes public signs and closes down democratic exchange into an aesthetically pleasing representation of that dangerous force. The black speaking body itself now provides a replicable, fungible, and commonly appropriable sign; posed before Stowe's readership, it becomes the basis of public knowledge and action. Stowe has now fully renounced her previous vision of democratic union based on the ties of sympathy. Should he wander by, Senator Bird will not see a body like Eliza Harris's that speaks to his own, but a mute statue with Stowe's pamphleteering narrative to further insulate him from its impact.

In this, "The Libyan Sibyl" forecasts a new discourse on charity, state welfare, and surplus embodiment. The essay concludes, like *Dred*, with a vision of moral citizenship tied to Stowe's artistic mediation. But, just as the 1863 version of Truth marks a change from Milly's sympathetic self-discipline, the 1863 model of national morality differs sharply from the sublime paternalism staged in Canada. In "The Libyan Sibyl," Stowe begins to describe dependence relations in terms of criminality and punishment. She signals this shift again in her 1879 report on the integration of freedpeople: "The miracle of our day," the writer announces, "is that *the ship is sailing on*, in better order than ever before... for that unwieldy stowage of oppression which she was obliged to carry has been thrown overboard, and she sails free!" (605). Stowe's overt meaning is, of course, that without slavery the democratic political economy progresses better than ever. But her metaphor, which hideously recalls the Middle Passage and the illegal slavers who jettisoned human cargo to evade prosecution, suggests a conception of "unwieldy stowage" far more immediate to white postbellum America, and pictures its violent disposal. Even as she appears at last to embrace racial assimilation, Stowe persists in imagining the erasure of black bodies.

In our own political culture, this recasting of oppressed as oppressor continues to inform the U.S. discourse on poverty. In its light, state welfare comes to be understood not as a form of just redistribution that corrects the failures of market capitalism, but as an "unwieldy stowage of oppression," a form of national thrall imposed by dependent bodies. This sense of injustice continues to congeal into what Robyn Weigman describes as "notions of hyperreproductive and socially vampiristic black maternity" and to provoke such responses as the forced sterilization campaigns aimed at African American women, or the punitive measures of welfare reform.[102] In the surplus and proliferating body of the Welfare Queen, abjection and menace appear as one, and acts of revenge take justification.

PRESIDENTIAL PRIVATION

Ironically, the very man who signed the vengeful logic of welfare reform into law himself became one of the most prominent figures of racialized privation ever to spill into public view. In more ways than one, Bill Clinton was, as Toni Morrison famously declared, "our first black President,"

> blacker than any actual black person who could ever be elected in our children's lifetimes. After all, Clinton displays almost every trope of blackness: single-parent household, born poor, working-class, saxophone playing, McDonald's-and-junk-food-loving boy from Arkansas.[103]

If Clinton's childhood poverty and adult appetites resonated with racist notions of hyperembodiment and failed self-containment, his putative advocacy of social programs and minority interests compounded that identification and made his "blackness" a dominant aspect of his political persona—particularly in the rhetoric of his opponents, who drew on the racialized rhetoric of privation to charge him and his policies with having allowed private needs and appetites to contaminate the democratic process. This tactic was not without precedent, as Illinois Congressman Jesse Jackson Jr. pointed out during the impeachment hearings. Likening his Republican colleagues to the Southerners who dubbed Abraham Lincoln "the black President" and his party "the black Republicans," Jackson argued that the campaign against Clinton was really an attack on his efforts toward a "second Reconstruction."[104] When the Lewinsky scandal broke, the rhetorical apparatus was already in place to frame it as yet another wave of spillage. To be sure, this characterization often encompassed the scandal as a whole; in his 1999 article for the *Economic Times* titled "Doing Away with Public Life," Neal Gabler begins: "If ever one needed an event to mark the end of privacy in America, Barbara Walters' recent interview with Monica Lewinsky would certainly qualify."[105] But at the root of the trouble stood Clinton's rampant body and the damage it had wreaked upon the nation. He became, in the words of critic Frederick Moten, "the black woman that every piece of poor white male trash holds deep within."[106] Moten elaborates, "Bill Clinton enacts modes of behavior that are tied both rightly and wrongly to the image of black women.... The danger to the state of this irruption/eruption is indexed in and by the identity and energy of the folks who are after him." Whether or not Moten is correct in attributing subversive power to the privative behaviors that Clinton exhibited (and of which black women are accused), it is certainly true that these were represented as an "eruption" and a "danger to the state." House Majority Whip Tom DeLay described the Starr hearings as a national "trauma" inflicted by Clinton. The *Chicago Tribune* scathingly compared the 1868 impeachment of Andrew Johnson, "having to do with the terms of Reconstruction and the political status of newly freed blacks," to its 1998 counterpart concerning only "a pathetic creature, slave to his enormous sexual appetites" (evidently concluding that U.S. slavery was less a matter of repulsively unmastered white appetites).[107] As intended, this portrait of injurious uncontainment generated its own backlash. Morrison was not alone in describing the response as "a lynching";[108] and, indeed, it did exhibit a familiar fusion of political strategy, economic anxiety, and sexual rage: as one Republican staffer put it in the days leading to the hearings, "we're going to nail his prick to the wall."[109]

However, if Clinton demonstrated that the logic of the black spill can cross racial lines, he also demonstrated its differential action. Which is to say that Clinton never lost the option of reasserting his white heterosexual masculinity as an inherent claim to—as identical *with*—democratic entitlement and belonging. When he went on television to finally acknowledge the Lewinsky affair, the majority of his remarks concerned his own sense of violation and dispossession: "Now, this matter is between me, the two people I love most—my wife and our daughter—and our God.... [I]t is private, and I intend to reclaim my family life for my family. It's nobody's business but ours. Even presidents have private lives."[110] Clinton simply inverts the terms of his own privacy crisis to shift its focus from his ill-contained privative body to himself as the victim of alienated privacy. Two years after signing the federal Defense of Marriage Act and Personal Responsibility and Work Opportunity Reconciliation Act—the latter of which required single mothers to report the names of their children's fathers in order to receive support—he appeals to the supposedly universal and sacrosanct rights of family autonomy, sexual privacy, and human dignity.[111] Unlike those punished by the legislation he authorized, Clinton need not earn these rights: to again borrow from Moten, "Bill Clinton is a black woman. Bill Clinton is not a black woman."[112]

But the tacit assertion of privilege that pervades Bill Clinton's apology derives from more than heterosexual and masculine normativity. It refers also to his status as U.S. president and to the problematic of executive privacy. Other critics have argued that Clinton used his televised address to distinguish between his personal and presidential selves, marking a zone of life exempt from public scrutiny.[113] Yet Clinton does not present himself as simply a private citizen but as *the* private citizen—as the one American individual who stands for all the rest of us. It is this double identity that lends a special national urgency and value to the sanctity of the president's private life.[114] The privacy that "even presidents have" is not theirs alone; it is also the (non)possession of their democratic subjects. This means, as Morrison points out, that Clinton's transgression against his own marriage could never be simply personal: "The root of the word, *adulterare,* means 'to defile.'...What is being violated, ruptured, defiled? The bedroom? The Oval Office? The voting booth? The fourth grade? Marriage vows? The flag?"[115] The citizen's stake in executive privacy was intrinsic to the case against Clinton. But he used that same stake to place himself and the American people on the same side of the conflict, mutually its victims. By airing Clinton's intimate secrets, Starr alienated something belonging to us all. Hence Clinton devotes a full third of his remarks to national injury, imperiled democracy, and national reclamation:

> It is time to stop the pursuit of personal destruction and the prying into private lives and get on with our national life. Our country has been distracted too long.... And so tonight, I ask you... to repair the fabric of our national discourse, and to return our attention to all the challenges and all the promise of the next American century.

In the chapter that follows, I examine the iconicity of presidential privacy at greater length, focusing on the Lincoln administration and its relationship to postbellum America. I explore the paradoxical nature of the president's simultaneous entitlement and nonentitlement to his own private life and demonstrate how—more than a century before Monica Lewinsky, in the throes of what Representative Jackson refers to as "the first Reconstruction"—this became the focus for struggles over democratic power, belonging, and meaning.

CHAPTER FOUR

Freedom and Ballgowns

ELIZABETH KECKLEY'S EXECUTIVE DOMESTICITY

> We were shown through the damp cold rooms into *the* drawing room. The nation's drawing room—where the mobocracy assemble by the light of beautiful chandeliers and circulating amidst rich furniture—great men and accomplished women fancy they live in a country of equality as well as liberty. Query: do they ever feel their inequality more than on such occasions?
>
> —Catharine Maria Sedgwick, journal entry following a visit to the White House

In 1866, while announcing his veto of the first American civil rights bill, President Andrew Johnson found occasion to remind Congress that intermarriage between blacks and whites was "contrary to law,... revolting, and... an offense against public decorum."[1] Johnson had a particular horror of miscegenation, which he had voiced on many occasions.[2] In this instance, however, its context was somewhat obscure, since the bill, drafted by Republican lawmakers to protect the newly acquired freedoms of ex-slaves from Southern legislatures, contained no mention of racial intermarriage. The president's speech marked a culminating point in his battles with Congress over how to deal with Southern state governments and other aspects of Reconstruction. Most specifically, it constituted a direct intervention into postbellum debates over how to define and delimit democratic freedom after emancipation. Radical Republicans argued that freedom had no meaning for anyone if not shared equally by all. As one proponent of the 1866 bill put it, the failure to legislate equal rights would not only nullify emancipation but render "all the principles of democracy and freedom upon which our creed of Republicanism rests...false."[3] The president, a former slave owner who believed blacks unqualified for the responsibilities of citizenship, opposed any move toward racial equality. In vetoing this bill he aimed specifically to prevent the convergence of black and white freedoms and to formalize the differences between them.[4] And it was toward this end that he invoked miscegenation and the threat it posed to sacred white domesticity.

Johnson acknowledges that interracial marriage is not addressed in the bill, but explains that he raises it

> to inquire whether, if Congress can abrogate all State laws of discrimination between the two races in the matter of real estate, of suits, and of contracts generally, Congress may not also repeal the State laws as to the contract of marriage between the two races? Hitherto every subject embraced in the enumeration of rights contained in this bill has been considered as exclusively belonging to the States. They are matters which in each State concern the domestic condition of its people...the safety and well-being of its own citizens. (75)

A staunch Jacksonian democrat, Johnson had long opposed the expansion of federal powers as a violation of state and popular sovereignty. Here he predicts a domino effect, whereby federal sovereignty would trespass further and further into the jurisdictions of state law until it overturned even prohibitions against marriage between blacks and whites. But, in offering this causal relation between black civil rights and miscegenation as his reason for mentioning the latter, Johnson also suggests a metaphorical relation. In the above passage, the intrusion of black bodies into white homes both results from and stands in for the intrusion of federal authority into the "domestic condition" of individual states. Furthermore, as Johnson continues, setting out now to demonstrate the chain of events that would inevitably lead from the bill's passage to the legalization of interracial marriage, another substitution takes place. At the point where Johnson's proof should arrive back at interracial marriage, he names a different outcome, interracial cosovereignty:

> If it be granted that Congress can repeal all State laws discriminating between whites and blacks in the subjects covered by this bill, why, it may be asked, may not Congress repeal, in the same way, all State laws discriminating between the two races on the subjects of suffrage and office? (75)

What Johnson's argument "returns" to, in the space logically designated for miscegenation, is the black vote. Rhetorically, miscegenation and cosovereignty come to occupy the same space, and Johnson places freedpeople at the bedroom door of the white body politic. With this, the president has arranged not one but two privacy crises. He has raised the specter of interracial marriage (rape always the implicit reference here) to conflate it with both an overpowerful federal government and the black vote and—one year after the Ku Klux Klan had formed to defend white Southern women from the "black menace"—to pose himself as the nation's guardian against both.

This chapter examines postbellum representations of imperiled white domesticity in order to investigate how these served, as in Johnson's veto speech, as tactical responses to the unstable political, economic, and racial relations of Reconstruction. Specifically, my arguments focus on how such representations were used to manipulate the discourse on democratic freedom. When the radical Republicans linked black civil rights to the symbolic integrity of white democratic liberty, they took their conflict with Andrew Johnson into the realm of abstract political ideals. Johnson responded cannily to this rhetorical situation by deploying the figure of white domesticity, one of U.S. democracy's most sacrosanct symbols. The power of domestic imagery in nineteenth-century America derived partly from its promise of what Lora Romero calls "a space insulated from politics."[5] This promise allowed that domestic iconography could stand for a corrective set of values in the way Jane Tompkins and Nina Baym have famously argued, but not necessarily as an opposition to—or, in Baym's words, "in competition with"—a public-political ethos.[6] The gynocritical gender binarism that informs this latter assumption obscures the way that nineteenth-century domesticity provided an idealized image of the political onto which utopian meanings could be projected and, at once, deferred, a horizon which informed the political sphere even while constantly receding from it. Closely related—and of particular interest in this chapter—is the paradoxical nature of domesticity as that place where the material conditions of privacy (shelter, solitude, bodies, and the paid and unpaid labor that sustains and produces all of these) came to stand for the fantasy of immaterial and inalienable private selfhood—where the democratic individual's property rights most overtly predicated the transcendent (non)property of that subject's individuality.[7] Finally, domesticity played a vital role in the discourse of imperiled privacy, where narratives of violation and dispossession served both to affirm an entitlement to democratic freedom and to identify particular threats to it. This is the mode in which postbellum references to miscegenation operated. Racial mixing was a personal obsession and persisting theme with Johnson, but it was not his alone. The idea of racial amalgamation had been used to discredit antislavery activists and politicians since the early 1830s.[8] By 1868, the term *miscegenation* had become a segregationist epithet used to sanctify ruling interests and demonize the emergent claims of black Americans. For Johnson it supplied a set of images—on one side the bestial sexuality of black men, on the other the revered purity of the white female body and home—through which to reify distinct freedoms, one black, one white, and to criminalize their union. Thus, domesticity, that which demands protection, became a kind of protection itself, a prophylactic against the movement of various others (most pointedly blacks, white women, and the working class) into the domains of white male freedom and power.

To get at the postbellum story of besieged domesticity and its role in the production of white national freedom, I turn to the White House. My analyses focus on one of its most infamous residents, Mary Todd Lincoln; on the autobiography written by her friend and employee Elizabeth Keckley, *Behind the Scenes; or, Thirty Years a Slave and Four Years in the White House*; and on the spectacle of executive domesticity that both women helped to create and compromise. As preceding chapters have emphasized, nineteenth-century privacy discourse always resonated at the national level—whether by framing the violation of one individual's privacy as an injury to the democratic community, or by warning that every failure at private self-containment endangered the entire political economy. Johnson's crisis narrative likewise speaks to his listener's sense of national selfhood, following in the tradition of Lincoln's House Divided speech, where the domestic metaphor solicits identification with national democratic ideals and the citizen's shared (non)possession of them. In executive domesticity—that which Catherine Maria Sedgwick refers to as "*the* drawing room[,] the nation's drawing room" in the epigraph for this chapter—the trope of national privacy takes interestingly literal form.[9] It becomes more prominently than ever a focal point for anxieties about property, (non)property, and dispossession. These anxieties play out in sometimes bizarre ways, as the Clinton-Lewinsky scandal demonstrated in 1998 (Toni Morrison summarized the nation's outrage thusly: "Lady, your husband is cheating on us"); and they always center around the grand themes of liberty and equality that, as Sedgwick observes, executive domesticity both symbolizes and destabilizes.[10]

In what follows I begin with Mary Todd Lincoln's controversial tenure as First Lady and representative domestic angel. This section focuses primarily on the "old clothes scandal," an episode that took place several years after her husband's assassination when Mary attempted to auction off the clothing she had worn during her years in the White House. In the ensuing public commotion, the intersection among executive domesticity, symbolic property, and democratic freedom came into sharp focus. In the midst of his own scandal, Bill Clinton famously insisted that "even presidents have private lives." Here I will argue that if the First Family has a private life, they do not own it; rather they provide it for the (non)possession of their citizens. Next I turn to Elizabeth Keckley's 1868 autobiography, *Behind the Scenes; or, Thirty Years a Slave and Four Years in the White House*. A successful entrepreneur, Keckley had risen from slavery to ownership of a thriving dressmaking business. Her friend and most famous client was Mary Todd Lincoln, and Keckley wrote her book in what she describes as an effort to save Lincoln's reputation after the ex-First Lady was discovered trying to sell the used finery that Keckley herself had created. For its first sixty pages *Behind the Scenes* reads like a conventional antebellum slave narrative, portraying physical abuse, rape, broken families, and, finally, freedom. The remaining three hundred pages provide an "as-told-by" exposé of the private lives of political figures, briefly recounting Keckley's employment with Mrs. Jefferson Davis, then detailing her four years as personal seamstress to the Lincoln White House. Thus, the majority of the autobiography concerns not Keckley but her privileged viewpoint of the most iconic of iconic domesticities: the First Lady and the First Home.

Much of the scholarship on *Behind the Scenes* approaches the text's lopsided structure as a defect and seeks to excuse Keckley for privileging Lincoln's affairs over her own struggles against the racial barriers of Reconstruction. Some critics emphasize the difference between antebellum and postbellum contexts, pointing out that after emancipation many black autobiographers shifted focus away from racial injustice and toward their own qualifications and desire for entry into dominant U.S. culture. Frances Smith Foster places Keckley at the origin of this new tradition of black life narrative, a tradition culminating with Booker T. Washington and characterized by portrayals of productivity, reliability, and loyalty to the capitalist system.[11] Key to my own argument is the fact that Keckley's focus on Mary Todd Lincoln enabled her to highlight her own prodigious output and success as a seamstress.[12] A more common and worrisome approach to *Behind the Scenes* is that which remedies Keckley's omission of personal information by conjuring the absent presence of her authentic voice. Such readings search out symptoms of suppressed "rage and longing" and infer "concealed scenes of personal mourning"; they find authentic black authorial intention in the "black mother-tongue" of "concealment, silence and secrecy."[13] Without discounting the value of reading between lines and within silences, I want to question this impulse to look, as one critic puts it, for something "more deeply recessed 'behind the scenes'" in order to locate (or produce) private black meaning.[14] One problem with this strategy is that it risks reinscribing logics of black privation—such as that examined in the previous chapter—wherein black expression and identity are encoded with a primitive and untranslatable authenticity that resists publication. More, this search for a hidden vein of private expression in black texts obscures how such writers demonstrate their own understanding of privacy as a strategic public construct and badge of power—as, for instance, in the astute materialist analysis of white domestic privacy that Harriet Jacobs presents in her 1861 autobiography, *Incidents in the Life of a Slave Girl.*[15]

Here I argue that Keckley not only rejects the authority and constraints of the always already private black voice, she also reveals the national function of iconic white privacy. In contrast to critics who worry that Keckley's focus on Mary Lincoln prevents her from addressing the postbellum struggle for freedom, I find that *Behind the Scenes* never ceases to examine what divides the black condition from the white, or to analyze how racialized divisions continue to inform concepts of freedom even after emancipation. For this, however, Keckley must adopt a new strategy, joining the radical Republicans and President Johnson in the battle over national symbolic meanings. She takes executive domesticity, a sign for an identity and freedom that specifically exclude her, and reveals it as a symbol (in her terms, a "surface") whose function is always conditioned by its material production (or "origin") in herself. Her narrative exposes the contingency of both white domesticity and white freedom, explicating the dependence upon enslaved and free black labor that compromises their transcendent aspect. She appropriates the category of domesticity from the dominant discourse, of which Johnson's speech forms a part, to write her own theory of freedom and of the intermarriage of white and black conditions that founds it.

Ultimately, however, *Behind the Scenes* was Keckley's undoing. In the final section of this chapter, I show that by explicating her relation to iconic domesticity she offered herself up as the indispensable threat to the inviolability that is its value. Her book was publicly denounced as the "back-stair gossip of negro servant girls" and its author accused of "opening other people's letters" and "listening at keyholes."[16] Shortly after its publication, a satire appeared called *Behind the Seams: By a Nigger Woman Who Took In Work from Mrs. Lincoln and Mrs. Davis.* Savagely racist, this text transforms Keckley's revelations into a means by which the image of white freedom could purge and rearticulate itself. In this, her book functioned much like the specter of the black body in Johnson's speech, and illustrated the effect that is the central concern of this book: the manner by which figures of imperiled privacy generate political value specifically by disavowing their own material and historical contingency, and the tendency of such disavowals to protect norms of racial and gendered political power.

"THE NATION'S DRAWING ROOM"

In September 1867, two and a half years following the assassination of her husband, Mary Todd Lincoln traveled incognito to New York City. Short on funds, thanks to delays in the settlement of husband's estate and her own disastrous financial judgment, she was on a mission to raise money. Lincoln intended to sell the extensive wardrobe she had acquired (along with debt amounting to more than $70,000) during her time in the White House. She was aided in this endeavor by her seamstress and confidante, Elizabeth Keckley, the ex-slave who had created much of the clothing now offered for sale. Their plan fell apart almost immediately. When Lincoln took her ballgowns and jewels to the commission brokerage of William Brady and Samuel Keyes, the two businessmen recognized their customer—both as the former First Lady and as a goldmine in free advertising—and persuaded her to let them manage the entire affair. They instructed her to contact various Republican politicians whom she had known during her days in the White House and ask them to buy her cast-off clothing on behalf of democracy's most beloved martyr. As Keckley would later remember, "[Brady and Keyes] argued that the Republican party would never permit it to be said that the wife of Abraham Lincoln was in want; that the leaders of the party would make heavy advances rather than have it published to the world that Mrs. Lincoln's poverty compelled her to sell her wardrobe."[17] The letter campaign failed, as did subsequent attempts to sell items at consignment shops. So Brady and Keyes followed up with two bold moves. They published Mrs. Lincoln's letters in the Democratic-inclined New York *World*, where her accusingly worded pleas would most incriminate their Republican addressees, and announced a public viewing and auction of her goods.[18]

The incident, which instantly became known as the old clothes scandal, failed to relieve Mrs. Lincoln's financial straits. The crowds who thronged the showrooms came to look, not buy. Worse, the affair called intense public censure upon Lincoln. She became, in the words of one reporter, "that dreadful woman" who had "thrust" herself upon "the open market with her useless finery."[19] Or, as the Rochester *Democrat* put it:

> Her fling at the three Republicans is probably an ebullition of female spite. Her letters are coarse and vulgar. From their publication a refined woman would have shrunk with horror.... She says

> these things were the gifts of friends. We do not believe it. She has lavished the money given her by the nation on diamonds, furs, and lace.[20]

The reporter from Rochester makes a typical move in attributing Mary Todd Lincoln's transgression to class ("coarse and vulgar") and gender ("female spite"). From her arrival in Washington, critics had portrayed the First Lady from rustic Illinois as an unrefined upstart and found her guilty of feminized self-interest and personalism.[21] The *Democrat* is also typical in interpreting Lincoln's act as embezzlement. In the opinion of the American public, "the nation" had prior claim to the "diamonds, furs, and lace" on view at Lincoln's auction. By trying to convert these to cash she had crossed a boundary between private and public ownership. She had commandeered for personal profit that which rightfully belonged to the democratic all.

The old clothes scandal was not Mary Lincoln's first difficulty over the property rights of First Ladyship. While in the White House she was frequently criticized for her vast overexpenditures on clothing and domestic furnishings. And she demonstrated from the outset her limited understanding of the presidential commodity. Mary correctly identified her husband's office as a marketable asset. Even six years before the old clothes scandal, she was trying to sell refuse from the White House stables at a price well over the going rate.[22] Lincoln reasoned astutely that even "useless finery" and horse manure became value-added products once touched by state iconicity. However, what she failed to recognize was that the value of the presidential commodity lay specifically in its incapacity for conversion to personal property and profit.

At the root of Lincoln's problem lay the paradoxical relationship among democratic governance, power, and freedom. On one hand, the conceit of popular sovereignty—of government "by the people, for the people"—requires that power be prohibited from taking a central location. On the other, democratic subjects require centralized representations of power in order to recognize and claim their own sovereignty. This double bind bears directly upon the American presidency, dictating that it serve as a repository of national power that is possessed equally and fully by all citizens and that does not, *must* not, possess itself. For in order that symbols of democratic power will belong simultaneously to everyone, they must belong to no one. Put differently, in contrast to a monarchical head of state in whom a body natural and body politic (particularity and representationality) may coincide, the democratic head of state must disavow his body natural.[23] As Claude Lefort argues in "The Image of the Body in Totalitarianism," "the democratic revolution... burst out when the body of the king was destroyed, when the body politic was decapitated.... [I]t is best recognized in this mutation: there is no power linked to a body. Power appears as an empty place."[24] Here is the central myth of democratic cosovereignty: that power resides with no one body, but with a body politic that functions as a unity, as one. Furthermore, in this function of representing-and-not-possessing power, the American presidency symbolizes also the ideal of democratic freedom. Freedom is possible only so long as the amorphous entity of national power refuses to particularize or belong more with one person than another. Like any utopian principle, democratic political freedom requires constant acts of representation—narratives and images to make visible that "empty place" of power that is available equally to all, and to none more than another. The institution of the presidency is one such empty place; it is the head of the headless state that permits democratic subjects to experience themselves as free. And executive privacy—in the form of the First Lady and the First Home over which she presides—plays a key role in making this work.

The rules surrounding the presidential commodity applied rigorously to Mary Todd Lincoln. Even by the time of the old clothes scandal, the Springfield *Republican* still demanded her adherence: "She will not let the people... only remember her as the widow of a beloved patriot but insists on thrusting her repugnant personality before the world to the great mortification of the nation."[25] Two years out of the White House, Mary Lincoln was still responsible to its iconicity, still coded with nationalist meanings, still barred from "personality" and individuation. Indeed, for many reasons the work of representing without possessing power is incumbent more upon the First Lady than the president himself. He, after all, must also act as head of government and wield power in very concrete ways. Being more remote from the operation of democratic power, the First Lady is more eligible to stand as its empty place. Then, too, she—along with her White House and her "diamonds, furs, and lace"—are the crucial, domesticizing accessories of the presidential spectacle. The First Lady, and the home life for which she metonymically stands, enable the president perfectly to resemble (without himself being of) the ordinary citizenry. She furnishes executive domesticity, the topological referent of those transcendent values of freedom and equality invested in the head of state.

As the nation's most prominent domestic space, the White House acquired utopian values with the spread of domestic ideology, as did other—albeit more middle-class—homes. By Mary Lincoln's time, the White House was a sort of nationalist creche scene in which the First Family performed their private lives in full view, both democratically visible and democratically accessible. Citizens walked freely in and out of its unguarded entrances, soldiers and vagrants slept in the parlors, visitors clipped souvenirs from Mary's new curtains and haunted passageways to shake Abe's hand. In the words of one historian, "the Lincolns promptly discovered that the Executive Mansion was as much a public building as it *was* a home."[26] The two functions are not incompatible, of course, but fully coincident: the White House was insistently treated as a public space because it was a home—the home of the body politic. This was not necessarily a comfortable arrangement, and Lincoln remarked that he "sometimes felt like a hotel keeper."[27] Nevertheless, it was regarded as a natural extension of democratic principles that "our elected president, living in a house that the citizens consider to be their gift and property, should be at ease with his people and give them easy access to his home."[28] Thus, when Mary Lincoln canceled public concerts on the White House lawn during the mourning period for her son Willie, public outcry against "The Illinois Reine" never ceased until the concerts resumed.[29] Lincoln's public reminded her of the distinction between democracy and monarchy, and claimed the executive mansion as a living monument to equality of power, government by the people, and political freedom.

After the fact and exercise of public ownership, there was still another way that the White House signified freedom to midcentury Americans. As Daniel J. Boorstin puts it, the

> "special democratic aura" of the White House derives not just from accessibility but also "representativeness." ... This distinctly American architectural metaphor ... offers the nation a scene of a president and his family leading lives not dissimilar from our own. It is a prosaic prospect, but one that elevates us citizens by reminding us that our president leads a life essentially like ours.[30]

In literal terms, of course, Boorstin is mistaken. The president's life, in the 1860s and today, bears no likeness to the vast majority of American lives; the White House resembles few other American homes. Nevertheless, in alluding to the determined banality of the First Family's image, Boorstin aptly characterizes the performance of sameness that permeates presidential domesticity. With its decades of camera-ready pets, children, and fireside poses, the executive mansion has never stinted on those scenes that dominant culture incessantly marks as universal and archetypal. Sameness, after all, is the surest guarantee of equality and thus of perfect freedom—freedom from difference, freedom from lack. It is not true that the First Family's domestic self-portrait actually reflects its constituency, any more than it is true that Americans are all, in fact, equal. Yet the White House signals the promise of equality through a set of images and meanings ideologically wired to provoke an illusion of self-recognition in a nation of consumer subjects. In that these "representative" images and meanings compose a "no place" of privacy that is highly particularized by whiteness and affluence, it begins to become apparent how such a commodification of political freedom serves to limit and protect that freedom.

In Mary Lincoln's day, the White House persona most responsible for dispensing spectacular sameness and accessibility was the nation's first domestic angel. No one else was (or is) expected to dish up quite so much banality. Nearly 150 years before Hillary Rodham Clinton's compulsory cookie bake-off with Barbara Bush, Sarah Polk was accused of alienating votes because the other candidate's wife made superior butter.[31] Here, too, it is worth noting that, like any other domestic angel, the First Lady did not represent or describe the actual lives of middle-class white women. Iconicity is not historicity, and the public representation of domestic womanhood signified ideals—such as freedom from contact with the public world of economic intercourse—which actual lives could never realize. But when Mary Lincoln displayed the First Lady's gowns at state dinners or sat at the First Lady's writing desk to sign her name to White House stationery, she, the costumes, the desk, and the signature stood alike as property of the nation. She offered a composite, commodified image of the power belonging to all democratic citizens, a representation of the free and equal—free *because* equal—body politic. When Lincoln tried to sell these same costumes and props for personal profit, she exposed herself as a body natural, "repugnantly individual" in the words of the Columbus *Sun*, and a threat to democratic freedom.[32] Mary Lincoln was slated as a commodity of the symbolic economy, not as a capitalist of the market economy. By auctioning her public body to feed her private one, she conflated the nation's symbolic and capitalist economies, and paid heavily for it.[33]

Finally, however, if Lincoln wore her iconicity badly, it was perhaps already determined that she should. She was required to uphold a myth that is inherently, usefully, precarious. As Lefort's decapitation metaphor suggests, democratic freedom is a chronically vulnerable condition of national being:

> As long as [power] presents itself as the power of no one, as long as it seems to move toward a latent focus—namely the people—it runs the risk of having its symbolic function canceled out, of falling [to] the level of the real, the contingent. [S]imilarly, those who exercise it or aspire to it are exposed to the threat of appearing as individuals or groups concerned solely to satisfy their desires.[34]

Here is the putative dilemma of democracy: it must prevent power from centralizing, but in doing so it leaves power vulnerable to division and co-option. Hence, to maintain its representational status the democratic state must incessantly reaffirm the ideal of collective freedom as separate from and endangered by the practice of freedoms by self-interested individuals. This predicament—the instability of a democracy's symbolic economy—is not necessarily meant to be resolved. It is productive. Democracies must constantly reenact their own fragility, conjuring new enemies for banishment. In Lefort's words, it is essential for the body politic "to assure itself of its own identity by expelling its waste matter."[35] In this respect, Mary Lincoln still played a central part in disseminating democratic fantasies of freedom. If she failed in her role as national domestic angel, another was already scripted for her as the "waste matter" of antidemocratic interest that would allow the body politic to rediscover its own free selfhood.

As we have already seen, the public attributed Lincoln's transgression to female and lower-class character: "She was neither a woman of great refinement nor of high intellectuality," observed the Albany *Argus*.[36] Early in her first term, Mary's class background gave off a democratic aura and even offered what one admiring journalist termed "a refreshing change to our Northern hothouse blooms."[37] But that background stood ready to be invested with antidemocratic significance. So did her gender. When the president openly practiced patronage and indulged a constant stream of supplicants, he was praised for democratic accessibility.[38] Meanwhile, the same newspapers repeatedly accused Mary of asking and bestowing political favors to promote her own agenda. The negative aspects of patronage took form in her "womanly desires" and "powers of persuasion." Dubbed the president's "kitchen cabinet," the First Lady became what historian Jean Baker describes as the "tainted alter ego of Honest Abe."[39] What Mary Lincoln's expulsion demonstrates, then, is how this bod(il)y politic(al) function serves to maintain precisely that which it professes to expunge—interested power. It benefits ruling interests by coding new claims to political power as inimical to freedom—hence the gendered and class-inflected rhetoric of Mary's condemnation; hence, too, the public censure that would fall upon the ex-slave and White House insider, Elizabeth Keckley, when she wrote her account of the old clothes scandal. Like Lincoln's auction, Keckley's autobiography could be conveniently deployed as a menace to the symbols of democratic freedom. In this, *Behind the Scenes* both aggravated the original offense and extended its utility.

ELIZABETH KECKLEY'S MULATTA BODY POLITIC

The juxtaposition of Lincoln's old clothes scandal with the Johnsonian logic of apartheid freedom brings into relief two features of Reconstruction discourse—both of which frame Keckley's arguments in *Behind the Scenes*. First, as we have already seen, both the scandal and the veto speech reinforce the fantasy of democratic political freedom by portraying embodied threats to iconic domesticity—Mary Lincoln's feminized body natural and the freedman's sexualized invasion. Second, as the following discussion demonstrates, both episodes also draw upon an ideological distinction between material and symbolic economies. In Lincoln's case this consists in an imagined disjuncture between individual private property and the citizen's (non)property in executive privacy. Correspondingly, Johnson's attempt to truncate black political rights relied on an ability to separate the possession of market freedoms from the possession of political freedoms.

Johnson knew his veto of the civil rights bill opposed strong majorities in both the Senate and the House (indeed, Congress later passed it into law along with the Freedmen's Bureau bill, overturning his vetoes in both cases). In order to justify his move he set out to naturalize a distinction between black and white freedoms; and for this he turned to the rhetoric of free labor and market autonomy. There are two classes of freedom, Johnson argues in his speech: one white, one black; one political, one nonpolitical. The latter obtains exclusively within the economic sphere:

> The white race and black race of the South have hitherto lived together under the relation of master and slave—capital owning labor.... They stand now each master of itself. In this new relation, one being necessary to the other, there will be a new adjustment, which both are deeply interested in making harmonious. Each has equal power in settling the terms, and if left to the laws that regulate capital and labor, it is confidently believed that they will satisfactorily work out the problem.[40]

For blacks, Johnson stipulates, freedom begins and ends with possession of one's labor. It derives from the free dynamics of the market and the absence of government intervention such as that called for by the Republican bills. Here, Johnson fights his opposition with their own rhetoric. Posed as the antithesis of slavery's dependence relations, free labor had been a prominent component of abolitionist arguments. Now it stood at the heart of Republican plans for economic and racial reconstruction. In fact, as discussed in the previous chapter, many Republicans and Democrats believed that market capitalism was guaranteed to bring prosperity and equality to the nation and to the war-torn South in particular. However, free labor discourse comprised many conflicting tendencies: it was by no means inherently egalitarian or dedicated to the cause of racial equality. It could also serve, as in Johnson's speech, to circumscribe black freedoms and civil rights. One version of free labor rhetoric held that blacks did not require material aid or supportive legislation, for once they possessed their own labor the market would certainly supply the rest. Another free labor argument resisted even this logic—which at least assumed, if disingenuously, an ascension from labor to the capitalist's economic self-determination and consequent political powers—by presupposing a permanent racialist segregation of those two conditions.

Johnson draws on this latter thread when he asserts that the opportunity to negotiate as "equals" with white capitalists satisfies the full extent of freedpeople's needs and aspirations.[41] If he aligns white freedom with the full exercise of civil and political rights, the freedom he envisions for blacks begins and ends with ownership of labor. Indeed, in the above passage, the term *laborer* replaces the term *freedman* completely, as the term *capitalist* replaces *white*. These substitutions persist throughout the speech, so that labor and capital transform from functions into identities and form a permanently racialized opposition.[42] Back in his days of championing poor whites against plantation owners, Johnson had once imagined democracy "as a ladder...up which all...may ascend."[43] Now, as blacks began their climb, he removed the middle rungs in an effort to replicate the old black-white dependence relations within the context of the new contract equality. He was not alone in this endeavor. As W. E. B. DuBois first demonstrated in *Black Reconstruction*, postbellum legal, economic, and social barriers did much to maintain an apartheid system of racial freedoms.[44] And yet, the conceptual distinction between capitalist and laborer proved unstable at best. Under slavery, black and white conditions had been clearly distinguished by laws that made one person the property and dependent of the other. Now, even despite the black codes passed by Southern legislatures to preserve white control, the new ambiguities of this relation were impossible to contain. The wider possibilities of black economic freedom had already been illustrated by a small but influential class of black entrepreneurs like Elizabeth Keckley who had fought through the obstacles of the white economic infrastructure to establish businesses and acquire land. With "self-right," or ownership of their own labor, the black bodies that had once been commodities in a white-controlled market economy now threatened to gain control over white bodies—first as agents in that market economy, and eventually as cosovereigns in the symbolic economy.[45]

In response to the instability of postbellum racial relations, racialist discourse turned back to the logic of natural and absolute racial difference to legitimate and secure political apartheid. Johnson demonstrates this tactic, asserting that blacks lacked the "capacity to exercise with safety the highest rights of the Anglo-Saxon."[46] A Thomas Nast cartoon from the period echoes his claim (see figure 4.1), depicting the houses of Congress overrun with Sambo caricatures whose distorted bodies and faces look grotesquely out of place amid a group of distressed white politicians. Both texts deploy ethnographic and anthropological "knowledge" regarding

Figure 4.1. "Colored Rule in a Reconstructed (?) State," *Harper's Weekly*, May 1874.

the immutability of racial types and hierarchies. Once an essential justification for slavery—as in such works as John Van Evrie's *Negroes and Negro Slavery: The First an Inferior Race: The Latter Its Normal Condition*—the "science" of embodied difference now served to legitimate and naturalize arbitrary limits, buttressing the Johnsonian segregation of freedoms.

Antimiscegenation discourse added a new and formidable twist to this line of reasoning. In rhetoric that insistently pictured its violation in embodied terms, the "truth" of racial division could be made even more true, inevitable, and required. And that division was most potently reinforced by the juxtaposition of black male and white female bodies. In Nast's cartoon, the figure of Lady Liberty who brandishes her sword from the top right corner looks more like a statue than a part of this human gathering, and seems nearly as out of place as the sambo legislators. Yet her difference places her above rather than below the political scene, and provides authority to bring "peace" by banishing the blacks. Likewise, the domestic angel protected white freedom through her utter difference from the imagined hyperembodiment of blacks. This is the force behind Johnson's reference to intermarriage and in the question, put repeatedly to those calling for black suffrage, "Would you have your daughter marry one?" In fact, the very term *miscegenation* originated in service to this strategy, in a pamphlet titled *Miscegenation: The Theory of the Blending of the Races, Applied to the American White Man and Negro*. Written during the 1864 presidential campaign, the pamphlet advances a bogus argument for improving the American population through racial amalgamation. The two antiabolitionists who anonymously wrote it intended to malign the Republican Party by pushing the emancipation agenda to an "absurd" conclusion. Here again, black and white bodies are forced together as an argument for their incommensurability.[47] For the postbellum United States, the idea of miscegenation and its mixed-race progeny signaled the nation's worst failures, recalling the depredations of slavery. By aligning these images with a potential future of cosovereignty, white supremacists sent a devastating message.

In April 1868, two years after Johnson's civil rights bill veto and in the wake of Mary Lincoln's old clothes scandal, Elizabeth Keckley published *Behind the Scenes: Thirty Years a Slave and Four Years in the White House*.[48] The autobiography takes as its focus those relationships at stake in Johnson's veto and the Lincoln scandal—relationships between white and black freedoms, between white middle-class domesticity and black labor, and between symbolic and market economics. As we have seen, the dominant political discourse posed each of these relationships as an opposition between mutually exclusive terms. Keckley turns these oppositions inside out. She reveals that the white ideal of political freedom relies intimately—in both its material and symbolic manifestations—upon the enslaved and free labor of blacks. In Lefort's terms, Keckley insists on precisely that possibility which haunts democratic culture: she exposes the proximity of private bodies to democratic power. In the terms of postbellum racialist discourse, Keckley asserts that white freedom is and has always been the offspring of some form of miscegenation. She performs her own ethnography of white supremacist America to expose it as a mulatta body politic.

As a black woman Elizabeth Keckley stood outside of most postbellum debates regarding the meaning and distribution of political freedom. She was black but not male, so the radical Republicans overlooked her in their work for "universal" civil rights. She was female but not white, and therefore soon to be excluded from the campaign for "woman" suffrage.[49] Yet as an ex-slave and intimate of the Great Emancipator's household, Keckley lived in close proximity to those spectacular events and symbols through which Americans imagined themselves as a nation dedicated to political freedom. As representations of domesticity, these symbols resisted her direct identification. In the South, after all, black women who left the fields to care for their children and homes after emancipation were criticized for "acting the lady."[50] Northern domesticity likewise marked the difference between freedom and slavery, acting in conjunction with what Laura Wexler calls "the imperial project of sentimentalism" to organize working-class and black subjects within white supremacist consciousness as an economic complement and ideological foil.[51] Yet, as Rafia Zafar notes, "the fact that Keckley... and others like [her] were employees within an intimate female world gave them a peculiar entree into, and a kind of power over, white women's lives."[52] In Keckley's case, this power had both material and symbolic dimensions. That is, the fact of her material relation became significant at the symbolic level because, as seamstress to the First Lady, she was the origin of one of white America's foremost symbols of political freedom. By re-presenting the domestic spectacle in the material context of her own life and labor, Keckley subverts its performance of noncontingency. She reveals the very thing the First Lady's image strives to suppress: the racialized conditions of its production.[53]

In her preface Keckley represents her relation to domesticity and freedom as a relation of origin to surface. She begins: "Through me and the enslaved millions of my race, one of the problems was solved that belongs to the great problem of human destiny.... A solemn truth was thrown to the surface, and what is better still, it was recognized *as a truth* by those who give force to moral laws" (xii). In Keckley's reckoning, it was suffering and unfreedom like her own that finally gave content to the concept of liberty, nearly a century after the Declaration of Independence. Enslaved bodies, that is, stand as the origin of freedom's truth—a status that Keckley characterizes as a service on behalf of "human destiny." Opposed to, but supported by, those bodies is the superficial "surface," a public veneer of white language, law, and imagery. Slavery is not the only context to which Keckley applies her origin-surface binary. In the passage immediately following that quoted above, she resurrects it in relation to very different circumstances. Having changed topics abruptly from slavery to the old clothes scandal, Keckley is explaining her reasons for writing the book: "The people knew nothing of the secret history of [Mary Lincoln's] transactions, therefore they judged her by what was thrown to the surface.... The veil of mystery must be drawn aside; the origin of the fact must be brought to light with the naked fact itself" (xiii–xiv). Practically speaking, this second application of the origin-surface conceit alludes to the premise that markets the autobiography: Keckley has exclusive possession of secret, authenticating information—truths that are the origin of "naked facts" regarding the First Lady and the old clothes scandal.[54] At the same time, however, the second passage refers back to the first. The word *surface* repeats less than a page from its first appearance, an unmistakable echo that establishes a connection between the two topics of the autobiography: slavery and the White House. This connection strengthens with Keckley's reference to the "drawn veil"—a common metaphor in slave narratives for the exposure of concealed truths.[55] Used in relation to the First Lady, the veil signals a correspondence between her "secret history" and the undisclosed crimes of slaveholders. Further, it implies a continuity between Keckley's two primary roles in the book: the formerly enslaved body that gives meaning to the word *freedom*, and the laborer who decodes the "naked facts" at the surface of the White House.

This logic of origin and surface provides the structure through which Keckley will define her position throughout the book. She is a site of origination, located somewhere "behind the scenes" and beneath a surface of meanings that stand as incomplete, vulnerable, and incomprehensible without her (one of the book's fundamental if unstated claims is that America is unqualified to read its own political theater and requires interlocutors such as herself). Keckley's claim to origin-ality is not simply a device to establish the veracity of her revelations, although certainly this is part of its import.[56] More centrally, she aims to reveal the means by which "truth" is produced. Her narrative traces the dialectic between material origin and symbolic surface that generates political concepts like "freedom." Within this dialectic, a claim to foundationalist authority can become a liability—particularly when that claim refers to the authenticity of black embodied experience. For, as we have already seen in relation to portrayals of Sojourner Truth, the trope of black embodiment was easily appropriated and deployed on the white-controlled surface.

The spectacle of the suffering black body is a common source of authority in slave narratives and, initially, Keckley draws upon it to construct her enslavement as a devastating physical reality that teaches whites to understand freedom and justice. Chapter 2, "Girlhood and Its Sorrows," portrays Keckley being summoned by a neighbor named Mr. Bingham who, at her mistress's behest, orders the girl to strip and begins to beats her. When she resists, her assailant only becomes more determined to "conquer" her (37). At the end of a third beating, however, he abruptly bursts into tears and vows never to beat a slave again, "declar[ing] it would be a sin." Keckley attributes this sudden change of heart directly to her body, explaining in the classic reformist rhetoric of sympathy, "As I stood bleeding before him... my suffering at last subdued his hard heart; he asked my forgiveness, and afterwards was an altered man." The following day, Keckley's master takes up where Bingham left off and assaults her again. This time his wife begins to weep and begs him to desist. As he administers a fourth beating, the master himself is finally converted, vowing, "with an air of penitence, that he should never strike me another blow" (38). At the center of this parable on liberty—in which arbitrary and cruel power attempts to "subdue" the victim's "proud, rebellious spirit"—is Keckley's body. Repeatedly, freedom's negative image is enunciated by her physical state: the humiliation of standing naked before a man as "a woman fully developed" (33), the "terrible, excruciating agony" of the whip upon her back (34), the carefully enumerated injuries that disable her for weeks to come. In each scene of injustice, Keckley's body is the vividly rendered picture of oppression. In each moment of conversion to the principles of freedom and justice, that body, "the sight of [Keckley's] bleeding form," is what teaches the truth (37).

Such scenes occur frequently in antebellum slave narratives where, like the white domestic angel, the enslaved black body could pose as a source of prepolitical authenticity and national value. Of course, the two modes of identification differ fundamentally. The white, feminine domesticity signals the promise of democratic freedom by encoding itself as disembedded from history and radically noncontingent. The trope of the suffering black body generates a related effect by encoding itself as *hyper*embedded, wholly subject to contingency. So that, as the absolute of unfreedom, the black body presents an inverted signified of the political signifier, freedom. As Mary Lincoln's case demonstrates, the strategy of drawing authority from transcendent privacy came with constraints. Likewise, the trope of martyred embodiment could become what Houston Baker describes as a "linguistic prison" that reidentified black autobiographers with enslavement and lack (256).[57] By the time Keckley wrote her autobiography in 1868, many black authors had recognized for themselves the treachery of embodied authenticity. In *My Bondage and My Freedom*, Frederick Douglass de-emphasizes the physical suffering that pervades his first book—a process that Ben Slote describes as "revising toward disembodiment."[58] Always a shrewd manipulator of democratic codes, Douglass exchanges the rhetoric of privative embodiment for that of public disembodiment. Keckley's origin-surface formulation of slavery—set out in her preface and illustrated in the conversions from chapter 2—seems to participate in the earlier tradition of corporeal authority. However, she will soon leave this tradition behind.

If "Girlhood and Its Sorrows" concluded Keckley's theorization of the relationship between bodies and surface, *Behind the Scenes* would do little to revise pre-emancipation racial constructs or to disrupt the new strategies of postbellum racialist discourse. Fortunately, the autobiography has more to say on both topics. Even as her preface sets out her initial interpretation of slavery and freedom—"a truth was thrown to the surface"—she adds to it this crucial observation:

> What is better still, it was recognized *as a truth* by those who give force to moral laws. An act may be wrong, but unless the ruling power recognizes the wrong, it is useless to hope for a correction of it. Principles may be right, but they are not established within an hour.... [E]ach principle, to acquire moral force, must come to us from the fire of the crucible.... [I]t purifies and renders stronger the principle, not in itself, but in the eyes of those who arrogate judgement to themselves. (xii)

This qualification is an early hint that Keckley's origin-surface device will work toward more than the appropriation of authority to her own person. Although she anchors the principle of freedom in embodied experience, she acknowledges too that meaning is always contingent, always subject to power. Meaning, she suggests, resides in neither the origin nor the surface but in the historical contexts and power relations that mediate their interaction.[59]

Keckley illustrates this more dialectical view of the intersection among meaning making, black bodies, and "ruling powers" with a later episode. Now recounting her life with the Lincolns, Keckley describes a spelling lesson between Mary and Tad. Tad, whose "book knowledge was very limited," is relying on the pictures and cannot be convinced by his mother or Keckley that A-p-e does not spell "monkey" (217). He defends his position at length.

> "An Ape! 'taint an ape. Don't I know a monkey when I see it?"
>
> "No, if you say that is a monkey."
>
> "I do know a monkey. I've seen lots of them in the street with the organs. I know a monkey better than you do, 'cause I always go out into the street to see them when they come by, and you don't."
>
> "But, Tad, listen to me. An ape is a species of the monkey. It looks like a monkey, but it is not a monkey."
>
> "It shouldn't look like a monkey, then." (218)

Keckley's recollection offers a pointed satire of white "knowledge" as a species of childish and tyrannical ignorance—a judgment that also implicates the sciences of ethnography and anthropology where the identities of both apes and Africans were objectified and, frequently, conflated. Yet Keckley also signals a deep recognition of the power that white knowledge production wields—specifically, over herself. At the conclusion of the scene she reflects wryly, "Whenever I think of this incident I am tempted to laugh; and then it occurs to me that had Tad been a negro boy, not the son of a President . . . he would have been called thick-skulled, and would have been held up as an example of the inferiority of [the] race" (219). Keckley's afterthought marks the graver implications of Tad's reading lesson. Acts of white signification may be arbitrary and even ludicrous. But, as practiced by Tad, Andrew Johnson, racialist "science," and the mob who spat the epithet "black ape Republican" at Abraham Lincoln as he arrived in Washington in 1860, they condition the national identity of her racialized person, right down to the thickness of her skull and the extent of her freedom.

The power of white signification is not dispatched by parody, moral condemnation, or any easy opposition between black authenticity and white inauthenticity. The embodying trope of originary martyrdom does not afford an identity that transcends its culture; nor does it remove black bodies from subjection to the surface. In this scene, where the domestic setting merges with the ethnographer's study, Tad's assertion of meaning-making prerogative resonates within the changing nationalist context of racial knowledge, where black bodies provided the ground upon which white supremacy affirmed itself with increasing violence. Whether by choice or not, Keckley must operate in this context. To do so most effectively, she leaves behind the originary status of her once-enslaved body for that of her paid labor.

Like Frederick Douglass, Keckley switches genres at the point where the rhetorical display of the martyred black body reaches its political limit. She drops the narrative conventions of the slave narrative and launches into as-told-by exposé with the Lincolns as her focus. This switch enables Keckley to exchange one identity for another among those available to her on the surface of white meanings. She continues to invoke the origin-surface binary and to associate herself with its first term by way of the body. But, by revising her narrative tactic, she re-encodes that body. The second part of *Behind the Scenes* constructs Keckley as what William Andrews calls a "superlaborer."[60] It details the growth of her business and quotes the praises of VIP customers. Always, it emphasizes her independence. Drawing on a different strain of free labor ideology than that which underwrites Johnson's apartheid logic, Keckley makes a great point of having bought her own freedom according to the terms of white contract law and market principles. She provides a long list of sacrifices, transactions, and sums, establishing the fact of her self-right with compulsive adherence to white standards.

This adherence seems to reach the point of excess in the chapter titled "How I Gained My Freedom," where Keckley negotiates terms of purchase for herself and her child. Her "master" responds to the request with "a petulant look" and tells her to escape across the river with her son: "If you really wish to leave me...[i]t is the cheapest way that I know of to accomplish what you desire" (48). Staring "in astonishment," Keckley delivers what Andrews describes as a pledge of "her unswerving fealty to the ethics of the marketplace":[61]

> "No, master, I do not wish to be free in such a manner....I can cross the river any day, as you well know, and have frequently done so, but will never leave you in such a manner. By the laws of the land I am your slave—you are my master, and I will only be free by such means as the laws of the country provide." (48–49)

This seems a strangely pious endorsement of the legal contracts by which whites defined black freedom. It could not differ more from the sentiments expressed on the same issue in Harriet Jacobs's *Incidents in the Life of a Slave Girl*, where her pseudonymous heroine Linda Brent declares, "The more my mind had become enlightened, the more difficult it was for me to consider myself an article of property; and to pay money to those who had so grievously oppressed me seemed like taking from my sufferings the glory of triumph."[62] For Keckley, writing in the postbellum context, the aim is not to preserve her suffering in a transcendent state of glory or triumph but to parlay it into a more advantageous position within the contingencies of market capitalism. With a series of carefully transcribed documents stating legal transfer of ownership, she transfers her body from one set of white codes to another, from commodity to economic agent—or, as Frances Smith Foster puts it, from "capital to capitalist."[63] It is important to note, however, that this move up the ladder of free labor remains within a relative frame of discourse that Keckley does not control. Like the category of "martyr," the category of "agent" could be appropriated and redeployed on the hegemonic surface. The paranoid attacks on freedpeople that pervaded postbellum discourse and journalism evince as much.[64] As we shall see, the parody *Behind the Seams* would participate in this publicity by recasting Keckley's economic agency as a violation of white entitlement. And, of course, Johnson's logic of apartheid freedoms reminds us that one could shed the status of "capital" without fully acquiring that of "capitalist." Nevertheless, within the discursive context of Keckley's autobiography, her new condition becomes integral to her project of resignifying the dominant understanding of freedom.

The chief advantage of Keckley's genre shift from martyred body to laboring body is not that it emphasizes a transition from dependency and enslavement to contract freedom, but that it underscores her relation to Mary Todd Lincoln and all that the First Lady represents. From this point on, Lincoln becomes the focus of Keckley's investigation into the phenomenology of white freedom. Here again Keckley diverges from the dominant slave narrative tradition, which always posits, in one form or another, a foundationalist concept of freedom. Whether in the transcendent authorities of Christian conversion, liberal self-possession, or human desire, freedom is always rooted in some authority beyond the control of white culture.[65] Even Harriet Jacobs and Frederick Douglass, who bitterly recount the failures of freedom in Northern society, point to a place beyond it. For Jacobs this is the metaphorical and material horizon of "home," for Douglass the utopian potential in universal suffrage and constitutional principles. Keckley's gaze falls somewhere short of "beyond" to focus squarely on that surface of democratic fantasy controlled by white culture. In sweeping and elegiac terms, Keckley describes the disappointments of Reconstruction for all freedmen and freedwomen; and she locates their source in Washington, DC:

> They came with a great hope in their hearts, and with all their worldly goods on their backs. Fresh from the bonds of slavery, fresh from the benighted regions of the plantation, they came to the Capital looking for liberty, and many of them not knowing it when they found it. (111)

In passages like this one, Keckley marks freedom as an empty promise around which real lives take disappointing shapes. And, increasingly, this emptiness converges with the empty place represented by Mary Todd Lincoln and the whole of the presidential spectacle.[66]

Many critics have pointed out that as Keckley settles her gaze on Lincoln and the White House she appears increasingly distanced from other blacks and complicit with white discourse.[67] Indeed, she seems to exclude herself from the "they" of the above passage. Yet this complicity is consistently and wonderfully double voiced. For, precisely where Keckley appears to espouse the master's logic, she exposes its contradictions and deceptions. One such instance is her story of meeting an "old freedwoman" who was unsatisfied with the terms of emancipation:

> "Why, Missus Keckley," said she to me one day, "I is been here eight months, and Missus Lingom [Lincoln] an't even give me one

> shife. Bliss God, children, if I had ar know dat de Government, and Mister and Missus Government, was going to do dat ar way, I neber would'ave comed here in God's wurld. My old missus us't gib me two shifes eber year." (141)

The ostensible purpose of this anecdote is to point up the other woman's mistaken view of democratic liberty and distance Keckley from it. "I could not restrain a laugh at the grave manner in which this good old woman entered her protest," recalls the writer. "Her idea of freedom was two or more old shifts every year" (141–42). This remark also echoes uncomfortably with contemporaneous critiques of the Republican-sponsored Freedmen's Bureau Program—a network of offices set up to support and advocate for freedpeople in the South. Speaking against a bill that would expand the bureau's powers and jurisdiction, Andrew Johnson argued thusly: "Pending the war many refugees and freedmen received support from the Government, but it was never intended that they should henceforth be fed, clothed, educated, and sheltered by the United States."[68] Here, as always, Johnson's first concern is increased federal power, and the compromise of universal sovereignty that would stem from federal interference into such matters as the widespread poverty and homelessness of newly emancipated blacks. By holding up the woman's mistake as ludicrous (in part by rendering it in minstrel-style dialect), Keckley seems to affirm both Johnson's condemnation of a Republican welfare state and his characterization of blacks as unqualified to claim the more valuable commodity of white political freedom.

Yet, this juxtaposition of official and unofficial ideas on freedom produces vital surplus effects. As Keckley recounts the old woman's theory, the identity of the presidency begins to waver:

> She thought, as many others thought, that Mr. and Mrs. Lincoln were the government, and that the President and his wife had nothing to do but to supply the extravagant wants of every one that applied to them. The old woman had been in the habit of receiving annually two shifts from her mistress, and she thought the wife of the President of the United States very mean for overlooking this established custom of the plantation. (141)

At one moment, the First Family is the preeminent symbol of universal power and freedom, disavowing private power, uncompromised by material relation to the welfare of individuals. At the next, read from the old woman's perspective, the White House becomes the Big House, and the First Family negligent masters. The scene recalls a similar moment in *Incidents*, where a "poor, ignorant woman" comes to Jacobs, begging for confirmation that the "queen of 'Merica" had forced the president to free the slaves. Jacobs explains:

> She said her husband told her that the black people had sent word to the queen of 'Merica that they were all slaves; that she didn't believe it, and went to Washington city to see the president about it. They quarreled; she drew her sword upon him, and swore that he should help her to make them all free.[69]

Lauren Berlant points out that such moments demonstrate "how the slaves misrecognized, in potentially and sometimes strategically radical ways, what constitutes the nation."[70] Like Jacobs, Keckley injects radical indeterminacy into the presidential icon by reading it through the gaze of black political unfreedom. She builds on this indeterminacy when she adds: "[The woman] thought, as many others thought, that Mr. and Mrs. Lincoln were the government." The comment raises some uneasy questions. For if Mr. and Mrs. Lincoln are not the government, what are they? There is one obvious answer to this question. The democratic ideal requires that Mr. and Mrs. Lincoln are not, as private persons, the government, and that the nation should not operate as a plantation, profiting neither a Big House nor a White House. Such an arrangement, thus translated from the market to the symbolic economy, would constitute monarchy. Although the market economy is imagined as a force of democratization within free labor ideology, it becomes violently antidemocratic upon contact with political transactions. The old woman's mistake forces this contact. It strips the Lincolns of what Berlant refers to as the "fantasy norms of democratic abstraction" and reduces them to private persons. As Berlant argues, Jacobs's president is embodied by a "cold tip of steel" against his throat that "educates him about his own body's boundaries."[71] Keckley's First Family acquires their embodiment by virtue of the "shifes" that she places in their hands and that transport them back from the symbolic into the market economy.

Yet, for all the similarities it reveals, this comparison of Jacobs and Keckley points again to a basic difference in antebellum and postbellum strategies. By invoking the "queen of 'Merica" and later the "Queen of Justice," Jacobs points to another external source of freedom. Her two queens constitute outside authorities to whom the president can be imagined as subordinate and who could force him to emancipate the slaves. Eventually this imagined possibility is undermined in *Incidents*: as Berlant points out, Jacobs introduces the queens only to bracket and even ironize their potential power.[72] Yet it is the transcendent authority of this possibility that informs the misrecognition of the presidency in her text. In contrast, Keckley exposes the presidency on its own terms. It is not misrecognized but recognized more fully, as the juxtaposition of white and black knowledges reveals the interdependence of symbolic and market economies. When Keckley turns her own gaze upon the white image of presidential power, she again marks its position at the intersection of symbolic and material systems of value, but with a different twist. Through Keckley's eyes it becomes apparent that, as symbolic persons who inhabit a surface of utopian meanings, the Lincolns are national commodities that circulate in the marketing of symbolic freedom. And she is the labor that produces them.

Using her vantage point as seamstress and servant in the nation's First Home, Keckley commandeers our view of presidential privacy. With her, we learn about the celebrated 1862 state dinner—not from the formal public dining room, but from the parlor where husband and wife negotiate arrangements. Later we worry with the couple at Willie's sickbed as ambassadors assemble downstairs. We review the various merits of cabinet members through the medium of household gossip. Most important, we come at every historical event through the focal point of what Mary wears: what fabrics make up the skirt, what types of trim adorn it, how many tucks go in the bodice, and so on. These scenes of "average" home life make up the nationalist spectacle signifying the "universal" freedoms of whites. Keckley makes them her privileged domain—a "surface" whose true significance can be explained only by her. She is the marginal but indispensable figure, an interlocutor like Raphael's angel, pointing at them but looking out toward us.

Significantly, Keckley installs herself just beneath this surface instead of within it, resisting identification with that domesticity and the ideas it conveys. As we have seen, Mary Lincoln's identification with both afforded her little freedom or power in either the market or symbolic economies. In *Behind the Scenes*, Keckley capitalizes on her relationship to Lincoln to control and exploit the value of the domestic spectacle without partaking of it. Like the freedwomen who rejected their "new right" to enter marriage contracts, recognizing it as another kind of bondage, she avoids the disempowerment of domestic identity.[73] Rather than seeking to resignify her own identity through relation *to* domesticity, Keckley sets out to resignify the identity *of* domesticity by explicating its relation to her. By extension, she will reveal the racialist, material basis of white democratic freedom and portend the full national significance of black economic freedom. It is her labor as a seamstress, after all, that places Keckley in the political households of Jefferson Davis and Lincoln; and the details of that labor—sums, hours, office space, clientele, and, of course, products—link her to some of the most significant political scenes of her time. She bids the Davis family farewell when they go south to Richmond, already predicting victory for the North (71–73). She listens to Abraham Lincoln review war strategy as she sews in Mary's sitting room and overhears him pondering state affairs as she passes an open door, arms full of silk. When questioned anxiously on whether Lincoln will be reelected, Keckley "look[s] up from her work" to assure Mary that he will (148–49). Not long after, she foresees the assassination two days before it occurs (178). Systematically, Keckley weaves her own labor and economic freedom into the fabric of U.S. political history.

Most important, as seamstress to the Davis and Lincoln families, Keckley is more than a uniquely qualified witness and translator of political spectacle. She is its creator and, as such, claims intimate relation to the scenes she interprets. A prominent focus of the public outcry against Mary Todd Lincoln was objects—the dresses she tried to sell, the sixty crates of furnishings she removed from the White House, a nightstand Abraham Lincoln had particularly liked that went to Chicago for Tad's use. The public was obsessively interested in these goods, reading article after article for their descriptions and cost. These objects were the props of Mrs. Lincoln's iconicity. Hinging between her symbolic function and her private personhood—between executive privacy and private self-interest—they became the natural focus of her guilt. At the heart of the public's obsession lay the question of possession: did these goods, and the power they symbolized, belong to Mrs. Lincoln or to the people? How could they belong to both at once? To the Rochester *Democrat* the answer was clear: "She says these things were the gifts of friends. We do not believe it. She has lavished the money given her by the nation on diamonds, furs, and lace."[74]

Keckley intervenes at exactly the crucial point, then, when she meticulously describes her role in creating and caring for the First Family's clothing and home.[75] As seamstress to the Davis and Lincoln households, she is quite literally the "origin" of the images "thrown to the surface" of America's political consciousness. She remembers, for example, having stitched a dressing gown for Jefferson Davis as he resolved to wage war for the Confederacy: "This very robe," she muses, "must have sometimes been on his back as he issued directions to the Confederate army" (67–69). Keckley's speculation is significant. For, at least in her own imagination, she is now not merely standing behind the scenes but costuming and staging that spectacular redemption of freedom—the Civil War. The full import of this claim only comes to light, however, when we discover that others corroborate it. While attending a charity fair in Chicago after the war, Keckley comes upon a waxen diorama of Davis's surrender. Adorning the statue is another of her creations—a chintz wrapper sewn for his wife. The story of "old Jeff's" capture in female disguise was, by then, a favorite national joke, widely repeated in cartoons, stories, and songs

Figure 4.2. "Jefferson Davis as an Unprotected Female!" *Harper's Weekly*, May 1865.

(see figure 4.2). Keckley first describes the diorama and the "great crowd" gathered around it—creating, in effect, a visual representation of the joke and the public attention it had garnered. She then adds herself:

> When it was announced that I recognized the dress as one that I had made for the wife of the late Confederate President there was great cheering and excitement, and I at once became an object of the deepest curiosity. Great crowds followed me, and in order to escape from the embarrassing situation I left the building. (75)

When the spectacle of Davis's humiliation is supplanted by the dressmaker who produced it, certain "naked facts" are "brought to light"—as Keckley's preface has promised they would. At one level, the scene reiterates her basic materialist argument concerning what lies behind the scenes of democratic iconography: the public searches for the reflection of its own freedom and unity—in the empty place of the presidency, or in the humiliation of slavery's defender—and discovers the origin of that surface in the laboring black woman. But Keckley also invites a deeper reading of these miscegenist material relations when she recalls the "great crowd" transferring its attention from her product to herself. The apartheid conditions of postbellum freedom prevented Keckley from standing with that crowd; that is, she would never reach the top of the free labor ladder to gain the political right of cosovereignty and join in full symbolic possession of the commodities she herself created. Relegated to the limited range of black economic freedom, she remained in some sense dependent upon the white capitalist-citizen. In the diorama episode, however, where the products of her black labor generate and regulate imaginary democratic communities, the terms of that relation shift. Johnson's racialized complement of labor and capital is displaced by a new pairing of production and consumption. With this re-vision of postbellum racial relations, the dynamic of dependence reverses—a point that hits home as the crowd attaches itself to Keckley and begins to follow her from the scene like the Pied Piper's spellbound children. The episode refers back to the First Lady—most obviously in that she stands among the nation's most prominent objects of consumer citizenship. It also recalls Lincoln as the infamously compulsive and profligate shopper who, regardless of the citizenry's harsh disapproval of her, emblematizes their own consumerist dependency.

As the narrative proceeds to its conclusion, the identity of the democratic state is repeatedly displaced onto its metonymic representation—that is, onto the objects created and controlled by Keckley that make up what Xiomara Santamarina aptly describes as her "sartorial publicity."[76] This process culminates in the seamstress's request that she be permitted to keep the glove worn by President Lincoln during his second inauguration. "I shall cherish it," she explains, "as a precious memento of...the man who has lifted [my race] out of bondage. I shall keep the glove, and hand it down to posterity" (154). Her promise identifies the glove as a signifier of the state and of the state's function as protector of freedoms in liberal democracy. Keckley says she takes the glove as memento of "the man" but, even as she speaks, the signifier "glove" floats free from its relation to him. To the democratic subject, the state resides in the glove—the spectacle—not in the man. The glove, furthermore, will remain when the man is gone, and its continuing power to signify "freedom" will draw from relation to Keckley rather than Lincoln. Indeed, as a teacher at Wilberforce University years later, Keckley became known among her students for distributing scraps from the fabrics she had used to make Mary Lincoln's clothing.[77] The hand of "manumission" extends not from the white man who wore the glove or the white woman who commissioned the gowns, but from the black woman whose laboring and once enslaved body radically conditions their transcendent promise.

If Keckley embraces the white surface of semantics and law that threatens to disempower her, she does so in order to expose its dependence upon herself. She demonstrates that although her freedom is a function of white laws and letters, the symbols of white freedom are equally functions of her labor. However, while Keckley's ascent from slavery to the White House allows her to reveal more effectively the dialectical nature of white freedom, it does not remove her from that dialectical process. Within a year of publication, her own narrative was appropriated and used against her in an 1869 parody by D. Ottolengul titled *Behind the Seams: By a Nigger Woman Who Took In Work from Mrs. Lincoln and Mrs. Davis.* The text gives a highly condensed version of Keckley's story, skimming through the pre-emancipation episodes before concentrating on the White House. The author's racism and paranoid hostility toward freedpeople are apparent throughout. But rather than venting these openly, Ottolengul borrows Keckley's own strategy, inserting himself behind the scenes of her autobiographical performance to revise its meaning.

Ottolengul's narrator ("Betsy Kickley, a Nigger") opens by pronouncing herself an imposter: "I made up my mind that if I could find a publisher who would engineer my book, I'd try the thing on as I used to do with Mrs. Lincoln's dresses."[78] The declaration discredits Keckley as an interpreter of the political events described in her autobiography. Her assumption of authorship, Ottolengul implies, was a presumption of power and identity not her own. Indeed, he rewrites Keckley as an illiterate who signs her statement with "X, her mark"—an insult that may also reflect the widely held theory that *Behind the Scenes* had been written by James Redpath, a Republican journalist (11).[79] At once, Ottolengul demotes Keckley from business owner and seamstress to servant, reinstalling normative racial relations in terms of social and economic power. Both revisions serve to dislodge Keckley from her position as the origin of the presidential spectacle. In a sense, "Kickley's" statement echoes and literalizes the way that Keckley's text reveals her presence within the presidential dress. However, where her text conditions the authority of executive domesticity by insisting on its materiality and identifying herself as its origin, his text resurrects that authority—reestablishing the White House as a symbol of transcendent freedom—by inventing the crisis of its invasion by Kickley.

As the parody proceeds, Keckley herself becomes the surface and Ottolengul her origination as he "tries on" her voice in a kind of blackface performance. Often the point is to ridicule, as when Ottolengul scripts her life for vaudeville. Her account of Mr. Bingham's assault, for instance, becomes "a matinee performance" by a "Mr. Bangley," followed by the next man's "debut...with a broom handle" (8). Yet, surprisingly, a majority of the parody summarizes its source with very few changes, as though Ottolengul's chief aim is simply to occupy Keckley's voice and thereby reverse her self-presentation as she who directs the spectacle of white power. Even where Ottolengul merely retells, he offers a glimpse of himself as the force that converts Keckley's black agency into a symbolic commodity controlled and circulated in his text. A crucial gap opens between the white and black bodies, the integrity and autonomy of the former reconfirmed as the latter is distorted, distanced, and, finally, expelled.

Eric Lott suggests that the antebellum minstrel show promoted a sense of equality and sociopolitical alliance among whites of different classes. By providing a common enemy-other, the minstrel created a "white egalitarianism that, for all its real instabilities, buried class tensions and permitted class alliances along rigidifying racial lines, a vital need in this period of seeming disintegration."[80] Thirty years later, Ottolengul's Reconstruction minstrelsy performs a similar function through "Kickley." "Mr. Lincoln was truly, a great and good man," she/he confesses, "and I almost feel ashamed of myself when I think of what I have still before me to write in this book, in relation to his widow" (14). Like the "domestic affairs" of state governments that require Johnson's protection, the domestic symbol of Mary Lincoln is cleansed by this presentation of Keckley's intrusive authorship. Even Mary's own misappropriation of presidential iconicity gets reassigned to "Kickley" when the latter confesses, "When Mrs. Lincoln left the White House, a great deal of furniture was missing—she did not take it, however—it was stolen by the niggers" (16). In her own text, Keckley had traced the dialectical production of truths and noted that "recognition" by "those in power" conditions all meanings (xii). Now that reflection seems prescient, as her own words function against her within the white-controlled public sphere. As Ottolengul reasserts the white sanctity of domesticity and freedom, the dialectic between origin and surface takes its next turn.

What, then, came of Keckley's involvement in these two economies—market and symbolic? Although the scandal damaged her business, she continued on and became known for training other black women as seamstresses, eventually accepting a position as head of Wilberforce University's Department of Sewing and Domestic Science Arts. Wilberforce, which had been part of the underground railroad before the war and shifted to all-black ownership and administration afterward, had always prepared its students for both economic and political self-determination—even inviting Susan B. Anthony to come lecture on woman's suffrage in the early 1870s. It seems likely that Keckley found new opportunities there for dismantling the postbellum culture of apartheid freedoms.

She also left us with a deep reading of executive domesticity that reveals how the intercourse of black and white identities engenders a mulatta body politic. The surplus value of this contribution is emblematized in Keckley's portrait of her own mixed-race son, George, a child born after Keckley was raped by a white neighbor in the town where she was enslaved. Musing upon the absurdity of racial politics when viewed through the lens of George's mulatto identity, she writes,

> The Anglo-Saxon blood as well as the African flowed in his veins; the two currents commingled—one singing of freedom, the other silent and sullen with generations of despair. Why should not the Anglo-Saxon triumph—why should it be weighed down with the rich blood typical of the tropics? Must the life-current of one race bind the other race in chains as strong and enduring as if there had been no Anglo-Saxon taint? (47)

Here Keckley voices the white American's horror of miscegenation—that "revolting . . . offense against public decorum"—and seems, initially, to confirm a view of race relations wherein the Anglo-Saxon body is "weighed down" by its African blood.[81] Yet by quoting white supremacist logic in relation to her son, Keckley subverts it. The burdensome (non)white blood results, not from a violation of the domestic angel, but from the sexual, economic, and political violence of whites. Keckley mocks antimiscegenation fears by juxtaposing them with the rape of black women by white enslavers. She completes the effect with her reference to an "Anglo-Saxon taint." For these closing words reverse the dominant narrative of racial purity and contamination, and—like Keckley's book as a whole—force us to reconsider its meaning. Looking back over the passage in the light of that final line, we discover that now it is the white blood that "bind[s]" and a black voice that "sings of freedom."

CHAPTER FIVE

The Cost of Self in Two Alcott Utopias

The true autobiography is written by one who feels an irresistible longing for confidential expansion.
—David Seed, "Rambles among Books, No II—Autobiography"

It can be truly said of Louisa Alcott that her words are a revelation of herself. She rarely sought for the material of her stories in old chronicles, or foreign adventures. Her capital was her own life and experiences.
—Edna Cheney, *Louisa May Alcott: Life, Letters and Journals*

In the final decades of the nineteenth century, the fantasy of inviolable privacy came to refer more explicitly than ever to the property and market relations against which it was defined, and to protect more overtly the forms of privilege and exclusion it disavowed. Previous chapters have shown that even while midcentury privacy discourse helped to exclude women and blacks from public authority and belonging, it also promised universal entitlement. In Fuller's Romantic nationalism, Stowe's moral economy, and even the aggressive white egalitarianism navigated by Keckley, privacy stands simultaneously as a site of individual autonomy and democratic inclusivity. By the 1880s this was no longer the case. Samuel Warren and Louis Brandeis aptly characterize this change in their 1890 essay, "The Right to Privacy," when they call for "a more liberal doctrine."[1] Although elements of republicanism still informed the end-century discourse on privacy, these had less to do with the common good than with social Darwinist theories on the ill-contained privation of nonwhites and the poor. The emphasis on privacy as an ameliorative communal experience that had characterized earlier representations now gave place to a portrait of beleaguered individuality and degraded mass publicity.

This chapter tracks the shifting tone of U.S. privacy discourse through the works of Louisa May Alcott, a writer who was intimately acquainted with both of its extremes. My analyses focus especially on the second and third installments of Alcott's March trilogy, *Little Men: Life at Plumfield with Jo's Boys* and *Jo's Boys, and How They Turned Out*. Both novels are set at the Plumfield School for boys, a "small world" of Alcott's invention where she experiments with both property and privacy relations to regulate her own ideal political economy.[2] Published in 1871 and 1886 respectively, the two works bracket the period that Stephanie Coontz identifies as the "apex" of U.S. privacy values. Their differences illustrate how privacy discourse both intensifies and shifts during those decades. *Little Men* demonstrates Alcott's strong allegiance to the utopianism of midcentury privacy discourse—including that of her father, Bronson Alcott—and to the postbellum creeds of free labor and market agency. Written fifteen years later, *Jo's Boys* reflects a very different set of attitudes concerning both property and privacy. In it, Alcott engages the same issues that would concern Warren and Brandeis four years later; but where they resent the loss of privacy, she resents the losses suffered for privacy. At the close of her career, Alcott confronts the exclusionary action of privacy discourse, and mourns its implications for U.S. democracy.

From 1870 until the early 1900s, laissez-faire capitalism dominated U.S. political culture, combining intense resistance to governmental intervention with aggressive confidence in the self-regulating institutions of the free market, free labor, and private property. Contributing to this mind-set was a discourse that has come to be described as classic social Darwinism. Proponents of social Darwinism advocated a political economy based on unrestrained competition, reasoning that groups who fared poorly under this system did so due to genetic inferiority and lacked those qualities that made an individual—and nation—successful. This "survival of the fittest" philosophy, largely derived from the midcentury writings of British philosopher Herbert Spencer, was one of many (mis)applications of Charles Darwin's evolutionary theory to human social patterns.[3] In the United States it gained currency as an exceptionalist narrative that affirmed the nation's "remarkable success in [converting its] forefathers from brute creatures into human creatures" and made evolutionary theory a precept for political and economic policy.[4] Elaborated in the 1880s by American sociologist William Graham Sumner, social Darwinism became a potent element of the laissez-faire attack on social welfare, economic regulation, and antidiscrimination legislation. Such measures, it was argued, prevented the natural elimination of "unfit" groups and weakened the nation as a whole. Spencer also applied his ideas to pedagogical theory, explaining that young children were developmentally equivalent to savages and must be guided along the evolutionary path in a manner that would not only preserve but also refine national and racial phylogeny. For both groups and individuals, laissez-faire and social Darwinism combined to form an ethic of elitist nationalism that identified progress with purification.

These theories merged with the discourse on privacy. In contrast to the midcentury period, when Americans who desired personal privacy were often accused of antidemocratic and aristocratic pretensions, late-century writers associated such desires with superior evolutionary development. In 1881, for example, J. V. Sears explains to *Atlantic Monthly* readers that the increased upper-class demand for "seclusion" and "impenetrable safeguards" is a recent social phenomenon indicating "progress from savagery to civilization."[5] Using this "scientific sociological" analysis to naturalize class privilege as a biological imperative, Sears predicts that it will soon be necessary to introduce telephones and electricity into upper-class homes in order to decrease contact with servants and tradespeople.[6] Meanwhile, like the laissez-faire economists who argued that savage and "unfit" groups lacked crucial instincts for acquisition and competition, others found that these same groups exhibited an uncouth taste for consuming other people's privacy and airing their own. The writer of an 1892 article titled "The Penalties of a Well-Known Name" envies the "obscure nonentities called Stubbs, or Stadge, or Briggs, or Bragg," who are fortunate enough to escape public attention; but, he adds, they "do not value it, do not appreciate it; do not, indeed, ever cease from dissatisfaction at it."[7] The writer then goes on to blame this group's "ill-bred interrogation," "vulgar taste," and "impertinent curiosity" for creating a market for gossip journalism. Repeatedly describing such desires in terms of "appetite" and "craving," he links disregard for privacy with the body's "baser" impulses, quoting a social evolutionary logic wherein groups display differing levels of progress along the continuum from a savage or animal condition dominated by bodily drives toward a higher state of civilized being.[8]

Race held a central place in the evolutionary narrative on privacy, particularly during the 1890s when anti-immigration sentiment, Jim Crow segregation, and lynching violence were most intense. Unsurprisingly, white writers found that nonwhites lacked the desire for privacy that distinguished civilized races. "Privacy," explains E. L. Godkin, "is one of the luxuries of civilization, which is not only unsought for but unknown in primitive or barbarous societies; the savage cannot have privacy, and does not desire or dream of it."[9] Working from this premise, others warned that the culture's failure to protect privacy amounted to a betrayal of Anglo-Saxon origins and would reverse racial advances. "Vulgarity will envelope the nation," warns the journalist John Gilmer Speed,

> and we will permanently deserve the reproach now put upon us by the nations of Europe—that in civilization we are on par with the half-reclaimed Slavs of Russia, and only a trifle higher in the scale than the mongrels who live in perpetual revolution in Central and South America . . . The individual citizen must cultivate to its highest development that confident moral courage which counts no sacrifice too great when made to enforce any atom of his rights.[10]

Like Godkin's, Speed's argument indicates how thoroughly the discourses on privacy and scientific racism were intertwined by the end of the nineteenth century. Speed also demonstrates that privacy was no longer championed as a universal right, but rather as an ontologically white and upper-class trait calling for aggressive "enforcement" against the imagined encroachment of alien others.

In "The Right to Privacy," Warren and Brandeis formulate two evolutionary arguments, both of which demonstrate how racialist theory merged with the discourse on privacy to naturalize an expanding zone of exclusion and privilege. The first echoes previous writers such as J. V. Sears who had interpreted upper-class reclusivity as a sign of national "progress from savagery to civilization."[11] Like Sears, the lawyers identify a developing sensitivity on the part of civilized Americans and theorize it as an elite adaptive strategy:

> The intensity and complexity of life, attendant upon advancing civilization, have rendered necessary some retreat from the world, and man, under the refining influence of culture, has become more sensitive to publicity, so that solitude and privacy have become more essential to the individual; but modern enterprise and invention have, through invasions upon his privacy, subjected him to mental pain and distress, far greater than could be inflicted by mere bodily injury. (77)

Here, Warren and Brandeis identify a desire for privacy with evolutionary success. They indicate the exclusive nature of this success by their mention of culture's "refining influence" as well as by posing it in opposition to public life and, specifically, to "modern enterprise" and "bodily" concerns. With this portrait of man's new and elite "sensitivity," Warren and Brandeis launch their case for a new form of legal protection.

The lawyers' second evolutionary narrative concerns the law itself, which by virtue of its "beautiful capacity for growth" is already moving in the necessary direction (76). The argument opens by tracing how far jurisprudence has already progressed in the "inevitable" expansion that is required to secure not just the material domain of the individual's person and property, but also the immaterial domain of his privacy (76). "In very early times," Warren and Brandeis explain, "the law gave a remedy only for physical interference with life and property" (75). It protected citizens from "battery" and "restraint," and from the loss of belongings such as "lands and cattle." As time passed, however, the law reached beyond the boundaries of physical well-being. From the law against battery grew the law against nuisance—a movement from bodily to nonbodily injuries, such as those inflicted by odors or noise, that staked out a wider zone of protection. Next, the legal defense against injury expanded to include fear of injury, a movement from physical to emotional jurisdiction. Finally this zone of "immunity" widened even more to accommodate what Warren and Brandeis refer to as "family relations": citing legal remedies for "the alienation of a wife's affections" and the parental pain suffered with a child's seduction, the essay positions wife and daughter at the outermost boundaries of a man's right to his person (76). The Darwinistic inflection of "The Right to Privacy" did not go unremarked. A letter written to the *Atlantic Monthly* soon after the essay's publication parodies its social evolutionary bent: "It seems that the great doctrine of Development rules not only in biology and theology, but in the law as well; so that whenever, in the long process of civilization, man generates a capacity for being made miserable by his fellows in some new way, the law, after a decent interval steps in to protect him."[12] The letter ends, however, with a less humorous response to this prospect of inexorable legal expansion—"But is there nothing left of liberty?" demands the writer. Together, the evolutionary narratives of "The Right to Privacy" characterize privacy as both a naturally broadening zone of immunity and a fragile cultural achievement in need of state-enforced protection. Warren and Brandeis failed to establish a new privacy tort, but they succeeded in shaping legal arguments into the next century and advancing the aggressive action of the U.S. privacy crisis.

At first glance, Louisa May Alcott seems not to concern herself with notions of imperiled privacy. Unlike Fuller and Stowe, she never tries to resurrect an imagined separation between transcendent selfhood and the encroaching pressures of property relations. And, although she often chronicles the hardships of wage earners, most trenchantly in her 1873 novel *Work: A Story of Experience*, her writing generally promotes free labor and reflects midcentury optimism about its democratizing potential—especially for women, blacks, and the poor. Alcott took great pride in her own working-class roots and literary labors. Even toward the end of her life, when her faith in free market principles had waned, she remained untroubled by matters of ontological instability or existential dispossession. Indeed, Alcott tended to view such concerns derisively. Her 1873 story, "Transcendental Wild Oats," offers a satirical portrait of Fruitlands, the commune at which her family attempted to achieve a life purified of property relations, spurning material interests to pursue spiritual ones. The piece was originally called "The Cost of an Idea" at the suggestion of the writer's father, transcendentalist reformer Bronson Alcott. He expected the story to glorify his own sacrifices for antimaterialist ideals. However, the provisional title clearly signified differently to Louisa, who used her sketch to recount the disproportionate demands placed upon female communitarians, illustrating the material costs of transcendent individualism and the politics of who pays them.[13]

And yet, if Alcott was not taken in by the promise of a selfhood disjunct from material relations, she nevertheless understood the power of this delusion and of the panic narratives that shaped it. This power, she recognized, could be benevolent or oppressive. Like Warren and Brandeis—and like her father, the failed communitarian—Alcott was concerned with the conjunction of privacy, property, and market capitalism, particularly as it implicated gender and race politics. Unlike these others, however, she recognized a priori selfhood as an effect, rather than a casualty, of the commodification and public circulation of selves. In her fiction Alcott exposes the ruse of privacy by explicating the ontological dependence of identity upon property and market relations. Moreover, she refused to regret that dependence. Indeed, in her early career Alcott saw the market-driven production of individuals as key not only to her professional success but also to an ideally reconstructed nation in which both gender and racial integration were to be achieved. Later, witnessing increased class conflict and racial intolerance, Alcott would lose her faith in the power of privacy discourse to generate a just ethic of belonging.

An early chapter from *Jo's Boys*, titled "Jo's Last Scrape," indexes Alcott's complex responses to U.S. privacy discourse. Significantly, Alcott approaches the problem through the lens of authorship, reviving Jo's lapsed literary career in order to examine a culture that commodifies not just books but also the people who write them. Jo, having famously disavowed her literary aspirations in *Little Women*, has since written a sentimental novel based on her own family and become a great success. In the words of the narrator, "the Ugly Duckling turned out to be, not a swan, but a golden goose, whose literary eggs found such an unexpected market that in ten years...Jo found herself famous in a small way, and, better still, with a snug little fortune in her pocket."[14] However, Jo's success has already begun to sour. Her audience, insatiable for that which she markets in her autobiographical fiction—access to an authentic, private self—persists in looking beyond the market for more of the same. This proves inconvenient,

> for suddenly the admiring public took possession of her and all her affairs....If she declined to open her heart to them, they reproached her...and if she preferred the privacy of home to the pedestal upon which she was requested to pose, "the airs of literary people" were freely criticized....Jo came to consider it the worst scrape of her life; for liberty had always been her dearest possession and it seemed to be fast going from her. (37–38)

As a popular author, Jo has become public property. Readers arrive daily to claim her time, her history, even her "heart." Hostage in her own home, Jo fends off throngs of autograph-seeking boys, girls who fall into her arms murmuring, "Darling, love me," and a reporter who thrusts himself through the door demanding "Mrs. Bhaer's age and birthplace, date of marriage, and number of children" (49, 45).

Initially it appears that Alcott, who hated being an object of publicity, uses this episode to illustrate and protest the same alienation of selfhood that Warren and Brandeis would protest four years later in the *Harvard Law Review*. But the tale of Jo's predicament is layered over in metafictional irony and ambivalence. Alcott, after all, made a hugely profitable career of marketing herself, thanks in part to her publishers, the Roberts Brothers, who advertised many of her works as unadulterated autobiography.[15] The strategy probably worked better than Alcott wished; but, although she resented the readers who chided her for not marrying Laurie (a favorite male character whose proposal Jo rejects in *Little Women*) or complained that her autographed photographs bore a poor resemblance to Jo, Alcott continued to sign "Jo" when responding to fan letters and to suggest titles such as "Jo March's Necessity Stories" for her books.[16]

The marketing of authorial privacy was not uncommon in nineteenth-century America—a situation that is perhaps not so much explained as promoted by the editor of *Female Prose Writers of America* when he writes, "It seems to be an instinctive desire of the human heart, on becoming acquainted with any work of genius, to know something of its author....The interest of the reader is often enlisted quite as much for the writer, as for the hero, of a tale."[17] This lucrative practice has been described by Richard Brodhead as "an organization of authorship...in which private, domestic women...courted an invasion of their privacy, exposing themselves to—if not in fact inviting—the public's vicarious consumption of their 'personal lives.'"[18] Of course, male authors also participated in the commodification of disclosure. But Brodhead accurately, if uncritically, re-presents the gendered terms by which literary practices were assessed. Gillian Brown provides a more analytical perspective on this question when she compares Jo's situation to that of the eponymous protagonist from Herman Melville's 1852 novel *Pierre, or the Ambiguities*. Another successful author, Pierre Glendinning also dislikes being made the property of his readers: "You lose your own sharp individuality," he complains, "and become delightfully merged in that soft social Pantheism, as it were, that rosy melting all into one.... [T]here no one draws the sword of his own individuality."[19] As Pierre's phallic imagery indicates, the model of individuality for which he grieves is masculine. His solution, Brown explains, is to reassert both masculinity and individuality through strategies that enact a priori personhood. Specifically, Pierre limits the sale of his works—a move that reclassifies the novels as original, nonreplicable literary property rather than mass culture commodity. He also prohibits the sale of his photographic image, thereby removing himself from the market.[20]

Pierre's complaint charts a gendered system of value wherein masculine a priority poses against a feminized ethic of accessibility and accommodation that is, at once, its idealized complement and despised antithesis. In "Jo's Last Scrape," Alcott steers between the two models of authorship that correspond to this gendered opposition:

> "There ought to be a law to protect unfortunate authors," said Mrs. Jo.... "To me it is a more vital subject than international copyright; for time is money, peace is health, and I lose both with no return but less respect for my fellow-creatures and a wild desire to fly into the wilderness, since I cannot shut my doors even in free America." (39)

Here, Jo seems at first to emulate Pierre (and anticipate Warren and Brandeis) by asserting a boundary between the literary marketplace and the writer's private life. And yet, Alcott does not exclude market relations from her zone of privacy and inviolate personality. "Time is money," Jo asserts, naming precisely that aspect of the labor contract that union activists theorized as an alienation of self-right.[21] Even her second equation, "peace is health," concedes the principle of exchange value. And when Jo objects to losing both time *and* peace "with no return but less respect for my fellow-creatures," it becomes even less clear whether she resents the presence of market forces in her personal life or merely her inability to control them. When Jo complains earlier in the same episode about the boy who has written "at least six" times to request autographs, his offense seems less to do with his excessive demand than with her suspicion that he "probably sells them" (39). Likewise, her chief objection to visitors is that they interfere with her ability to write: she calls upon the state to protect her conditions of production. The complaint is not entirely satirical; as we shall see, Jo's "wild desire to fly into the wilderness" signals a form of disenfranchisement that concerns Alcott very much. But this loss differs from the sort that troubles Pierre Glendinning. Even as Jo calls for a protected space that precedes market relations, Alcott suggests that no such place exists and begins to subvert the natural rights defense of privacy.

This subversion gains pace as we recognize the integral role that Jo's lament for privacy plays in Alcott's marketing of privacy. By turning fictional supplicants from Jo's door, Alcott enhances our sense of privileged access. The domestic scenes, family adventures, and personal struggles that follow in the remaining nineteen chapters are effectively labeled "private" by the presence of that avid and frustrated crowd on the doorstep of chapter 3. Moreover, this chapter contains the most conspicuously autobiographical portion of the novel—a point that Alcott slyly emphasizes when her narrator introduces a "sketch of one day [to] explain the state of things, offer some excuse for the unhappy woman, and give a hint to the autograph-fiend now rampant in the land; for it is a true tale" (39). Ostensibly these words refer to Jo, whose sufferings have just been outlined and whose struggles with "autograph-fiends" are to ensue. But the passage also makes the always implicit reference to Alcott explicit. For it addresses not the fictional readers described in the novel, but the actual readers who have bought Alcott's work. The "excuses offered" register on behalf of Alcott, not Jo, and the fiends in question turn out to be ourselves. In case we overlook this momentary slippage, the narrator adds that pointed final clause: "it is a true tale." In asking her own consuming public to leave her in peace, Alcott reaffirms the co-incidence of her self with her literary product—and so offers that self to the public anew.

This exercise goes well beyond the "organization of authorship" described by Brodhead. Where he imagines female authors "exposing themselves" to consumers, Alcott's striptease leaves us wondering where and how such selves exist.[22] Thus, the people who do manage to invade Jo's home never find what they came for. Exuberant ladies from Oshkosh arrive seeking "one peep at her sanctum" (47). But their desiring gaze is repeatedly frustrated. They admire her portrait only to discover that it immortalizes a different authoress. They gather at a desk to "rhapsodize that this is where such beautiful novels are created" and never notice that it belongs to Professor Bhaer (47). When they do find the right portrait and actually meet Jo, the ladies are disappointed by the "sad difference between the real and the ideal" (46). What they look for can only be "possessed" through the mediation of print. They can be sutured to the Truth of a self that precedes market relations only as consumers who encounter it alienated and made iconic by its public circulation. This is true for the ladies from Oshkosh. It is also true for us, the readers who only seem to access what our fictional counterparts do not because we read the book rather than the person. Alcott sidesteps our desiring gaze, refusing to supply herself as a site of feminized accommodation or to strike Pierre's pose as the masculine author who (supposes he) comes before the text he possesses. Instead, Alcott signifies upon both of these authorial models in order to criticize both the gendered politics of the literary market and the gendered social and economic dynamics they refract.

However, for all its arch cynicism, the story of "Jo's Last Scrape" does register loss, diminished freedom, and declining powers. Even Jo's new career is described as drudgery, and seems to lack the joyous energy that permeates writing scenes in *Little Women*. In this, the chapter provides a crucial additional clue into how Alcott came to view the discourse of privacy in her final years. Its ambivalent tone is particularly pronounced where we learn that "the success Jo valued most" came from providing her mother with a room of her own in which to die:

> As a girl, Jo's favorite plan had been a room where Marmee could sit in peace and enjoy herself after her hard, heroic life. Now the dream had become a happy fact, and Marmee sat in her pleasant chamber with every comfort and luxury about her, loving daughters to wait on her as infirmities increased, a faithful mate to lean upon, and grandchildren to brighten the twilight of life. (37)[23]

In this passage Alcott theorizes privacy in succinct terms. Jo sells her own stock in the stuff of privacy—the "capital of her own life and experiences" as Edna Cheney puts it—to buy privacy for her mother: even that which seems most originary—the site of maternal domestic autonomy—comes not before but after the subject's immersion in public economies.[24] But this scene of iconic privacy is also a scene of death—and of disturbing isolation, for even with the attentions of her family, Marmee has in a sense been put aside. Both implications echo disconcertingly with the characterization of Jo herself, who has become "too old and tired" to put up with her fans and retreats deeper and deeper into her home to escape them (38). Lucrative as it may be, privacy is also beginning to prove lonely and confining.

In her cheerfully cynical approach to the useful delusion of a priori selfhood and its origin in property relations, Alcott differs markedly from Fuller and Stowe, who engage privacy discourse in deadly earnest and toward antimaterialist ends. And yet, like them she views privacy relations as the key to a more free and democratic national community. Indeed, as I argue below, Alcott was more ambitious in this regard. For she hoped that privacy relations would engender a racially integrated America. Here I differ from those critics who ascribe to Alcott an impulse to eradicate nonwhiteness from normative subjectivity and sociality. In studies of Alcott's engagement with social Darwinism and racialist evolutionary thought, both Caroline Levander and Maude Hines show how the writer aligns education with the taming of childhood "savagery" and argue that this process entails an erasure of "brownness."[25] Elizabeth Young finds similarly that Alcott's fiction envisions a nation remade according to feminine principles, but in doing so "contracts the racial boundaries of femininity . . . into a nearly all-white world."[26] While I also explore processes of whitening and contraction in Alcott's novels, I propose that Alcott invokes these forces to reform them. *Little Men* presents Plumfield as an integrated polis, where interlocking systems of property and private personhood both enfranchise and incorporate the racial other. In *Jo's Boys*, however, the Plumfield economy has lost its reformist power. Here Alcott aligns privacy with modes of privilege and exclusion that provoke Jo's "wild desire to fly into the wilderness . . . even in free America" (39). For Alcott, U.S. privacy relations have failed at this point, not just at providing freedom but also at incorporating "wilderness" and "wildness"—crucial terms for her scheme of integration—within its doors. The image of Marmee, slowly dying in the "pleasant chamber" bought for her by Jo, suggests Alcott's own sense of imprisonment within the impoverished confines of whitening privacy.

I begin below by investigating the antebellum contexts that shaped Alcott's understanding of U.S. privacy relations. First I review her father's philosophical views and their application at Fruitlands, a commune dedicated to eradicating property relations for the cultivation of authentic privacy and individuality. The next section interprets *Little Men* as Alcott's response both to Fruitlands and to the larger problematic of national Reconstruction. Plumfield, I argue, is a pro-property utopia that links ownership to private selfhood as the joint bases of a democratic, racially integrated community. The final section turns to *Jo's Boys*, where Alcott reexamines the interlocking functions of property and privacy during a time when both are characterized by injustice, exclusion, and violence. Portraying the white ideal of privacy as denaturalized and imprisoning, Alcott laments the failures of her nation's democratic culture.

OWNING UP IN AMERICA

Antebellum Americans held ambivalent and contradictory attitudes about property and its role in the production of national subjects. Liberal contract theory began with the premise that self-ownership was simultaneous, even synonymous, with free personhood; and in the United States this theme infused Revolutionary discourse, making self-right a sacrament of liberty and the antithesis of slavery and political subjection.[27] Matters become less clear with the question of whether citizenship required property in more than one's self. Some early Americans celebrated the sanctity of legal property—and of land in particular—alongside self-right as equally indivisible from democratic individuality. This view was reflected, for example, in the fact that most states based suffrage on property requirements. However, there were many who challenged the conflation of citizenship with ownership, and disputed such voting qualifications—most memorably in the Dorr Rebellion of 1842. Meanwhile, the expanding market economy was transforming all relationships between property and citizenship. Where the concept of property had referred primarily to land—a very stable and literal marker for the individual's legal autonomy and political freedom—it now denoted the "dynamic, instrumental and more abstract" figure of capital.[28] To be sure, this new form of property generated its own narrative of democratic freedom through market agency, but it also undermined the ideals of independence and self-determination.

Linked to the first problem were questions concerning the relation between private property and the public good. From the seventeenth century forward, colonial and U.S. leaders had been at pains to establish that personal property should be regarded as a means of promoting the general social welfare. Calvinists taught that property came into the Christian's hands only temporarily and belonged, ultimately, to God. Ownership "provided a calling," as historian William Scott puts it; its rightful profits were not personal advantage but collective grace.[29] Later, the agrarian communities of the colonial and early national periods conceptualized ownership as stewardship: property holders had power and commanded deference from dependents, but were themselves obliged to make their property serve the community as a whole.[30] Similarly, republican ideology framed property as an opportunity for practicing political virtue, stipulating that self-interest should not be pursued as an end in itself but toward the higher aim of patriotic disinterest: "The order of nature," wrote Jefferson, "is that individual happiness shall be inseparable from the practice of virtue."[31] However, when the growth of market capitalism transformed the meaning of property, it likewise altered perceptions of the relationship between private ownership and public duty. Charles Sellers finds that during the most intense phase of market expansion and developmentalism, court records reveal a shift in emphasis from cases concerning the protection of communal welfare and morality to cases that focus on the protection of private property. It was in this period, Sellers notes, that Alexis de Tocqueville described lawyers as enemies of the democratic common good.[32] By the 1840s, the idea that private property rights should or even could serve political virtue was sufficiently rare for Tocqueville to report in *Democracy in America* that

> in the United States hardly anybody talks of the beauty of virtue. . . . The American moralists do not profess that men ought to sacrifice themselves for their fellow creatures *because* it is noble to make such sacrifices, but they boldly aver that such sacrifices are as necessary to him who imposes them upon himself as to him for whose sake they are made.[33]

In what Tocqueville describes here—a mind-set he famously classifies as "self-interest rightly understood"—moral or disinterested behaviors are instrumental, performed with the long-sighted aim of individual gain. In the antebellum United States political virtue and self-interest remained as tightly linked as before, but now their union was meant to serve the latter instead of the former.

The most immediate influence on Louisa May Alcott's ideas about property came from the reformist environs of Boston and Concord, Massachusetts, in which she grew up, and most specifically from the transcendentalist movement with which her family was closely affiliated. For all of their touted nonuniformity of opinion, transcendentalists concurred in their distaste for property relations. In their writings, both Ralph Waldo Emerson and Henry David Thoreau repeatedly oppose ownership—the materialist appropriation of nature—against the idealist apprehension of divinity in nature that is the transcendentalist's chief purpose. Thoreau's disgust toward devotees of possessive individualism is particularly emphatic; in *Walden* he ridicules neighboring farmers whose selfhood is so entirely dependent upon property that they seem to carry their barns upon their backs.[34] Alcott's father, Amos Bronson Alcott, enjoyed close friendships with Emerson and Thoreau and was intensely committed to philosophical investigations akin to theirs. In his view, property obstructed the moral welfare of both individuals and communities. Not only did it foster competition over cooperation (a problem that concerned even contract theorists) but, more gravely, it founded community upon the principles of mutual economic interest rather than higher conceptions of the good. Ever a man of action, Alcott responded to the property problem with Fruitlands, a short-lived experiment in nonproprietary existence. There he, Abigail May Alcott, and their four daughters joined other reformers to form a "consociate family" from the early summer of 1843 until the winter of 1844.

Many of the experimental separatist communities that sprang up during the 1840s and '50s blamed U.S. property relations for spreading corruption and disunity. But most communitarians also believed that, with reform, property could promote civic virtue and social equity in concert with individual freedoms. At Brook Farm—the only transcendentalist commune other than Fruitlands—members held shares in the land and its proceeds, and could increase individual holdings by contributing extra labor. To protect unity of interests and the integrity of the land, limits were placed on members' ability to disinvest and no one could draw off profit for personal use beyond an annual 5 percent. More radically (and much less successfully), the socialist New Harmony group made all property communal, endeavoring "to introduce an entire new system of society; to change it from an ignorant, selfish system to an enlightened social system which shall gradually unite all interests in one, and remove all causes for contests between individuals."[35] New Harmony founder Robert Owen believed that private property and self-interest could only corrupt virtue and impede social cooperation. He rejected both Jefferson's belief that self-interest was naturally linked with and mediated by virtue and Tocqueville's more cynical view that self-interest would, for pragmatic reasons, moderate itself to ensure instrumentally virtuous citizens. But even Owen viewed joint ownership as an instrument for just social change.

Bronson Alcott and his partner in utopianism, Charles Lane, went well beyond the reforms of Brook Farm and New Harmony by prohibiting—or at least disavowing—property in any form, private or communal. Charles Lane spent his life savings to purchase the land for Fruitlands, but neither he nor Alcott would consent to stand as legal proprietor and convinced Samuel May, Alcott's brother-in-law, to hold the property in legal trust. In a letter to the antislavery *Herald of Freedom* that would become the commune's unofficial manifesto, Alcott and Lane explained this condition of (not) having their cake and eating it too: "We do not recognise the purchase of land; but its redemption from the debasing state of *proprium*, or property, to divine uses, we clearly understand; where those whom the world esteems as owners are found yielding their individual rights to the Supreme Owner."[36] Here the reformers dismiss the very concept of property, framing it as a social delusion that one might simply refuse to "recognise"; yet they also blame that delusion for placing man in a false relation to nature and to the "divine" presence within it. The same document interprets Lane's purchase as "an arrangement... which liberates this tract from human ownership" and recasts farming as the "sober culture" of soil "consecrated to human freedom" and action in "union with uncorrupted fields" (428–29).

The prohibition against property at Fruitlands was integral to that community's general program of abstinence and self-denial, designed to remove obstacles from the individual's communion with Spirit. Avowing that "the pure soul, by the law of its own nature, adopts a pure diet and cleanly customs," Alcott and Lane imposed a rigorously minimalist economy. In their declaration to the *Herald* they explain:

> The greater part of man's duty consists in leaving alone much that he is in the habit of doing. "Shall I sip tea or coffee?" The inquiry may be. No... "Shall I consume pork, beef or mutton?" Not if you value health or life. "Shall I stimulate with milk?" No. "Shall I warm my bathing water?" Not if cheerfulness is valuable. (441)

Writing in response to a previously published inquiry, the two men engage their correspondent (and society at large) in Socratic dialogue—the pedagogical technique for which Alcott, a former educator, was already famous. Their letter proceeds systematically through a list of comforts and pleasures to be abjured, banning warm clothing, sugar, lamp oil, and other barriers to chaste spiritual knowledge. Their list concludes with property: "Shall I subjugate cattle? Shall I trade? Shall I claim property in any created things?" No, no, no, our instructors answer for us. "The pure soul" eradicates all desire for the outward world; ownership must go, along with bacon and hot baths. Indeed, the abolition of property and commodity lay at the heart of the Fruitlands regime(n) against private vice. For ownership was both paradigmatic of all desiring attachments and the institutionalization of them.

Bronson Alcott was especially fixated on the pernicious influence of property. In the spring of 1842, deeply demoralized by the failure of his pedagogical experiments at Temple School, the philosopher traveled to England to visit Alcott House, a school devoted to his educational principles. The trip did much to repair Alcott's ego and his faith in social progress, and—when he met Lane, one of the Alcott House founders—became the genesis of Fruitlands. Yet his letters and journal entries from this time convey a strong undercurrent of disappointment. As he met with various reformers and attended lectures on philosophical and spiritual matters, Alcott felt that everyone was missing the vital point:

> Neither people, delegates, nor leaders seemed at all aware of the remedy for the social evils under which they are now writhing in sorrow, disappointment, hunger. It is not bread nor wages... but property, gain, and the lust of gain.... [T]hese are the parents of the ills they suffer.... Property, property still, and the people still enslaved to their lusts and passions.[37]

For Alcott, ownership was the seed of all social ills—despair, starvation, poverty, slavery—because it was the beginning of desire's corrupting influence upon human spirit. Property was the point at which the individual began to look away from his true self and toward a proliferating array of secular attachments: "He loses the original perceptions with which he was wont to behold things, and terminates his vision in the reflex image of himself on surrounding things."[38] Years later, Louisa would illustrate her father's beliefs in the opening scene of "Transcendental Wild Oats." There we find the "consociate family" en route to their new home and being lectured on the evasive nature of Truth by one of their leaders. The mother clings to an assortment of possessions, trying to carry some aspect of the old life into the new, but as the group trudges along a mirror falls and shatters. Mother sighs, but the patriarch strides onward, crunching glass underfoot and muttering, "We want no false reflections here."[39] The scene concisely captures Bronson's stern critique: possessions are a place we look to for ourselves, and from which we receive an inauthentic self; they take us down a false trail in pursuit of a distorted, deceptive reflection ("the reflex image of himself on surrounding things") that only divides us more deeply from our selves.

According to Bronson's theory, ownership debased the thing owned by denying its divine status; at once, ownership damaged the owner, who was deluded and distracted from "original perceptions" of divinity. This is a familiar pairing of transcendentalist ideas.[40] But Bronson took the chain of effects a step further, revealing his deep imaginative involvement with the dynamics of market value and commodification. He argued that the soul was not merely neglected by materialist pursuits but corrupted at its core: "The narrow covetousness which prevails in trade, in labor, and exchanges, ends in depraving the land; it breeds disease, decline, in the flesh,—debauches and consumes the heart."[41] For Alcott, the damage that ownership inflicts upon the thing owned rebounds to damage—even consume—its origin. More, it disseminates the originary self into distorted copies. Lane and Alcott argue that "the notion of Property is the prolific seed of so many evils that there seems little hope for humanity so long as it is made a leading consideration, or is harbored in the human bosom.... From the midst of this sin and its consequences it is difficult to emerge without committing more sin" (438). Here property appears not as a natural right, an inherent feature of individuality, but as an unnatural social creation that penetrates and infects the individual to disperse his will into proliferating evils.

Seeking to remedy property's corrosive effects, Alcott designed his commune as a place where the individual could withdraw completely from material attachments and regain originary self-unity: "Outward abstinence," wrote he and Lane, "is a sign of inward fulness" (441). At Fruitlands, Bronson sought to cultivate a condition I have referred to as self-(non)possession. His goal, that is, was not self-possessive individuality, whereby the "I" owns the "me," but an individuality in which the "I" is exorcised of its shadow, its "false reflection" in the beloved object—the commodity, the mirror, the me. Here, too, Louisa captures the essence of her father's philosophy, recalling in "Transcendental Wild Oats" that "ten ancient apple trees were all the 'chaste supply' which the place offered as yet; but in the firm belief that plenteous orchards were soon to be evoked from their inner consciousness, these sanguine founders had christened their domain Fruitlands."[42] This exegesis plays ironically upon her father's ideal of immanent nourishment—or "inward fulness." It also tropes on his habit of referring to the commune as his New Eden: in the interiorized economy of Bronson's paradise it would be possible to taste the apple without committing the sin of appropriation; there would be no fall into the self-dis-unity of ownership; innocence would be regrown in the "plenteous orchards" of the soul.[43]

As with every narrative of dispossession and invaded self-unity examined in this book, Bronson's privacy crisis relies on the very logic of property that it resists. He identifies the inwardly full self through negative acts of withdrawal and denial, apprehends plentitude as the obverse of loss, and locates unity in resistance to invasion. As Richard Francis puts it, "Alcott's life can be seen as a sequence of zeroings-in on an ever-retreating utopian possibility."[44] This is nowhere more clearly illustrated than in his own near suicide. As the Fruitlands community disintegrated, a despairing Bronson Alcott put its principles of self-denial to the ultimate test by retreating to his bed and refusing to eat, drink, or speak. Still on a mission to eradicate desire, he would have at last succeeded in reversing alienation by achieving, in death, the perfect (non)possession of self. In the words of his daughter: "This dreamer, whose dream was the life of his life, resolved to carry out his idea to the bitter end."[45] Instead Alcott eventually consented to take nourishment, and so lived on to burden his family for years to come.

A key aspect of the Fruitlands method—and one that profoundly shaped Louisa's future career—was the practice of journaling. For Bronson, journal writing was a lifelong compulsion. As he reflects on its meaning in his autobiography, *Concord Days*, it becomes apparent that language is another medium for his pursuit of seamless selfhood:

> Was it the accident of being shown, when a boy, in the old oaken cabinet, my mother's little journal, that set me out in this chase of myself, continued almost uninterruptedly, and now fixed by habit as a part of the day, like rising and setting of the sun? Yet it has...made me emulous of attaining the art of portraying my

> thoughts, occupations, surroundings, friendships; and could I succeed in sketching to the life a single day's doings, should esteem myself as having accomplished the chiefest feat in literature.[46]

Here Bronson imagines himself entering the symbolic order. His impetus is the mother's "yes" rather than the father's "no," but the result is the same: ever since his glimpse into an imagined plenitude of feminine interiority—as fracturing as that other primal scene—Bronson has been in pursuit of self-unity. In a journal entry from January 1851 he laments,

> If the pulses would but fasten our sensations on some indelible scroll, and become our faithful Diarist from the first systole to the last diastole of their motions, that would be an autobiography, and portrait of the invisible worth having, and spare the writing and editing of much nonsense and dullness.[47]

Journal writing was not just analogous to personal reform at Fruitlands; it was also a much emphasized component. All of the associationists devoted significant daylight hours to the labors of writing. The four Alcott girls in particular learned to use their journals as their father did his, as vehicles for self-pursuit. Louisa kept a diary from first learning to write until two days before her death. In the Fruitlands months, Abba wrote a note in Louisa's journal to commend a particularly pious entry: "Remember, dear girl, that a diary should be an epitome of your life. May it be a record of pure thought and good actions, then you will indeed be the precious child of your loving mother."[48] From childhood Louisa was trained to strain after that "chiefest feat in literature"—a nonalienated relationship to self through text. On one hand, the diary was to offer a perfect account—a "sketching to the life"—of Louisa's self; on the other hand, it was to instantiate a perfect self, a "pure" version of Louisa that she should strive to resemble in life. Together, the two efforts close the gap between the writing subject and her textual object: as Louisa writes "pure thoughts" she becomes more pure, interpellated by her own self-representation. In this way, the journal provides another mechanism for extricating the self from sin and serves, ultimately, as a space of privacy—of unmediated, unalienated self-relation.

The Alcott journals also served as mechanisms for ideal association—that is, for mediating unmediated union with others. Thus, although it seems contradictory for Abba to invade Louisa's process of textual self-unification, it is not. The family's tradition of exchanging and reading from each other's diaries is well known. As several critics have suggested, this practice indicates a panoptic mode of parental surveillance, a way of installing self-surveillance by training the child to read over her own shoulder.[49] But the Alcotts' consociate journaling can also be read as a strategy for cultivating privacy as a communal space, not unlike the space of "private relations" that Fuller envisions in *Woman in the Nineteenth Century*. Here we find a similar principle of publishing one's privacy as a public resource that reforms by interpellating others into its pure space. Bronson frequently offered his own "chase of self" for such community use, reading portions of his journal aloud to family members and pasting and transcribing passages into family letters. By this same logic, we might regard Bronson's habit of reading his daughters' journals as an attempt to access *their* immanent selfhood, to peek once again into his mother's cabinet.

Looking back at "Jo's Last Scrape" and the autobiographical marketing campaign it simultaneously examines, subverts, and advances, we can see that in some ways Louisa's career reverses her father's efforts at Fruitlands. In her constant plundering of autobiographical material for inspiration and profit, she sends the "me" away instead of chasing it down. She explores the economy of alienation instead of renouncing it. This impulse is evident from an early age, where her journaling speaks not inward, but outward, toward the desiring gaze of her parental audience: a Fruitlands entry reads, "I rose at five and had my bath. I love cold water!"[50] Later, Louisa would become her own audience as she read through her old journals in search of saleable material.[51] The writer frequently annotated past entries, sometimes commenting wryly on old troubles, sometimes jotting a character's name beside mention of its real-life model: "Jo in her garret" appears by an entry that describes eating apples and reading in the attic of Orchard House.[52] Such marginalia reveals Alcott reading the journal as—and, in a sense, for—the general public, clearly anticipating that her annotations would themselves become public fare with the inevitable publication of the journals after her death. Here the author manages her property, packaging it for consumption. This is not the voice of someone "in chase of [her]self," not an author seeking continuity with her text. Indeed, the alienation of writer from text is formalized by her use of the third person. Unlike her father, Alcott never saw the commodity—nor even the commodified self—as a false reflection that might rebound destructively upon its owner. By her reckoning, the commodified self was imbued with life and life-giving powers that, if she was lucky, would return like the "literary eggs" from "Jo's Last Scrape" with an "unexpected cargo" of "gold and glory" (35–36).

As we shall see, this same faith underwrites the narrative of *Little Men* where property relations are key to the curriculum at Plumfield School, specifically because of the way they alienate, circulate, and reconstitute the selfhood of Jo's students. And yet, even as it betrays aspects of Bronson's core belief, Louisa's career—and Plumfield in particular—was also loyal to his vision. Louisa embraces property and market principles in *Little Men* precisely in order to realize her father's ideal community of self-(non) possessive subjects. Plumfield is Alcott's post-Romantic utopia, dedicated to the idealist principles of her own postbellum context—specifically, the faith that free labor and a free market could reempower the democratic individual and extend that status to formerly excluded groups, while also healing the nation's wounds. Louisa's use of property and trade principles as a means of correcting and fulfilling her father's transcendentalist program deeply informs her approach to the inclusion of women and nonwhites. On these topics her ambivalence toward Bronson's influence is particularly acute. For, although he instilled Louisa with abolitionist, integrationist, and suffragist convictions, his own attitudes on race and gender were often contradictory.

In many ways Bronson was unusually attentive to the forms of disenfranchisement structured by race and gender. More than any other transcendentalist, he was committed to rectifying these problems with institutional change. He and Abba joined William Lloyd Garrison to form the first white abolitionist society in New England, and supported full racial integration throughout their lives. Bronson was also a charter member of the Boston Committee of Vigilance, risking his life more than once to protect fugitive slaves from recapture, and his insistence upon enrolling a black student at Temple School contributed to its failure.[53] Influenced by Abba and by his friend Elizabeth Peabody, he also believed in full equality between the sexes and strongly supported women's rights. But Bronson's theories on property stand oddly divorced from his social politics. Like most transcendentalists, he believed that change would stem from personal rather than public reform. "The evils of life," he and Lane wrote, "are not so much social or political, as personal; and a personal reform only can eradicate them" (437). In Bronson's philosophy, even property reform was essentially a personal matter, lifted from its "social or political" context. Thus, even while he viewed the abolition of property as key to ending slavery and sex inequality, he failed to consider how the relationship between property and individuality was itself shaped by race and gender.

This meant that he also overlooked the gendered and racialized dynamics of privacy relations, even while employing both race and gender as metaphors for self-(non)possession. In the Fruitlands texts, Bronson invokes slavery repeatedly as a figure for the self-alienation inflicted by material attachment. Sounding very like Fuller in his references to "people still enslaved to their lusts and passions" or "a servile slave of his own folly," he posits ownership as the opposite of that freedom acquired through divine truth. Perversely, he reduces slavery to a metaphor for ownership—

a condition that categorically excluded enslaved people.[54] Also significant here are Bronson's racialist beliefs. As Sarah Elbert shows, he proudly viewed his own Aryan looks as a sign of spiritual election, and ascribed Abba and Louisa's quick tempers—that is, their distance from spiritual freedom—to their dark skin, referring to the latter as a "true-blue May, or rather, a brown."[55] Like Fuller, Bronson appears to align whiteness with the capacity for self-(non)possession.

Gender features even more prominently than race as a structuring principle—and neglected actuality—in Bronson's antiproperty philosophy. For he viewed the ideal of self-(non)possessive self-unity as an inherent aspect of womanhood. This belief led Bronson's first biographer, Odell Shepard, to pronounce the philosopher a "gyneolater," explaining,

> His worship of women was one of his most decided American traits.... [H]e... never lost the conviction that women had somehow monopolized "purity." He never theorized purity. That was what women were, always and by nature—or, at any rate would be if men would let them alone.... It was what men might aspire to be, rather hopelessly and from far, far away.[56]

Woman defines purity, purity defines woman. But Shepard is mistaken in claiming that Bronson never theorizes purity: Fruitlands is that theorization. What Bronson never theorizes is Woman. Therefore, while a conception of femininity shapes his ideal of self-denial and nonownership, Bronson appears simply to disregard the gendered material relations that make this ideal possible—and keep it the privileged domain of white (and propertied) men. When he takes up his practice of "being, in preference to doing," his wife and daughters take up the labor of house and farm (441). None of this was lost on Abba, whose own materialist gender analysis was always incisive. Visiting a neighboring Shaker settlement, she returned more angry than ever about her own situation: "There is a fat sleek comfortable look about the men, and among the women there is a stiff awkward reserve that belongs to neither sublime resignation nor divine hope. Wherever I turn I see the yoke on woman in some form or other."[57] Even Lane noticed the problem of Abba's overwork; needless to say, his solution was to send for more women. But Bronson remained obtuse to the last. His own response to the Shakers was to marvel that "the only really successful extensive community of interest... was established by A WOMAN."[58]

Louisa corrected her father's oversights by using her fiction to examine the ways that race and gender mediate both property and privacy relations. Sometimes this correction was rather pointed, as in her portrayal of beleaguered female communitarians in "Transcendental Wild Oats." But it is also important to recognize that the writer's passion for racial and gender justice stemmed from parental influence. Louisa was bred to activism. She participated directly in the family's abolitionist doings, even organizing her own vigilante group to protect one of the Harper's Ferry conspirators.[59] She marched alongside her mother to demand women's suffrage and civil equality. In *Little Men*, Louisa pursues these same political commitments by imagining Plumfield as what Ebert calls a "post-civil war feminist dream [that] reconstructs the nation as an extended democratic family."[60] Through the combined economies of privacy and property, Alcott suggests, America could open its borders to a new, nonwhite, nonmale citizenry.

MOTHER BHAER, OR, HOW I LEARNED TO STOP WORRYING AND LOVE THE MARKET ECONOMY

Having survived nine months of utopian living at Fruitlands, Louisa May Alcott went on to imagine her own ideal community in *Little Men*, the 1871 sequel to her best seller *Little Women*. As if signaling an intention to revive and reinvent her father's social vision, she gave her commune a name that simultaneously references and revises his: Plumfield.[61] However, like most midcentury utopian projects, Plumfield also revises the culture at large—hence Jo's yearning at the novel's conclusion for "a new and charming state of society in which people lived as happily and innocently as her flock" (328). *Little Men* tells of life at a school for boys run by Jo Bhaer (née March) and her German philosopher husband, Fritz. Plumfield operates as a self-contained polity. It comes equipped with heads of state in Jo and Fritz Bhaer; a treasury in Mr. Laurence (*Little Women*'s Laurie, all grown up and come into a seemingly bottomless inheritance); a spiritual leader in Jo's father, Mr. March; and a population of students for its subjects. Jo's niece Daisy provides "the domestic element, and [the boys] feel the charm of her quiet, womanly ways" (327). Reinforcing this structural insularity is a narrative that focuses so exclusively within the school that Jo seems to speak for the reader when she confesses, "One of my favorite fancies is to look at my family as a small world [in which] to watch the progress of my little men" (327). In keeping with its postbellum genesis, the novel gives special emphasis to the intersecting projects of reconstructing both racial and property relations. For many Americans, free labor and a free market represented the keys to economic recovery and national reunification. For workers, women, and newly emancipated blacks, the rights to claim and trade one's labor on the open market were tickets to a better life and proof of national belonging. Such hopes were often disappointed by the realities of postbellum material relations, as previous chapters have shown. But in the first blush of postwar optimism, faith in self-right and free labor was widespread. This faith also pervades *Little Men* and its creation of what Young describes as "Alcott's reconstructed America."[62]

Readers discover the centrality of property relations to Plumfield society in the very first chapter of *Little Men*, when a new boy called Nat Blake arrives on the scene. Nat's introduction into his new community is carried out primarily through its market economy. Within his first twenty-four hours, he has toured Plumfield's financial district—a barn referred to as "Wall Street"; formed a partnership with an owner of pet hens, Tommy Bangs; and become "the proud possessor of one egg" (38). He has also borrowed a violin—his particular means of production—and resolved to earn enough money to buy his own instrument for future profit. Finally, he has received a parcel of land, "his own farm," so that he can grow a crop for sale. In all three cases, ownership engenders belonging. The other boys also possess trades, livestock, and farms, and by acquiring his own Nat goes on the books as one of the little men. Indeed, as though deliberately emphasizing the aspect of ownership that most troubled her father, Alcott makes property and identity indivisible at Plumfield. The farms are particularly evocative in this regard, for each crop represents a child's personality and its function within the community. Stuffy, the fat greedy boy, grows watermelons that upset stomachs; Tommy, "who tends to get into scrapes," grows nettles for the Plumfield donkey; and, inevitably, Daisy grows flowers to adorn their communal home (267).

Characters are also incessantly identified by what they collect and consume. A basket of cookies from Mrs. March comes custom-designed in shapes particular to the recipients: Nat, the musician, gets a violin, Stuffy a "fat pig," and so on (161). Each self is insistently reflected back to itself in the things it acquires, and to such an extent as to beg the question of whether identity obtains anywhere but in the thing owned. Thus, if *Little Men* embraces market idealism in the style of other boy books from its period, it differs from works like *Ragged Dick* in that it does not celebrate an American individuality that rises from nature to express its self-identity in acts of appropriation and production. When Nat first enters partnership with Tommy, he acquires property simultaneously with identity as, with one gesture, Tommy bestows the egg and chalks the title "T. Bangs & Co." on his bank (38). These words "& Co." seem the more important of the two acquisitions, for "Nat [finds] them so fascinating that he [is] with difficulty persuaded to go and deposit his first piece of portable property in Asia's storeroom" (38). The phenomenon of self-revelation/self-recognition literally fixes him in place. The egg provides a fitting symbol here, for it marks a kind of natality wherein it is impossible to decide which came first, Nathaniel or his first property—a conceit that *Jo's Boys* will reprise when the "golden eggs" of Jo's literary works circulate to bring about her rebirth as a rich and famous authoress. Alcott embraces property, market, and labor in *Little Men* for the very reason that her father rejects them: because they act recursively upon the self, providing mirrors in which the Plumfield subject may recognize—or discover—his self. In her small world, this process is critical to the production of little men and to the stability of the polis they form.

And yet, property almost destroys Plumfield when four quarters are stolen from the secret hiding place of entrepreneur Tommy Bangs, "a moral earthquake [that shakes] Plumfield to its center" and breeds strife and distrust throughout its economic sphere (202). As the narrative climax of *Little Men*, this event illustrates precisely those aspects of the capitalist economy that concerned socialist communitarians: divisive competition among individuals and the corrosive influence of self-interest upon personal morality and the public good. Yet, more serious than this crisis in property relations is the crisis it provokes in privacy relations. As suspicions shift from one boy to another and economic arrangements fall apart, so too do normative patterns of identification and association. Plumfield's chief industry, the production of selves, gets disrupted. Briefly it appears as though Alcott means to prove her father right after all. For the event demonstrates how ownership can alter and "consume" the owner's heart, and reveals the insecurity of identity and belonging that rely upon "false" reflections in property.

Eventually the Bhaers discover their thief in Jack Ford, "a sharp, rather sly lad," characterized by "unboyish keenness and money-loving" (26). Before Jack's guilt comes to light, however, suspicions fall first on Nat and then on his closest friend, Dan Keane. Both boys lose their standing on Wall Street and within Plumfield society. When Nat is the suspect, the inscription that he so values is erased by his former business partner: " 'I don't mean to hurt you, Nat, but you see I can't afford to lose my money, so I guess we won't be partners any longer,' and with that Tommy rubbed out the sign 'T. Bangs & Co.' " (212). Nat's identity is literally erased from the economic sphere. He becomes "bankrupt in honor and an outlaw from the business community.... The barn, which was the boys' Wall Street, knew him no more" (212). Nat becomes something of a pariah; the other boys "let him severely alone" (208). But his plight goes beyond ostracism; for without the reflection of his proprietary name to recursively bestow civic personality, he is truly a "ruined man," "rubbed out" and known "no more" (212). This doubled effect also extends to Tommy, who has effaced his own name with Nat's and whose hens stop laying immediately after. Soon not only Tommy's business but all of Wall Street begins to fail. The economy no longer lays eggs—neither the kind to eat, nor the individuals to eat them—and Plumfield as a whole is endangered by its constipated productivity.

When the Plumfield economy founders, Jo responds, not—as Bronson would have counseled—by severing market and social relations, but by deepening their interdependency. Although property was the problem to begin with ("Tommy's hens were at the bottom of the whole trouble," 202), property remains the fundamental principle of social organization at Plumfield. Thus, when Jack seeks forgiveness and reentry into the Plumfield circle, he is immediately reimmersed in market logic: "Father Bhaer led the bankrupt boy back into the little world, which received him coldly at first, but slowly warmed to him when he showed that he had profited by the lesson and was sincerely anxious to go into a better business with a new stock in trade" (240). On one level, Jack's rehabilitation seems little more than a lesson in the pragmatic nature of market ethics—he moves from unmediated self-interest to that quality of "self-interest rightly understood" admired by Tocqueville. Indeed, we know from an earlier episode that Professor Bhaer has tried previously to temper Jack's unscrupulous business practices by lecturing him on honesty and integrity, and that Jack has decided "he cannot get on without these virtues" and tried to comply (120). Here is self-interest as Tocqueville describes it, an "irresistible force" that "disciplines a number of persons into habits of regularity, temperance, moderation, foresight, self-command; [that] if it does not lead men straight to virtue by the will... gradually draws them in that direction by their habits."[63] Yet when Jack undertakes a "better business" he must learn a different kind of market ethics (240). In this new venture, Jack's "new stock in trade" is his own chastened self, for which he must now seek a market among the other Plumfield boys.

In *Little Men*, Alcott literalizes and extrapolates from the trope of self-possession by depicting a process in which boys learn to relate to their selves as property, as something alienated or separate, in order that they may offer it to others and receive it back. In Alcott's economy, as in Tocqueville's, self-interest plays a central role. But in her version, self-interest is acquired and cultivated—not the inexorable and originary force that he imagines. More important, it seeks gratification not in objects outside of the self but by turning in upon the self. Self-interest for Alcott is interest in self. Where Bronson wants to reunite with his "me" by recalling it from its separate existence until it merges with and restores the "I" to plenitude, Jo teaches her boys to alienate the "me" in order to acquire an "I." Self is the result, not the origin of property relations. In this, Alcott violates one of her father's most cherished principles. But she also organizes a "chase" of selfhood that pursues and achieves a similar goal. She corrects the method of Fruitlands while paying homage to its aims, arriving at Bronson's dream of seamless selfhood through her own unorthodox means.

In Plumfield, Alcott suggests that the combined circulation of property and privacy can accomplish what neither the nation's capitalist economy (based exclusively on property and self-interest) nor her father's transcendentalist economy (based exclusively on privacy and self-denial) could. She unites the subject with his moral self to create an ideal, self-(non)possessive citizen. More significantly, Alcott also proposes that her system can serve the higher purpose of public good by integrating the production of individual subjects like Jack and Nat within a larger exchange economy to create a community of interdependent, mutually replenishing members. It is within the context of this latter concern that Alcott's vision of racial integration comes into focus. The ideal of ownership pervades postbellum discourses on racial reconstruction and black uplift. It ratifies the emergence from slavery into self-right, and underwrites the hope that free labor will enfranchise and assimilate displaced peoples. Emerging from this context, Alcott's own focus on property—including her hyperliteralization of property in self—inevitably unites with her integrationist convictions. She had for years been what she described as a "fanatic" on the emancipation and integration of black Americans into U.S. culture and had already written several stories including "My Contraband" and "Hospital Sketches" against slavery and racial prejudice.[64] When she sets out to devise a "new and charming state of society" in Plumfield, Alcott naturally makes that society coracial. Thus, our very first glimpse of Plumfield, at the close of *Little Women*, includes a "little quadroon" among its students.[65] In an early scene from *Little Men* where the household sings a hymn together, the narrator observes that the black cook "joined at times with the sweetest voice of any, for in this family master and servant, old and young, black and white, shared in the Sunday song, which went up to the Father of them all" (46). In *Jo's Boys* it is similarly asserted that the Bhaers "believed so heartily in the right of all sexes, colours, creeds, and ranks to education, that there was room for everyone who knocked," including "the awkward freedman or woman from the South" (247). To be sure, these integrationist claims are not reflected in the principal casting of the novels: the "little quadroon" never reappears in *Little Men*, where the only black characters are Asia—the aforementioned cook—and Laurie's anonymous driver. No freedpeople are ever visible among the student body of *Jo's Boys*. Such omissions prompt critics to suggest that Alcott's vision of coracial community is more talk than action.[66] Yet integration stands at the heart of both plot and thematics in both of her Plumfield novels.

Alcott's treatment of racial integration focuses on characters who are coded nonwhite in subtle and sometimes only symbolic ways. Displaced representations of race appear frequently in Alcott's writing, as Elbert and Maude Hines demonstrate in their respective discussions of *Moods* and *Jack and Jill*, two novels featuring characters whose dark coloring combines with immigrant histories and, often, black American tropes. In *Jack and Jill*, for example, the eponymous heroine is of French-Canadian derivation, has black hair and eyes, is referred to as both "gypsy" and "indian," and addresses her mother as "Mammy."[67] More, in such characters, darkness nearly always aligns with wayward behavior—a pattern both Elbert and Hines link to Alcott's own dark skin tone and her father's reading of it as an outward sign of excessive will—and with the problematic of integration. The Plumfield novels feature three such characters: Nat, his friend Dan Keane, and Nan Harding. Both Dan and Nan are marked with dark complexions and willful spirits; and although presented as ethnically white, Dan clearly reprises the character of Robert Dane, the heroic escaped slave from Alcott's 1863 story, "My Contraband." Nat breaks with the pattern in being emphatically pale and passive, yet he too is racially encoded. He arrives at Plumfield a refugee, having grown up on the streets among immigrants. One of these, Nicolo, has stolen Nat's violin, and this loss adds to a pattern of dispossession and alienated labor that seems to align Nat with newly emancipated blacks: after the boy has borrowed the school violin his first song is "a simple negro melody"; and when he begins fiddling for pay, he finds it "so much nicer than fiddling in the street, for then I got none of the money, and now I have it all" (16, 54). All three of these racialized children are introduced in *Little Men* as Plumfield newcomers and must master their blemished temperaments while also finding—or creating—places for themselves within the school's insular structure. Nat and Dan are especially important here. Their struggles to assimilate—and Plumfield's struggle to incorporate them—provide the primary throughline for the two novels; their arrivals open *Little Men* and they are the final concerns of *Jo's Boys*.

As she depicts the process of self-mastery and integration for her racialized child protagonists, Alcott turns to the ideas of social Darwinism and plots an evolutionary progression from animalistic or primitive behaviors toward a more civilized or "tamed" condition. In 1871, Herbert Spencer's theories of social evolution, wherein disadvantaged groups were said to have proved themselves genetically "unfit," were just beginning to shape U.S. discourse in ways that would culminate in the eugenicist movement in the 1890s. Alcott, however, was most interested in Spencer's ideas on educational theory. The philosopher argued that children—and boys in particular—resemble savage or primitive peoples in their lack of development. Educators were to guide children through the evolutionary stages already achieved by the race as a whole—and, indeed, to help them improve on that achievement by refining away unwanted traits from the national character. As critics including Hines, John W. Crowley, and Caroline F. Levander have demonstrated, Spencer's ideas about childhood development appear throughout Alcott's works for children.[68] In *Little Men*, evolutionary logic applies to all of the children to some degree. But its special focus falls on Dan and Nan, who are repeatedly described as "wild" or "savage" while endeavoring to overcome their primitive ways, and on Nat whose education, as Levander ingeniously observes, "uncannily mimics human evolution itself, as his 'bent shoulders slowly straighten' (52)."[69]

But while Alcott relies on the social evolutionary narrative, she also adapts it to her own purposes. Specifically, she resists its linear structure and monological account of value and success. Most previous scholarship overlooks this resistance, finding that the evolutionary plots of *Little Men* reflect a racist and racialist belief that poses whiteness as the only standard of development. It is true that as Alcott's children evolve they often also whiten: boys are cleansed of their dirt, girlish complexions recover from excessive (uncivilized) exposure to sun; even genetically brown skin tone blanches—as when Dan turns white with pain from an injury that proves integral to his taming. For critics such as Hines and Levander, this pattern correlates character growth with assimilation to whiteness. Elizabeth Young similarly finds that Plumfield "contracts…into a nearly all-white world."[70] However, not every "savage" impulse or "animalistic" trait in Alcott's fiction receives negative coding. Although Alcott presents temper, heedlessness, and excessive resistance to restraint as "savage" qualities that require conversion, there are other aspects of "wildness" that she clearly wants to incorporate into her small world. In particular, the children's "animal" characteristics usually represent playfulness or other favorable traits that are encouraged to develop, thereby disrupting the notion that evolution is a linear progression from the untamed to the tamed. In a related discussion, Michael Moon reads the "taming" of Plumfield's little men as a fall narrative. His argument refers back to the conclusion of *Little Women*, where Jo first conceives her Plumfield plan and exclaims, "Think of what luxury: Plumfield, my own, and a wilderness of boys to enjoy it with me!"[71] For Moon, this declaration "represents a utopian moment in Alcott's writing about Jo's adult life that is never fulfilled" because the "wilderness" thusly imagined in *Little Women* starts to be domesticated immediately upon its arrival at Plumfield.[72] Moon's analysis helpfully underscores the attractions of savagery in Alcott's worldview—the persistence of which is indicated by Jo's own desire to "escape into the wilderness" when beset by admirers in *Jo's Boys* (39). Yet he too reads Alcott's scheme one-sidedly. Indeed, Moon's identification of utopia with a condition prior to Plumfield socialization smacks of the same chimera that Bronson pursued at

Fruitlands (and that Jo's readers seek when they invade her home): a pristine originary selfhood. Additionally, he, like Levander and Young, overestimates the scope of Jo's taming program in assuming a total eradication of wildness and brownness.

Alcott's ideal community contains elements from either end of Spencer's developmental continuum, incorporating both wild darkness and whitened civilization. And, although she reinscribes the fundamental racism of his theory by aligning wildness with darkness and whiteness with civilization, she refuses to place these in hierarchical or linear relation to each other.[73] Rather, Alcott merges the social evolutionary narrative with her progressive theory of ownership and comes up with a scheme for integration. Spencer cites an "ill-defined" sense of property on his list of primitive traits and makes ownership integral to his prescribed process of self-mastery and development.[74] Alcott adheres to this plan, as we have seen. But she also extends it to propose that self-possession can become a mechanism not just for mastering but also for investing one's self—wild or otherwise—into the social economy. At Plumfield the exchange of boys' selves, their "stock in trade" (240), results in an intermingling of traits that is Alcott's version of amalgamation.

At the heart of Alcott's integrative economy stands Dan. He is constantly referred to as Plumfield's "wild boy" and his darkness is more emphasized than any other child's. Jo considers him to be her most challenging project and her "best work" in the business of taming (41). When Dan seems ready to become a docile Plumfield citizen, Jo introduces him into the same system of ownership that incorporates and produces Nat. But where Nat has been dispossessed by others, Dan's problem lies in his failure to take possession of himself. The headmistress begins, therefore, by teaching him a proprietary relation to the things he has collected in his pockets during rambles in the woods. The strategy is comparable to that employed by the U.S. government in "giving" private property to Native Americans as a mode of installing them in stable relation to, if not within, U.S. national sovereignty—a significant resemblance, given how frequently Dan is likened to Indians.[75] He has been one with nature; now Jo teaches him to objectify his beloved wilderness and exert proprietary will over it. On the first day of training she points to a cabinet and asks, "Now Dan, if you really love these things... don't you think those drawers would be good places to put your eggs, and stones, and shells, and lichens?" (148–49). The offer is partly a bribe: Dan is required to "earn" the drawers through good behavior. But the cabinet is a highly disciplinary form of reward. As he formalizes his possession of and distance from his wild goods and creates systems of value and meaning among them, Dan learns to impose order on his own wild self.

Dan's lineage from Robert Dane, the escaped slave from "My Contraband," is especially apparent in this process. Both characters struggle to achieve self-mastery through self-possession, and both receive help from a female protagonist. Dan's relationship with "Mother Jo" recapitulates that between Robert and Nurse Faith Dane, exhibiting a similarly odd fusion of erotic tension and filial attachment. More important, Dan's presence at Plumfield generates a challenge analogous to that which arose with the infusion of fugitives and freedpeople like Robert Dane into the nation's democratic collectivity. Both test principles of justice, liberty, and inclusion. Both require accommodation and change. Hence the novel's dramatic climax occurs with Dan's implication in the theft of Tommy's quarters; his own welfare is at stake but also that of Plumfield: can Jo's system of privacy relations incorporate Dan's wildness?

Initially, the outlook is grim. When Dan falls under suspicion, the market's power to alienate and distort personality appears more powerful than ever. Although he is innocent, Dan takes on a criminal aspect, for himself as well as for others. When Nat defends Dan, asserting, "You don't lie, and I don't believe you'd steal," Dan replies, "I've done both. I used to fib like fury . . . and I stole things to eat out of gardens . . . so, you see, I *am* a bad lot" (210). He begins to speak "in the rough, reckless way which he had been learning to drop," as though the stolen property is reflecting its image back upon him, in spite of his innocence, displacing the newly developing Dan (210). Like Nat, Dan becomes a pariah and in his case the exile is so extreme that he threatens to resume his savage state; in a kind of evolutionary regression he avoids the house and spends "his leisure hours roaming about the fields and woods, trying to find playmates in the birds and beasts" (218). Contrary to Moon's identification of wilderness with fulfillment, Dan's feral stage brings suffering—he is isolated, "lonely," and "wistful" (211, 218). Most important, Dan's regression signals a breakdown in the state's ability to produce and manage its subjects. Jo tries to comfort him, but he "shun[s] her more than anyone else, and only look[s] at her with the half-imploring, half-fierce eyes of a wild animal caught in a trap, when she trie[s] to talk to him alone" (218).

Once Jack confesses and Dan is reinstated in Plumfield society, Jo secures his membership with more training in property and privacy relations. This time she takes her method a step further by teaching him to possess *and* exchange the self for full integration into the economy of little men. This begins with a conversation between Dan and the school's resident child-philosopher, Demi Brooks. Demi has recently received his own training in self-possession by learning to regard his interiority as a kind of storage closet. He explains:

> I play that my mind is a round room....The walls are full of shelves and drawers, and in them I keep my thoughts, and my goodness and badness, and all sorts of things....Every Sunday I put my room in order, and talk with the little spirit that lives there, and tell him what to do....[G]randpa likes this play, and gives me nice things to put in the drawers, and tells me how to shut up the naughties. (234)

Demi has learned to relate to his own personality—made up of "thoughts," moral behaviors, and "all sorts of things"—as property that he must manage. The parallel to Dan's own curio collection is obvious; we do not require the reminder that Alcott provides when Dan worries that he cannot take part in this new "play" and Demi responds, "You keep your drawers in the cabinet all spandy nice; why can't you do the others?" Demi's drawers make overt the function of Dan's: both boys are cultivating self-interest of the Plumfield variety. At this juncture, however, the training advances to a new stage. When Dan asks Demi to teach him the game of the round room, he promises, "I'll pay you for it by telling all I know about my sort of things" (234). The possession of self opens onto the exchange and amalgamation of selves. Having objectified and compartmentalized their respective personalities, Dan and Demi now trade them as commodities for profit. At Plumfield, boys are fungible. Thus, in an ensuing discussion with Jo, when Dan worries that he should not be trusted to make the exchange with Demi because the younger boy "is so kind of precious" (236), Jo replies that Dan, too, has value (indeed, in *Jo's Boys*, Dan is deemed "worth a dozen Jacks and Neds," 12). She explains that she means to trust him with Demi as a way to "give [him] the best reward [she has]." Jo often speaks of plans to "give" or "lend" her little men to the world; and at the conclusion of *Little Men*, Dan is to be "loaned" to the local naturalist: "Mr. Hyde will ask for him soon, and I mean to give him a...little servant" (319, 325).

In the bargain struck among Dan, Demi, and Jo it becomes clear that Dan's wildness is not erased by his newly "evolved" ability to alienate and possess it. Rather, it is invested into the community economy. Jo approves the deal less because Dan needs to be tempered by an infusion of Demi's personality than because Demi and others need to partake of Dan.

> "I'm going to trust not only Demi, but also my own boy, to you, because you can teach them some things better than any of us....[H]e needs just what you have—knowledge of common things, strength, and courage....Then you know a great deal about natural objects and can tell him more wonderful tales of birds, and bees, and leaves, and animals than his storybooks give

him. . . . Demi will unconsciously strengthen your moral sense, you will strengthen his common sense." (237)

In this economy, Dan's wildness is not an obstruction to communal progress or a weakness to be eradicated in a competition for survival. It is a valuable resource to circulate and increase through amalgamation with other resources. Dan's investment matures in Demi as the latter abandons his childish ways and begins to exhibit "manliness," a quality incessantly attributed to Dan (288). Especially significant, as Demi takes on extra chores and hard manual labor to help support his family, his body roughens and acquires the uncivilized mark of "three small hard spots in his little palm" while Dan remains brown as ever (306).

The infusion of Dan into the Plumfield economy increases significantly with the founding of a Plumfield museum, funded by Laurie but filled with items donated by Dan or discovered with his guidance. This is not a movement of "contraction" but of integration. To be sure, as Levander points out, nineteenth-century museums of natural history reinforced notions of Anglo-Saxon cultural superiority and formalized the civilized man's mastery over his savage past (42). The Laurence Museum, however, complicates such implications when it becomes the setting for a round of show-and-tell lectures in which students share what they have discovered about nature. Several of these lectures challenge the division between human civilization and the untamed world. Nan, for example, criticizes her fellow students while instructing them on the uses of the sponge and, when accused of straying off subject, replies, "No, I ain't; we are to write about vegetables or animals, and I'm doing both: for boys are animals aren't they?" (253). More important, the episode demonstrates the novel's motif of exchange and reciprocal consumption by concluding with a scene in which the boys present Dan with a telescope "to kind of pay for" his having been suspected of the theft (263). When Dan thanks the other boys, "his language was anything but polished" and "many paws were given, and heartily shaken": here again, wildness is not refined but valued and disseminated by exchange (263).

Plumfield passes Dan's test by successfully integrating his wildness; it learns to accept possession of him even as he has learned to possess himself.[76] Early in the novel, when Nat asks if Dan can come to Plumfield, Jo nearly refuses, saying, "I like to know something about them first. I have to choose them, because there are so many" (81–82). Jo's protest evokes the reluctance expressed by many of Alcott's contemporaries toward receiving the postbellum influx of immigrants and freedpeople into the U.S. body politic. In *Little Men*, however, nationalist and white supremacist resistance is quickly cast in a negative light—by Nat's dismayed surprise:

"I told him to come because I thought you'd like it!"—and by the ensuing narrative that proves the value of newcomers like Dan (82).

This is certainly a happy resolution for little men. But what of women—made to stand for the ideal of seamless selfhood by Bronson Alcott, and for the accommodating function of privacy by the culture at large? Nan, remember, is another wild child whose brownness and savagery disrupt Plumfield and who, like Dan, must achieve self-mastery. Their plots follow parallel courses. He spends a month breaking in a colt so as to learn that there is greater liberty in friendly restraint than in running dangerously free. Nan, meanwhile, receives her lesson by spending a day tied to the parlor sofa by a cord that she could easily unknot. In this way she learns to "curb her frantic desire for entire liberty" (225). Like Dan's, Nan's wildness is a resource that will be integrated into the Plumfield economy. Jo invites the unruly girl because Daisy is "getting prim and Bettyish, and needs stirring up a bit" (102). Nan is also an agent of sex integration, brought to help Jo "make little gentlemen" of the boys by cultivating their gentle side (107). But here Alcott also sounds a note of warning. *Little Men* frequently suggests that the fungibility of girls is less equitable than that of boys. For example, in one episode the girls host a tea party at which the boys steal food and refuse to repay the girls' efforts by performing as gentle guests. And in *Jo's Boys*, Jo exclaims, "It takes three or four women to get each man into, through, and out of the world. You are costly creatures, boys; and it is well that mothers, sisters, wives, and daughters love their duty and do it well, or you would perish off the face of the earth" (16–17). This seems a lighthearted and normative portrait of gender relations. But later Nan, now a young adult, instructs her fellow women to bargain carefully so as to avoid "making slaves of ourselves and tyrants of [men]" and attributes Demi's prosuffrage stance to his recalling that he "owes much to [his] mother, sisters, and aunts" (91). Also, of course, *Jo's Boys* features the problem of Jo's own commodification by invading readers—for which, she complains, she receives no compensation at all. Women risk more than men when they become objects for consumption in the economy of privacy. They have less hope of full inclusion and more risk of depletion and dispossession. Thus, it is significant that, through Jo, Alcott imagines a place for herself that is not within this economy of privacy relations but outside and above it. In Jo's role as headmistress, as in Alcott's role as author, a woman can profit from the production of privacy without subjecting herself to its gendered terms.

In seeming contradiction with its oft-stated philosophy of possessive individualism, Plumfield is a place where property and property relations are entirely controlled by the state. In one respect the novel appears to reflect its historical context of continental expansion: there is always something available to be apportioned to new boys for activating their identity and belonging. However, in contrast to the frontier myth, Plumfield contains no virgin territory, and entitlement to property is never inherent. The violin, the cabinet drawers, the gardens, the Wall Street barn—everything is explicitly on loan from the Bhaers. Ownership is not a natural but a vested right proceeding from a benevolent state, granted and revoked in a pattern designed to modulate behavior and collective identification.

Like the violin, farms, and cookies, the selves that Plumfield boys acquire are also on loan and controlled from without. And it is in this regard that the problem of Jo's (and Alcott's) authorship enters the world of *Little Men*. After Jo famously surrenders her fledgling career as a sensation authoress in *Little Women*, Alcott waits until *Jo's Boys* to revive it. Yet the issue of authorship is not quite elided from *Little Men*, for it registers in Jo's management of privacy relations among her students. "I really don't know which I like best," Jo remarks at one point, "writing or boys" (33–34). Happily, she never has to choose, for as headmistress she authors the characters of her little men and plots their development. The analogy comes into relief where Jo employs actual literary procedures, such as the stack of diaries she keeps with other toys in her "play closet." Apparently, not even these items belong to the boys who write in them—an arrangement recalling Alcott's own childhood training in self-relation via her parentally surveilled journal. The same closet also contains Jo's "conscience book," which she shows to Nat on his first night, explaining, "This is one of the ways in which I try to help my boys":

> [It] opened at a page on which there was one word at the top.
>
> "Why, that's my name!" cried Nat, looking both surprised and interested.
>
> "Yes, I have a page for each boy. I keep a little account of how he gets on through the week, and Sunday night I show him the record. If it is bad I am sorry and disappointed, if it is good I am glad and proud; but, whichever it is, the boys know I want to help them, and they try to do their best for love of me and Father Bhaer." (33)

As with Alcott's Fruitlands diary, the conscience book is designed to generate a double movement in which both child and "account" progress toward "purity." But Alcott adds a strange twist to her parents' strategy. Besides the fact that it is Jo and not the child who writes the weekly account, there is also the eerie appearance of Nat's name on one of the pages just a few hours after his arrival. Both details demonstrate Jo's always already possession of the boys and the recursive action of her possession upon their selfhood. For just as Nat's name in the conscience book seems to precede his membership at Plumfield, each week's record of his character will precede his apprehension of it. Jo writes him into a being that he will then experience as originary and a priori. Helpfully, this episode occurs immediately before the one in which Nat receives his egg and "& Co." designation, so that the recursive logic of identification through property echoes loudly with the recursive logic of identification through literary self-revelation, a connection reemphasized by the double entendre of "account."

Once again, circulation is an essential part of the transaction by which the "I" is formed. Although Jo promises that "only you and I will ever know what is to be written on the page below your name," Nat's tale goes public soon after he sees the conscience book (33). First, when the boy's illiteracy is discovered during the next day's lessons, Father Bhaer calls the other students to attention and recounts Nat's previous hardships for the benefit of all (51). Near the end of the novel, Nat's story again features as public fare that benefits each listener and provokes a recursive flash of self-recognition in Nat. As Jo begins a story titled "The Suspected Boy," "Nat look[s] up from the nuts he was picking.... [H]e feel[s] a peculiar interest in this tale and [thinks] it open[s] well" (300). He has learned to invest "interest" in the commodity of self. More, he has evolved from the episode in which he was so transfixed by the public inscription of "& Co." that he could not conduct the business of carrying the egg to the cook. Now Nat understands the importance of continuing exchange and circulation: "Suppose you tell another story," he cries out at the end of the parable, "that was such an interesting one" (304).

Nat's request is granted at the novel's conclusion, when the boys feast on the proceeds from each other's farms—the same farms that Alcott has used earlier to symbolize students' differing personalities, and which Father Bhaer has developed into yet another parable on character. The professor instructs his boys to plant that which they lack—patience, steadiness, and so on—and to tend and raise good crops (44). Initially, the parable makes rather commonplace use of the self-culture paradigm, but further on Alcott develops it into another example of mutual self-propriety. Boy-selves again become commodities for exchange when Professor Bhaer strikes a "little bargain" with Stuffy and Demi that if they grow good crops of moderation he will build a new cricket ground for the school (46). And at Plumfield's Thanksgiving celebration both sorts of crops are harvested and consumed together in a strangely cannibalistic turn of metaphor. Everyone ends up stuffed—with themselves and each other—and the process that begins with self-alienation finishes by swallowing the worm of negation into itself.

As headmistress-author, Jo creates and manages the economy of identification that produces little individuals from her wilderness of boys; she deploys the ruse of privacy toward the benevolent end of community. However, even while Jo's authorship cultivates privacy relations, she remains free of them. This brings us back to the two models of authorship discussed at the beginning of this chapter—on one side, the female writers that Brodhead describes as "court[ing] an invasion of their privacy...inviting the public's vicarious consumption of their 'personal lives'"; on the other side, the ideal of premarket author-ownership that Gillian Brown finds epitomized by Pierre Glendinning.[77] Through Jo, Alcott locates a position in relation to the promotion of self-(non)possession whereby she is neither its masculine subject or feminine object, neither consumes nor allows it to consume her. Years later, when asked to provide an autobiographical essay for *Female Prose Writers of America*, Alcott jotted three short sentences about her birth and childhood, followed by a list:

> 87th 1000 of Little Women—now selling fast,
> 47th 1000 of Old Fashioned Girl—" " "
> 48th 1000 of Little Men—which came out in June last.[78]

The story of Alcott's "I" resides not in her "me," but in the action of disseminating and profiting from it. To locate Alcott in relation to the circulation of her autobiographical fiction, we must look to the empty category of authorship-as-function that enacts labor and market freedoms in their purest form.

Little Men responds with a fusion of irony and adherence to the longing for self-(non)possession that shapes both the doctrine of possessive individualism and Bronson Alcott's resistance to that doctrine. In Plumfield, Alcott creates a world in which market relations can be made to generate an experience of selfhood that precedes property. Thus, even as she violates her father's principles, Alcott realizes their ultimate aim—a community devoted to "goodness" and inclusivity, nourished by the reciprocal exchange of selves. Here, Alcott's authorship, represented by the efforts of Headmistress Jo, creates a reconstructed image of the nation-state wherein integration and inclusion prevail over the drive toward whiteness and contracting boundaries. Fifteen years later this picture will change radically. Writing *Jo's Boys* in 1886, Alcott no longer exhibits supreme faith in the power of property *or* privacy to serve the public good. More, she no longer affirms the power of her own authorship to create a space of democratic inclusivity and justice.

"THE RIGHT TO BE LET ALONE"

By the final years of Alcott's career and life, the promises of social justice through free labor and market idealism had proved false. With more than 80 percent of workers living in poverty and workplace conditions that were more hazardous than ever before, few Americans still believed that the market's invisible hand could guarantee equitable labor relations, much less class harmony.[79] In 1886, the year *Jo's Boys* was published, a decade of violently suppressed labor activism climaxed with Chicago's infamous Haymarket riots. The event was followed by a wave of nativist violence, as police sought scapegoats from the socialist enclaves of German and Eastern European immigrants. Meanwhile, for black Americans free labor had failed even more severely to deliver opportunity for uplift. Since emancipation, blacks had been systematically excluded from white economic infrastructures, and in the 1880s and '90s this exclusion was reinforced by the terrorism of white lynch mobs and by a series of crushing legal setbacks. These decades saw what Eric Sundquist describes as "a long assault on the Fourteenth Amendment," a methodical dismantling of black Americans' civil and political rights that began with the 1877 withdrawal of federal troops from the South and culminated in the federal ruling on *Plessy v. Ferguson* in 1896.[80] Through economic, political, and physical violence, blacks were driven back from the long-desired goal of national membership. Once again, their freedoms—and lives—were sacrificed to the cause of white national union, as the removal of federal protections appeased Southerners and helped restore North-South alliances. Literary culture contributed to this trend with fiction and poetry that romanticized the preemancipation South, circulating images of aristocratic white Southerners served by happy, faithful "darkies." *Uncle Tom's Cabin*, the antislavery manifesto that had once influenced Alcott's political and literary ideas, was now appropriated to promote the racist discourse of plantation nostalgia.[81] In addition to the blighted hopes for class justice through democratic property relations, the dream of a reconstructed biracial democratic family that Alcott and her father had once cherished seemed lost.

The campaign for white political and economic hegemony went hand in hand with a more openly elitist discourse on privacy. Indeed, for the leading U.S. advocate of social Darwinist laissez-faire, William Graham Sumner, property interests and privacy converged as synonymous values in the promotion of a white national supremacy. Arguing against government action on behalf of economic and social justice, Sumner famously declared that the state's purpose was exclusively to protect "the property of men and honor of women against the vices and passions of human nature."[82]

His assertion reflects the classic laissez-faire stance against governmental intrusions into the private affairs of citizens. Pairing private property with feminine sexuality, it encodes the former with similar values of virtue, innocence, and fragility. Building upon this association, Sumner invokes the threat of "vices" and "passions" to align those who might benefit from government regulation (at the expense of property interests) with the idea of sexual excess. This strategy was not unique to Sumner. As chapter 4 has shown, during the late 1860s Andrew Johnson likened federal aid for freedpeople to racial intermarriage. Similar reasoning underwrites the Supreme Court's 1883 decision to overturn the 1875 Congressional Civil Rights Act—legislation that had attempted to remedy flagrant noncompliance with the Fourteenth Amendment by specifying forms of prohibited discrimination. The Court's primary argument against the congressional act was that it empowered the federal government to regulate private persons, overreaching federal authority by invading not just state sovereignty but also the sovereignty of individual citizens. Sumner differs, however, in that while he defends feminized white privacy from political coercion, he also calls upon that political authority to "defend" it. That is, he makes the endangered sanctity of white privacy a weapon against emergent claims to political and economic justice and a way to legitimize—and, ironically enough, enlist government support for—the expansion of white upper-class privilege.

Less than a decade later, Warren and Brandeis would attempt to establish privacy as a formal legal right. Defining privacy first as a "right to be let alone" and next as "rights as against the world," their argument shifts in tone from defensive to aggressive (76, 86). This shift is echoed by their use of an evolutionary legal narrative that presents the expansion of personal immunity as natural and inevitable. The privacy tort called for by Warren and Brandeis never came to be. But the defensive-aggressive force of white privacy continued to exert itself within U.S. legal and political culture. One of the most infamous examples would follow just a few years after "The Right to Privacy," when the Supreme Court deemed that blacks and whites were entitled to "separate but equal" domains of civil freedom.

The *Plessy v. Ferguson* case began in 1892 with the arrest of Homer Plessy for refusing to vacate a white-only railway car while traveling through the state of Louisiana. Plessy had staged the event deliberately along with a group of activists, including the lawyer who would eventually argue the case, Albion Tourgée. They sought to expose Louisiana segregation law as an unconstitutional violation of Fourteenth Amendment rights and privileges. They also wanted to show that segregation was unworkable. Able to pass as white, Plessy actually had to self-identify as black to provoke arrest. As critics such as Sundquist and Amy Robinson show, Plessy and Tourgée challenged more than racial segregation. They also took on the hegemonic fiction of racial difference by forcing the binary logic of Jim Crow to confront the actuality of Plessy's mixed-race person.[83] The case went to the Supreme Court in 1893 and concluded in 1896 with Chief Justice Henry Billings Brown's disastrous validation of separate-but-equal entitlements. Brown framed his decision with the same laissez-faire argument that had informed the Court's ruling in 1883, reasoning that the judiciary could not intervene into the conduct of private citizens and businesses. But the ruling signals more than a simple refusal to overreach jurisdiction. For the ratification of "separate but equal" intervened deeply into racial relations to produce and protect white entitlement under the aegis of privacy.

The centerpiece of Tourgée's argument was that Louisiana law violated Plessy's rights by depriving him of his property in the status of whiteness and the economic benefits to be derived from it: "The reputation of belonging to the dominant race, in this instance the white race, is property," the lawyer reasoned, and the law enabling "an officer of the railroad company to ask a person to a car set apart for a particular race, enables such officer to deprive him...of this property—this reputation—which has an actual pecuniary value."[84] Here, by equating whiteness to property and reputation, Tourgée points out that racial identity does not precede but derives from social recognition. He denaturalizes not only race, but also white racial privilege—as the reference to the "pecuniary value" of whiteness emphasizes. More important, he frames whiteness as a form of dependence, an aspect of self that is established from without and subject to determinations of social—and even market—value. In his ruling, Brown grants Tourgée's notion of whiteness as property, but contends that this is not a property that Plessy can legitimately claim and, in fact, that by passing for white Plessy was the bearer of stolen or misappropriated goods.[85] With this, Brown reasserts the coherence and a priori truth of racial difference. As Robinson persuasively argues, Brown turns Tourgée's own device against him by accessing the Lockean principle of a presocial property in self, restoring whiteness to a place of privilege—and, I would add, productive peril—within what Robinson terms the "discourse of natural ownership."[86]

Here I want to push Robinson's analysis a bit further. For in the full logic of Brown's ruling, Plessy's case becomes illegitimate not because he appropriated whiteness from its rightful owners, but because he mistook it for a fungible commodity. When referring to the 1883 precedent that prohibits the Court from empowering the federal regulation of private persons, Brown extends the earlier argument by elaborating upon its theme of invasion. Specifically, he marks a line between public acts of discrimination and private "racial feeling" and places the latter beyond the state's jurisdiction. Brown writes that it is the government's role "to enforce the absolute equality of the two races before the law, but, in the nature of things, it could not have been intended to abolish distinctions based upon color, or to enforce social... equality, or a commingling of the two races upon terms unsatisfactory to either"; in Brown's judgment, "legislation is powerless to eradicate racial instincts."[87] Here, an ethic of laissez-faire government merges with a psychoevolutionary theory of "natural" racial feeling to characterize legislated integration as an invasion of affective privacy and an alienation of whiteness itself. In other words, Brown responds to Plessy's staging of a racial crisis by staging a privacy crisis. His evocation of racial feeling reinforces a theory of race as a priori Truth—but not as property. Rather, by posing an aversion to blacks as inextricable from whiteness, he presents them together as a thing—like Warren and Brandeis's figure of "inviolate personality"—that simply ceases to exist *as* itself if divided *from* itself. The threat here is not the theft but the destruction of whiteness. Brown deploys imperiled white privacy against integrationists and, more particularly, against blacks. More, he legalizes the expansive evolution of white privilege by effectively privatizing vast tracts of public space as zones of white immunity.

As privacy discourse becomes more openly affiliated with what Sundquist describes as "the nation's rush toward racial extremism in law, in science, and in literature," Alcott's approach to it changes.[88] The earlier discussion of "Jo's Last Scrape" has shown that she continues to treat anxieties about privacy with derision, staging Jo's authorial alienation to reveal that alienation is precisely that which generates privacy and possession of a unified self. This time, however, Alcott's tone is not lighthearted. In *Little Men*, the discord caused by Tommy's quarters is an intra-Plumfield problem that empowers Jo. It activates her status as benevolent author, headmistress, and head of state, and enables her to produce more self-(non)possessive little men. Conversely, in *Jo's Boys* the trouble emanates from outside of Plumfield and encompasses the whole school, Jo included. She can no longer escape or oversee the dynamics of alienation. Privacy no longer registers as a useful delusion that can be manipulated to create inclusive community. Rather, it aligns with a narrowing zone of privilege and exclusionary ruling interests. In 1886 Alcott regards privacy as destructive to the just community she had envisioned in 1871 and confronts her own diminished power to shape its use.[89]

The first sign of Alcott's new pessimism is Plumfield's embattled relation to the market economy. As Gregory Eiselein notes, *Jo's Boys* breaks the insularity of *Little Men* by sending many of its characters out to engage life beyond Plumfield; they travel to a range of foreign countries and pursue ambitious careers. However, this process is often troubled and, if Jo's "small world" now acknowledges its wider context, it also seems in danger of being overwhelmed. While Jo struggles with print culture, her students narrowly escape the perils of sea travel, frontier life, dissipated European society, and extra-Plumfieldian romance. Most significant, Jo's immediate family gets displaced by urban-industrial developments that have "shut in the old house, spoilt Meg's nest, and dared to put a soap-factory under Mr. Laurence's indignant nose" (2). Marmee and the sisters have retreated to Plumfield and built replicas of their old homes on its grounds—a flight from invasive economic forces that is echoed a few pages on by Jo's own withdrawal deeper and deeper into the confines of her home. Gone is the incessant affirmation of free labor and possessive individualism we witnessed in *Little Men*. Capitalism no longer appears a beneficial system that serves, under Jo's benevolent management, to constitute home and community. She and her fellow utopians are, literally, refugees from it within a Plumfield whose insularity ultimately feels more intense and claustrophobic—in part because it seems enforced—than in *Little Men*. Most of Jo's cherished wild boys and girls go out to tackle the big world. But this only leaves Jo more bereft—left behind with the remaining students, whom even Eiselein describes as "passive and a bit boring."[90]

Even more notable than Alcott's withdrawn endorsement of property relations is the withdrawal of her corollary endorsement of privacy relations. Like *Little Men*, *Jo's Boys* dramatizes the production of self-(non)possession. More, the novel acknowledges its own role in providing that fantasy of private selfhood to readers. But now Alcott betrays deep ambivalence toward this process and its end result. We can begin to track this new stance by considering the fate and role of "wildness." In *Little Men*, Dan and Nan must surrender their wild desire for freedom outside of society to acquire a place of self-(non)possessive citizenship within it. Both discover there is more freedom in self-mastery and belonging than in autonomy. Jo's "wild desire to fly into the wilderness, since [she] cannot shut [her] doors even in free America" clearly recalls the savage yearnings of her former students. But for her the loss of savage freedom does not yield, as for Dan and Nan, a more capacious civilized freedom. Indeed, Jo's liberty seems "to be fast going from her" with no compensation in sight (38). Alcott does, of course, satirize Jo's desire for privacy and autonomy: there is no such thing as a closed door (Alcott opens these herself, and invites the reader in); nor, as we shall find, does there exist a wilderness into which one might escape. But the sense of loss and damage are real, for the uninvited visitors also prevent Jo from writing. In a journal entry written soon after *Little Men*'s publication, Alcott refers to this predicament with irritation: "People *must* learn that authors have some rights. I can't entertain a dozen a day, and write the tales they demand also."[91] In *Jo's Boys* the problem is more grave. By disabling the very thing they pursue, Jo's demanding readers impair her power to author a just and diverse community. As the U.S. government overturned its own safeguards for social justice and equality, Alcott ceased to imagine a heroine capable of creating an alternative in her own "small world."

In *Jo's Boys*, as in *Little Men*, our investigation into the intersecting discourses on privacy, race, and belonging focuses on Dan. He returns to Plumfield twice in the course of the novel. The first homecoming is triumphant: Dan has been ranching and prospecting out West and tells of befriending a tribe of impoverished Montana Indians. Delighted with his adventures, Dan's friends begin to plan a new utopian community, a kind of Plumfield-West to be called Dansville. Dan then lights out for the territories once again, but this time he accidentally kills a man in a barroom brawl and serves time in a prison. By his second return to Plumfield he has been "tamed"—or perhaps broken—by his experiences. Recovering at the school, Dan reveals an impossible romantic love for Bess, the jealously guarded daughter of Laurie and Amy. To this point, Dan's 1886 plot mirrors the one from 1871: two homecomings, the second in a humbled condition that attaches him to a female character. In 1886, however, the wild boy is not permitted to stay. In the ten fictional (and fifteen historical) years since we last saw it, Plumfield has lost its power to accommodate and integrate Dan's wildness. Sent back to his Indians, he dies defending them.

Dan's first homecoming occurs at the end of "Jo's Last Scrape" and puts a finishing—and racializing—touch to that chapter's portrait of violated privacy. In this chapter, Alcott has already several times alluded to the social evolutionary theories that aligned privacy with endangered whiteness. Alcott refers to the invading journalists as a "tribe," and the ladies from Oshkosh speak in a pronouncedly quaint dialect to indicate their uncultured status.[92] Also, Jo resignedly "offer[s] herself up on the altar of juvenile literature"—as though her privacy has been made an object of primitive worship. The most overt allusion occurs with Dan's arrival. Jo, who has retreated upstairs to hide, learns from her maid that there is a gentleman downstairs who "wouldn't take no for an answer" and has "walked right in as bold as brass" (52). "I guess he's another crazy one," adds maid Mary, "I declare I'm 'most afraid of him, he's so big and black." Jo at first refuses to meet this new intruder, but when she hears Mary cry out and "remember[s] the ways of reporters and also that her maid was both pretty and timid, Mrs. Bhaer [flings] down her pen and [goes] to the rescue" (53). Here Alcott stages Dan's first appearance as the culminating and most egregious attack on Jo's privacy. His intrusion is racialized obliquely by his affiliation with "the tribe" of reporters (borne out in the chapters to come by his frequent identification with Indians). But the scene's racial narrative obtains primarily in its insistence upon Dan's "blackness" and in how that blackness is linked to the suggestion of a sexual threat to Mary—a jarring note in this period when lynchings were so often justified by rumors of black rapists and endangered white womanhood. This insinuation persists, even after Dan's true identity is established, with the story of his forbidden interest in Bess.

In fact, our initial impression of Dan as the dark invader of white privacy never quite dissipates. He is, of course, an extremely welcome guest at Plumfield: after "one keen look" through the shaggy black hair and beard, Jo "complete[s] Mary's bewilderment by throwing both arms around the brigand's neck" (53). But while this reversal casts an ironic light on the racial tropes that Dan has seemed to embody, it does not quite displace their effect. Dan's racial inflection is far more pronounced in 1886 than in 1871. Alcott never lets him enter a room without noting his brown skin, black hair, or black eyes. He is likened to Mexicans (55, 78), Spaniards (77), Native Americans (54), and Egyptians (58), and linked to both blackface minstrelsy (Ted promises that as a Dansville farmer he would use "'de shubbel and de hoe' like a good one," 59) and Shakespeare's Othello (84). Dan's brownness is associated, as of old, with his desire for freedom—as when "his keen dark face" and "love for a wild, wandering life" cause Jo to surmise he "[has] Indian blood in him" (54). However, his savage otherness is now also strongly associated with criminality. Jo compares Dan to Mexican banditti and her niece, Josie, exclaims that he looks "as big and black as a villain in a play" (58). The comparison to Othello comes soon after, and here Dan is cast opposite Bess: spying on the pair, Jo and Laurie find "little Desdemona . . . looking up with moonlight full upon her into young Othello's face" and worry that "his 'grand, gloomy, and peculiar' style will be too much for our simple maids" (84). Alcott also employs darkness as a recurring metaphor in the story of Dan's actual crime. Imprisoned for murder, he looks "with a shudder at the brown fist he clenched involuntarily as he remembered what it had done" (229). Once released, he tries vainly to "get the prison taint off him" before returning to Plumfield (287). Here Dan's color symbolizes not just the temper he has failed to control—as in *Little Men*, or in Bronson Alcott's estimate of his dark-skinned daughter—but also a deeper stain of criminality and nonbelonging.

There is a determining logic to the way that brownness marks both crime and criminality in *Jo's Boys*. As the "involuntary" clenching of Dan's brown fist suggests, his racial aspect seems to control and render him unfree in a way that recalls the trope of self-imprisoning blackness discussed in previous chapters. Here, however, Dan's color seems to act upon rather than within or from him. Its insistent and unsettling visibility in the narrative gives it a causality of its own, as though it is not Dan but a force outside of him that ultimately necessitates his expulsion. Dan's initial misidentification as an intruder and sexual threat, and its persisting trace in the narrative, lead the reader to interpret the conclusion—Plumfield's tragic inability to receive Dan as one of its own—as simultaneously inevitable and mistaken. "[He] says you'll be sorry if you don't see him," reports the maid to mistress Jo; and when Jo finally recognizes Dan, he laughs and asks, "Won't you be sorry?" and again, after they embrace, "Now won't you be sorry if I go away?" (53). Alcott repeats the point three times, and it merits the emphasis because it names her central theme of loss. Jo *will* be sorry when Dan is gone—her grief is the focus of the novel's final scene—for his exile reveals the impoverished nature of the privacy that imprisons her but cannot accommodate him.

A related ambivalence shapes the account of Dan's taming. It is important that once he is no longer mistaken for an invader, Dan begins to feel trapped at Plumfield. He paces like a restless animal, gasps for fresh air, and "glance[s] about the room as if he already f[inds] it rather confined and long[s] for all out-of-doors again" (55–56). This is the Dan from *Little Men* who resists the constraints of middle-class domesticity and the cozy compromise of self-(non)possession. It aligns him with Jo and her desire (expressed just a few pages earlier) to escape into the wilderness. As with many of Alcott's racialized heros, Dan stands both for a desired object (the liberating and erotic wildness that will disappear from Plumfield with his exile) and for a mode of desire that white women could not display for themselves. Dan, that is, represents Jo's forbidden desire to escape white middle-class belonging and the mourned absence of wildness within white middle-class belonging.[93] Hence, while his taming follows a path similar to that taken in *Little Men*, this time the process is much more equivocal. Like Jo's, Dan's impulse to flee stems in part from an encumbering market economy. He has made a good investment and the resulting "little fortune" seems to "rather oppress him." Jo, in a flash of her old possessive-individualist ethos, advises Dan to "be prudent and invest your money... for rainy days come to all of us, and dependence would be very hard for you to bear" (55). But she also reflects happily that "the money-making fever had not seized her lucky boy yet" (55). Jo's response contradicts itself, posing the freedom of having money against the constraint of being "oppressed"—or "seized"—by money. In the intersecting economies of the first Plumfield novel, this contradiction would have resolved itself with a happy and sensible compromise. Here it stands as one of many places where Alcott presents U.S. freedom as a double bind and seems to partake of Dan's longing for a free space, a wilderness where neither dependence nor wealth can possess him.

It jars our ear, therefore, when immediately after this conversation the other Plumfieldians arrive to lay claim to Dan's otherness. First Josie and Bess block Dan's exit: "'Here!'" calls Jo, "'we can't allow any monopoly of Dan.... Bring him back and keep an eye on him'"; and "led by these agreeable captors, Dan return[s] to the parlor" (57). The conceit of entrapment and appropriation continues in the discussion that follows. As the Dansville plan is introduced and enthusiastically developed, Josie objects that she wants Dan to continue "the wandering life which brought her thrilling tales and pretty things at each return" (60). Nan, now a medical student, asks Dan to let her feel his arm: "'Splendid biceps! Now, boys, see there: this is what I call muscle.' And Nan deliver[s] a short lecture with Dan's sinewy arm to illustrate it" (61). Each person makes Dan an objectification of exoticism, freedom, or power that can be possessed.

The scene almost reprises the integration of wildness that occurred in *Little Men* through the drawers in Dan's curio cabinet, his contracted exchange with Demi, and the museum exhibition. Indeed, Dan participates in this home economy by opening a box of Indian artifacts and distributing gifts until everyone is wearing Native clothing, sketching buffalo heads, lying on bearskin rugs, or singing "plaintive Indian songs written on birch bark" (76). He seems to have resumed his old function of investing Plumfield with his own wildness. But this time, the community's attempt to consume Dan seems excessive and even ironically framed. Laurie, for example, offers to buy his way into Dansville—"I shouldn't mind investing in a few prairies and cowboys myself" (59)—and then, upon learning that Dan's "old friends the Montana Indians" are starving on their government reservation, expands his investment plan by "privately resolving to people his as yet unbought prairies with Montana Indians" (63). Laurie's plan hyperbolizes the logic of Plumfield's privacy economy, where fungible boys possess and are possessed by each other, and renders it grotesque. It also reflects back ironically on Dan and Jo's desire to flee to a wilderness, and reinforces Dan's identification with the Montana Indians. They are the very symbol of dispossession, of wildness appropriated by the nation-state but not integrated or reimbursed: "Hundreds have died of starvation because they didn't get their share," explains Dan. "[They have been] driven from their own land to places where nothing will grow" (62). Introduced amid the household plundering of Dan, this image is prophetic of his future. Like the Montana Indians among whom he will die, his offerings will be received but not reciprocated.

If the process of Dan's appropriation is unsettling and unrewarded, his actual taming is even more so. In *Jo's Boys*, taming is represented chiefly through acts of confession: Dan and others must disclose their transgressions in order to progress. This rite recalls the principle of evolution from *Little Men*: one gains possession of oneself only by giving that self away. Here again, Dan's initial resistance is seen as symptomatic of his savagery: "It was always hard for him to show his inner self," explains the narrator, "and he took pride in hiding it as an Indian does in concealing pain or fear" (111). A similar connection is drawn when Dan is in prison and will surrender "no cry for help," exhibiting "the dumb despair of an Indian at the stake" (182).[94] Dan's reticence is not a sign of self-possession or self-(non) possession, nor even of the noble savage's stoicism, but of his undeveloped, unassimilated state. According to social Darwinists, one of the savage's identifying traits was his resistance to being known.[95] Dan's secrecy also reinforces his criminality, for his initial refusal to confess his failings gives them power over him that leads to murder. When Dan begins at last to disclose the secrets of his personality—first to the prison confessor and later to Jo, trading wildness for belonging—it appears that we are resuming the taming that began in the previous Plumfield novel. This time, however, the process is portrayed with ambivalence. In *Little Men* Jo patiently waits until a boy elects to confide in her. In *Jo's Boys* she pressures and ambushes Dan, wryly comparing herself to "an old spider" waiting to catch him out: "They always open their hearts sooner or later" (96). When Jo discovers Dan's feelings for Bess by watching the two in a mirror, she feels ashamed, "like a thief who has stolen something very precious" (307). This reaction marks another significant change from *Little Men*, where scenes of accidental overhearing occur constantly, giving Jo her reassuring air of benevolent omniscience and allowing Alcott to present readers with more privileged access to privacy. But with Dan's taming in *Jo's Boys*, confession and discovery come to seem invasive or presumptuous, as though Alcott has ceased to accept the sentimental legitimization of her own disciplinary intimacy.[96] In the revelation of Dan's love for Bess, it becomes especially clear that the Plumfieldian tradition of dispossession is no longer seamlessly benevolent and redemptive in its outcomes, and that self-unity and community belonging are no longer its promised returns.

Dan's desire for Bess signals both his readiness for full membership in the Plumfield body politic and the impossibility of his ever achieving it. Bess represents those aspects of a fully evolved self that Dan lacks—a role established in *Little Men* where, as Levander notes, the girl symbolizes the "exclusive association of whiteness with bourgeois culture" and functions as an "object of desire [that] tames all the students" (41). In *Jo's Boys*, Bess is posed repeatedly against Dan's blackness—in their Othello/

Desdemona tableau, at the dance where we find him "rolling his black eyes admiringly" at her blonde beauty (80), and in the image of his death-dealing "brown fist" with her "white hand... laid in it confidingly" (229). As an artist and cultural connoisseur, Bess also represents civilization in contrast to Dan's wildness—a point made explicit when the two debate the relative merits of Rome and the Rockies (68). When Dan seems ready to flee Plumfield during his first visit, it is a glimpse of Bess's white shape in the darkness that stops him. Later, her photograph sustains him in his struggle for self-mastery while in prison. Bess symbolizes for Dan the possibility of white, civilized self-unity via (non)possession of this other ideal self. Jo recognizes this fact, likening his infatuation to a "hunger for food neglected or denied" (305). She also attributes Dan's feelings to the early loss of his mother, a wound that elsewhere explains his undeveloped emotional and moral faculties—and here we might think back to "Jo's Last Scrape," where Jo's own mother symbolizes the privacy and originary selfhood she has acquired recursively from her writing. For Dan, however, Jo never imagines that attaining his desire will be possible—and here the narrative's inexorable black-white opposition reemerges as she sadly reflects that "light and darkness [are] not farther apart than snow-white Bess and sin-stained Dan" (305). Through Bess, Alcott demonstrates that while Dan is ready to evolve into full Plumfield belonging, Plumfield is not ready or able to accommodate him.

With Dan's expulsion, the narrative's ambivalence becomes more pronounced and the novel's critical voice more distinct, as Alcott asks readers to share in her bitter disappointment over the era's multiple failures and losses. Both Elizabeth Young and Michael Moon read Dan's departure as a failure of Alcott's imagination: in Young's words, Alcott can find "no place in her disciplined and whitened body politic" for Dan's blackness.[97] I find that *Jo's Boys* portrays—rather than participates in—this failure. The narrative cultivates conflicting expectations. On one side, it strongly favors Dan as a walking display of patriotism, heroism, and "manliness" and marks him for success. A marriage between Dan and Bess is encoded into what Moon describes as Plumfield's "utopian scheme": "Bess," Moon observes, "was supposed to have grown up and become the mate of the author's favorite male character, Dan."[98] On the other side, the absolute necessity of Dan's exile is established from his very first appearance by that mark of criminalized nonwhiteness. Ostensibly, Dan's crime explains his banishment. Yet the narrative presents the murder unambiguously as an accident resulting from Dan's attempt to protect a naive young friend. Dan is a victim of circumstances—and, indeed, of his own heroism. The murder does not adequately account for his categorical disqualification from Bess and Plumfield. Thus, his expulsion derives not from moral causality but from the criminal stigma that exceeds and, more important, precedes the crime. He is driven out by the narrative's insistent black/white reasoning that, like the arbitrary legal application of absolute racial difference, enforces its own consequences. In our regret over Dan's expulsion and the fatal indelibility of the mark that causes it—and in our disappointment that the novel has not pursued the course that, as Moon points out, the author herself "seems to have her heart set on"—we partake of Alcott's own response to her racially segregated culture and the violent forces of U.S. apartheid.[99]

Finally, *Jo's Boys* laments not only Dan's exile, but also the diminished and denaturalized model of U.S. selfhood that it secures. The novel presents two critical examples in Nat Blake, Dan's old friend and fellow supplicant for Plumfield belonging, and the wealthy Mr. Laurence. As Dan leaves without Bess, Nat returns from his own travels to claim his love interest, Daisy, and official admission into the Plumfield family. This conclusion is surely part of Plumfield's "utopian scheme"; it gratifies an expectation that was established in the very first scene of *Little Men*. However, the perfect closure of Nat's induction rings hollow. For Jo is mourning Dan's departure—as Dan himself predicted she would. She refuses to view Nat's homecoming as "the silver lining of that cloud" (320) and persists in "clinging fast to her black sheep although a whole flock of white ones trotted happily before her" (322). As for Laurie, Jo's erstwhile "head boy . . . the first boy Mrs. Jo ever had to take care of," he is the prototype of Plumfield citizenship (*Little Men* 160). He is also Bess's extremely protective and possessive father. And if owning fair Bess constitutes the state of whitened selfhood and belonging that excludes Dan, Laurie epitomizes that state in an unsettling manner. Both parents feel "that the most perfect lover they can find will hardly seem to them worthy of their precious daughter" (311), but it is Laurie whom the narrator repeatedly describes as a Pygmalion with Bess as his Galatea (21). This recurring association reflects suggestively on the ideal that Bess represents and that Dan is denied, identifying it as a mode of solipsistic self-gratification whereby the individual achieves completion by jealously monopolizing an ideal that he himself creates. Here, white male self-(non)possession appears incestuous, empty, greedy, and paranoid—not unlike the (non)property of whiteness that the U.S. Supreme Court would protect, one decade later, from wrongful appropriation by the likes of Homer Plessy.[100] And, as though anticipating the aggressive expansion of white immunity that would ensue under "separate but equal" law, this father who keeps his daughter for himself is also the entrepreneur who plans to expand his holdings into the very wilderness of Dan's exile. For Alcott the better individual is the one who dies defending the dispossessed Indians and "the green wilderness he loved so well," rather than the one who means to purchase them, prairies and all (322).

In *Little Men*, Dan's otherness is integrated to enrich and transform Jo's small world and its inhabitants; in *Jo's Boys*, Dan is eliminated to protect an ironically idealized community—a "whole flock of white ones"—that fails to satisfy Jo. That Alcott uses her novel to criticize the culling of non-whites from the national flock is confirmed by her concluding scene. There Nat celebrates his homecoming with the same song he played as a child on his first night at the school. The violin performance reemphasizes that the narrative has come full circle, and establishes Nat's long-awaited Plumfield membership. But the meaning of the song—and thus of that belonging—is tragically revised. In its 1871 rendition the song is described as "a negro spiritual." It signals Plumfield's commitment to inclusivity and Alcott's postbellum faith in racial reform. In 1886 the song is reintroduced on the heels of that community's failure to make a place for black Dan. This time Nat's piece is referred to simply as "an old street melody"; however, as the family sings along we find that the reference to slavery remains:

> Oh my heart is sad and weary
> Everywhere I roam,
> Longing for the old plantation
> And for the old folks at home. (321)

These lyrics undermine the very closure they offer, by reminding us that Dan is "roaming" homeless even as we listen. More disquieting still is the song's reference to the nostalgia for plantation "folks" and a preemancipation world that was at this time a popular literary theme. Once a symbol of postbellum optimism, the song now becomes an ironic anthem to the old order of race relations that resignifies both the plantation tradition and the Plumfield family circle that has succumbed to it. If *Little Men* is Alcott's utopian vision of a reconstructed America, *Jo's Boys* is her tragic portrait of Jim Crow nationalism.

CHAPTER SIX

Epilogue

REBIRTH

"We have a product on the loose!"
—*The Island*

In the century since Samuel Warren and Louis Brandeis demanded their "right to be let alone," U.S. privacy has grown vastly more complicated.[1] Legal debates have shifted focus from the civil entitlements that concerned Warren and Brandeis to the more encompassing arena of constitutional privacy and the controversial matters of reproductive, sexual, and marital choice. Social phenomena like the Internet blogosphere, YouTube, and reality television have made the production and consumption of self-disclosure a major cultural preoccupation, and heightened anxieties about eroding boundaries and deteriorating public values. Perhaps most significant among these developments is government surveillance. With the emergence of wiretapping, electronic monitoring, and other means of tracking citizen activity that were unimaginable in the nineteenth century, what legal scholars refer to as "front door invasions" have become a dominant focus of twenty-first-century political discourse.

Needless to say, U.S. privacy is still in crisis. And if present-day panic narratives focus on new threats such as the domestic activities of the CIA or same-sex marriage, they also continue to shape conceptions of democratic freedom and belonging that—whether expressed in a bumper sticker exhorting fellow citizens to "Keep Big Brother *Out*" or in the insistence that heterosexual marriage is a divine mandate rather than a material privilege—emphasize disengagement, passivity, and transcendence.

Moreover, concerns about property and market relations continue to play a vital role in contemporary privacy discourse. Much of the recent scholarly and popular commentary on the relationship between privacy and property is characterized by what Miranda Joseph calls "Romantic anticapitalism," an approach that posits two "hostile worlds"—one governed entirely by market value and exchange relations, the other by human value and care relations—and assumes these cannot come into contact without mutual contamination.[2] Scholars taking this view divide human functions into commodified and noncommodified domains and denounce the marketization of sex, reproduction, or health care as a violation of a sacred boundary. As a number of social theorists suggest, this paradigm can be traced back to nineteenth-century separate spheres ideology, and has a similar effect of distorting—by polarizing—the arenas of market and so-called nonmarket activity.[3] And, as the preceding five chapters have argued, this polarization is not only distorting and limiting; it is also productive.

This book has explored the consequences of imagining human existence in terms of two antagonistic and simultaneous conditions—we are owned, we are not owned—and of incessantly rehearsing the drama of passage between them. Most particularly, it has investigated how such representations, and the fantasy they project of self-(non)possession—that is, of self-possession without self-alienation—intersect with questions about democratic freedom and nationhood. In this concluding discussion I revisit those questions in a twenty-first-century context by looking at biotechnology—a major source of modern "commodity anxiety" and a place where market pressures come to bear on personality and life narrative in their most fundamental form, DNA. My analyses focus specifically on Michael Bay's 2005 clone-action movie, *The Island*. In many respects, the film pursues a familiar account of privacy relations endangered by property relations. At its conclusion, however, something different emerges—an ideal of private selfhood that is progressive rather than nostalgic, produced rather than salvaged from market culture. This, I argue, represents a new development in the narrative of imperiled privacy that enhances its power to suture democracy with capitalism and resolve contradictions between the modes of individuality and freedom imagined within them.

A clone movie may seem incongruous, coming at the conclusion of a study that has concentrated on biographical and autobiographical writing from the 1800s. Yet, in the twenty-first-century imagination, biotechnology raises many of the same questions and anxieties that haunt nineteenth-century life writing. Biotechnologies trouble belief in the inviolability of human personality, individuality, and life; and this trouble intensifies when the market enters the equation, as with the patenting of genetic materials or the sale of Ivy League eggs and third world organs. Interestingly, these concerns often come into focus in relation to life narrative. Indeed, for the President's Council on Bioethics, life and life narrative coincide: their 2002 report on "Human Cloning and Human Dignity" states that the use of cloned embryos for biomedical research "denies the continuous history of human individuals from the embryonic to fetal to infant stages of existence."[4] For others, the problem is that DNA represents autobiography at its most elemental—constituting what one critic describes as a "genetic diary"—and that with genetic technology this story can circulate to unknown locations to perform unauthorized functions and disclose "sensitive personal information about the individual and his or her family."[5] Over the past decade, legislators and activists have raised concerns about the DNA samples kept over from criminal investigations for use in "DNA dragnets." In addition to protesting this violation of prisoners' privacy rights, some predict that pressure from commercial interests will lead to the uncontrolled dissemination of such databases, making them available to insurance companies, employers, political opponents, and so on. Pointing to the analogous case of Social Security numbers, critics warn that although the justice system promises to keep DNA databases to limited and confidential use, these too will inevitably become widely accessible sources of detailed personal information.[6] Added to such fears about the misappropriation of genetic life narrative are fears regarding the narrative itself. As Priscilla Wald explains,

> the genome sciences make it possible for people to return—literally—to a transformed past to learn from their DNA, for example, that they are not who they thought they were: that they are not the children of their presumed biological parents, perhaps, or that they do, or do not, have biological ties to a particular racial or ethnic group.[7]

The disquieting possibility of self-defamiliarization that Wald describes here recalls many nineteenth-century complaints about violated privacy. Like the unauthorized photograph or exposé, the uncanny self revealed by genetic code threatens to destabilize the self from which it has been alienated. It is not surprising that among the causes championed by proponents of genetic privacy is "the right not to know."[8]

The biotech privacy crisis also echoes its nineteenth-century antecedent in the intersecting questions it provokes about gender, race, and embodiment. Given the significance of biotechnology to reproductive options, it is inevitable that concerns about the disruption—or abrogation—of motherhood and femininity figure prominently in the controversy around it.[9] The racial politics of biotechnology take myriad forms. Issues include the disproportionate number of blacks in the prison population that results in disproportionate representation in DNA databases; the collection of DNA (or "bioprospecting") from indigenous groups whose genes are of special interest to medical researchers but who rarely benefit from the financial profits or medical discoveries that follow; and the convoluted racial politics of the markets for eggs, sperm, and surrogacy.[10] These aspects of biotech practice inevitably remind us of the longtime denial of self-right to nonwhites in America. But they do so in ways that are diverse and complicated; so that, as both Wald and Robyn Weigman argue, the oft-used analogy to slavery generally obscures more than it reveals.[11] That said, I would argue that the prevalence of the "bioslavery" trope is significant precisely because of the way it reduces the old problematic of privacy, property, and embodiment to manageable form. Genetic engineering might, as the President's Council on Bioethics claims, represent the ultimate act of mastery over the body.[12] But it also disables the cherished dream of an immaterial—and therefore free—selfhood that transcends its body. Cloning (at least in its popularly imagined form) particularly emphasizes the physical basis of personality and its consequent vulnerability to alienation, replication, and commodification. Expressing this dilemma through the metaphor of slavery displaces it historically and, in many cases, racially, and overresolves it into a state of absolute unfreedom—a setting from which the possibility of absolute freedom seems easily discernible.[13]

Like *Total Recall*, *Blade Runner*, and *The Matrix*—its predecessors in the sci-fi action genre—*The Island* translates biotech anxieties for popular culture. Grounded in the hostile worlds paradigm, where property and privacy relations contaminate each other with disastrous results, all of these films explore the violation of selfhood by a market-driven political economy. They feature protagonists who discover that they are not humans but products (specifically: clones, replicants, coppertops, and cyborg slaves) and that their memories and life stories are nothing more than embedded computer programs, virtual realities, and the like. In the rare case of a film like *Blade Runner*, the prospect of ever decontaminating the commodified self is left in profound doubt. More typically, crisis narratives generate liberation narratives, with the separation of commodified and noncommodified worlds restored, and human individuality rooted firmly in the latter. *The Island* opts for both liberation and decontamination. But rather than achieving these through retreat and restoration, it describes a forward movement through and beyond commodification. Its vision of self-(non) possession not only requires market capitalism for a foil but also reimagines market capitalism as birthplace.

The Island establishes its story of violated privacy with a series of revelations, each placing alienation in a new light. The film opens with a dream sequence in which a man glides over turquoise waters in a futuristic yacht, receiving sultry looks from a beautiful woman who lies draped across the foredeck. Both are white and clothed entirely in white, their perfect bodies rendered more perfect by a trick of overexposed film that causes their shapes to dissolve, ethereal and weightless, into light. The man, as we soon discover, is Lincoln Six Echo, and this is his wish fulfillment of transcendent freedom and autonomy. The dream girl is Lincoln's friend and her name, Jordan Two Delta, confirms her symbolic function in this scene and in the narrative arc: she is the promised land, the desired object of our hero's yearned-for self-completion. But Lincoln's dream is brutally interrupted when men appear from nowhere to capture Jordan and toss him overboard, alienating his desired object and expelling him from paradise. At this point Lincoln wakes alone in a futuristic room—everything still white, but now lit for sterility instead of transcendence—and is confronted by an overhead LED readout that registers the fact of his restless sleep and instructs him to report for counseling. In the bathroom, a second LED reports excess sodium in his urine and orders a high-fiber diet; a camera watches him get dressed. In short, Lincoln wakes into an Orwellian scenario of surveillance, a reality of invaded privacy and unfreedom that accounts for his dream. This reality is further established as he emerges from his room and proceeds through what one film reviewer describes as his "highly organized and scrutinized" day, moving about within an enclosed compound that looks and operates like a high-end health spa—white surfaces, high-tech exercise rooms, and beautifully groomed white people pursuing a regimen of healthy diet and light activity—under the close supervision of the colony's director, Dr. Merrick.[14] Lincoln and his fellow colonists believe themselves the only human survivors of an environmental catastrophe that has turned Earth into a toxic wasteland. One by one they are being chosen by lottery to go live on the only remaining earthly location to have escaped toxic contamination—the island. Meanwhile, their lives are constantly surveilled and regulated by prohibitions including one against "proximity" that forbids physical touch between Lincoln and Jordan.

Up to this point, Lincoln's unfreedom appears to be explained by the system of invasive governance represented by Dr. Merrick's sinister paternalism. Soon, however, Lincoln's situation takes a turn for the worse—or for something the film encodes as worse. Our hero discovers that he and his fellow "survivors" are actually clones, manufactured by the Merrick Corporation to provide backup body parts for the fabulously rich (a revelation that presumably explains the colony's nearly all-white demographic). Dr. Merrick, we learn, is not merely an evil scientist but also an evil CEO, and winning the lottery means that your body has come due for "harvesting." This information revises the nature of the film's central conflict. Subjection to state surveillance now seems a mere annoyance in comparison to this more profound subjection to marketization—to prove it, Lincoln is suddenly able to roam the compound undetected. The focus now falls on the body. In obedience to the mandate of normative self-(non)possession, Merrick's clients have divided themselves from the plight—or "contamination"—of corporeality and the contingency to which it binds them ("The human body is perfect," observes Merrick's sales pitch, "except like all machines it wears out"). They have displaced the body elsewhere. Now it is the clone who finds himself trapped in flesh that, because it can be owned, divides him from himself. The good news is that this information actually alleviates Lincoln's predicament by shifting the impact of invasion from the immaterial to the material self. What has begun as a movie about inescapable state authority and mind control turns into a simple escape plot—escape from the colony (with Jordan in tow), but, more important, escape from the body. The clone must replicate the act of his owner, or "sponsor," to restore the community norm of self-(non)possessive individuality.

To enunciate this change the film turns, inevitably, to the trope of slavery. The viewer first discovers the clone plot (earlier than the clones themselves) from an overhead shot of bodies developing in plastic sacs, composed so as to suggest the nineteenth-century schematics of slave ships loaded for the Middle Passage; meanwhile, Lincoln and Jordan get the news from an informant who explains, "They, like, own you." The slavery motif includes Lincoln's name—and he will indeed prove himself a great emancipator. Jordan's name also resonates with U.S. history by evoking the exodus myth so significant to American slaves. And all of these allusions are reinforced by the character of a bounty hunter who pursues Lincoln and Jordan after their escape; besides turning out to be the son of an African slave insurrectionist—information we learn when he shifts allegiance to the clones—he is played by the actor Djimon Honsou, who imports an allusion to American slavery with his fame from *Amistad*. With these references, as with the symbol of Jordan's white femininity, *The Island* draws with striking consistency from a vocabulary first developed within nineteenth-century privacy discourse.

And yet, even while faithfully adhering to its codes, *The Island* takes the narrative of imperiled privacy in a strange and unprecedented direction. Its hero is, after all, a clone—not an originary self that has been injured by alienation, but the result *of* alienation, the uncanny copy. He has no premarket psychospirituality to reclaim. In fact, his consciousness only exists as an afterthought, added when Merrick's first attempts to develop inanimate body parts failed. No aspect of Lincoln's psychology belongs originally to him. He and Jordan learn that their childhood memories—the bicycle, the grandmother, the warm cookies, all the treasured recollections of life before the apocalypse—are implanted. Nor are these false histories particularly particularizing, since Merrick's technicians work with only a few stories and "mix up the pieces." More significant, it turns out that, like their bodies, their tastes, talents, and predilections all originate from and replicate their sponsors'. In Lincoln's case, this means not only his "inborn" mechanical aptitude and reckless personality; within the Lamarckian logic of the film he is also indebted to his sponsor for acquired skills in mechanical drafting, Latin grammar, and hovercraft operation. Even Lincoln's dream—the film's inaugural statement of freedom and autonomy—derives from the adult experiences of his sponsor, who designed and owns the boat—called the *Renovatio*—and has often watched Jordan's supermodel sponsor in a Calvin Klein perfume advertisement that the dream closely resembles. Lincoln Six Echo is entirely product—a fact that should position him as the story's antihero. He *is* the alarming uncanny that we have seen previously in Margaret Fuller's paranoid sense of vulnerability to the public version of herself ("How is it that I seem to be this Margaret Fuller? What does it mean? What shall I do about it?") and in Bronson Alcott's dread of property as an externalization of selfhood that threatens to rebound upon and destroy the true self.[15] Indeed, Lincoln seems to justify such fears when he seeks out, kills, and assumes the identity of his sponsor.

Amazingly, *The Island* never quite acknowledges that what its protagonist yearns for is someone else's authentic selfhood and a freedom designed by Calvin Klein. The film should be parodic. At its fingertips lies the very metanarrative that Sojourner Truth, Elizabeth Keckley, and Louisa May Alcott access in the nineteenth century to ironize the liberal democratic ideal of unencumbered individuality, a metanarrative that some of Bay's own sources clearly understand well. Bay, however, takes it up for style points alone, omitting any satirical or critical content. Even as his film explicates the constitutive mediation of private selfhood, it never ceases to pursue perfectly nonironic resolution in self-(non)possession. When Lincoln returns to the compound to free his fellow clones, Merrick marvels, "You came back. You truly are unique, Six Echo," and Lincoln retorts, "My name is Lincoln." This moment works in *The Matrix*, where Bay found it. When that hero rejects the false name assigned to him by enslaving computers and asserts his self-chosen hacker identity ("My name is Neo!") he declares his dis-interpellation from the oppressor's imprisoning fiction. But, although the name "Six Echo" (indicating manufacture date and model) does signify subjection to the political economy of the clone compound, "Lincoln"—the name of his sponsor—does nothing to establish authenticity or particularity external to that system. The movie, however, celebrates this defiant announcement in deadly earnest. As it champions Lincoln in his struggle toward (non)possession of his sponsor's white, masculine privacy entitlement, its tone is triumphal—vive le product!—its ethical sense equal parts corporate personhood and snowflake baby. When reviewers criticized *The Island* for its remarkable number of product placements, Bay acknowledged initially that these had been a necessary concession for financing. By the release to video, however, he had devised what he evidently regards as a more principled response:

> People complained that we were whoring out the movie. We were making a commercial. Now let's face it, guys, the world is focused on products. Products surround us. And for us to be thinking that in the year 2019 that we're not going to still be focused on products—labels flying at us from every different vantage point—is just unreal. It's not a true world.[16]

Bay has missed the point, of course. Critics were not concerned with verisimilitude, but with the colonization of art for advertising—with the same forces of invading commodification that *The Island* professes to view with such horror. Perhaps Bay is "especially dim and literal minded," as the *Village Voice* suggests.[17] If so, this may be precisely what enables him to reveal the cultural imaginary in the fullness of its inconsistent, simple-minded, inhumane sentimentality.

Interwoven with *The Island*'s exodus narrative is a genesis narrative in which Lincoln and Jordan play Adam and Eve, and their fresh-minted perfection provides the blueprint for a brave new world. Here, as Alys Weinbaum has predicted, the genome becomes the new Garden of Eden.[18] To be sure, the clone factory presents that garden in a dystopian light—"another day in paradise" one inmate grimly remarks—and the clones' childlike affect (engineered for docility) makes for a creepy state of grace. However, if the film encodes the escape as a fortunate fall, it does not value experience as a higher achievement. Rather, Lincoln and Jordan's manufactured innocence prevails as a new ideal of "originary" selfhood: as their informant puts it, "I'd trade in your [implanted] memories for my shitty childhood any day." The purity of the product also trumps the too-knowing, too-compromised ethics of its consumer: Lincoln and Jordan wield a second-grader's nonrelativistic sense of morality, presumably learned from *Fun with Dick and Jane*, the reading primer for Merrick's clone classrooms. And, above all, they correct the corrupt embodiment of their sponsors. If the "originals," Sarah Jordan and Tom

Lincoln, exemplify the ideal of mastering and transcending embodiment when they purchase their replacement bodies, they do so out of failure. As a supermodel, Sarah sells her body for a living, and Tom has contracted hepatitis C—the outcome, he explains, of "lots and lots of sex," and an emblem of uncontained (and contagious) bodily excess. They—their promiscuous, commodified, and diseased bodies—coincide with the contaminated outside world that Merrick has taught his clones to fear. Indeed, as clone owners, they are responsible for the film's central conflict: they have forced the hostile worlds of commodified and noncommodified relations into mutually contaminating contact.

It is up to Lincoln and Jordan to wield their purity against this corruption. They do so by replacing their sponsors' bodies with their own bodies—bodies that have no history and, thanks to Merrick's "no proximity" rule, no sin; bodies that seem to transcend physical laws, wandering unscathed through the incessant dangers of the outside world—a rattlesnake, a speeding motorcycle, the interminable chases and high-casualty explosions that are Bay's specialty; bodies, that is, that are *not* bodies. And, with this, they recover fully from the disease of commodification. In this triumph of blankness-as-innocence we might recognize a version of what Lauren Berlant terms "infantile citizenship"—an ideal of liberal democratic subjectivity symbolized by the child or fetus, its blankness passing for democratic virtue, its passivity for freedom.[19] Discussing the sentimental discourse of child labor reform, Berlant criticizes the way that child exploitation is taken up as a "visible sign" for the violent and systematic action of capitalism upon human beings. This figure of the infantile—the innocent and involuntary—organizes a public experience of righteous indignation, or "true feeling," that culminates in catharsis when the child is restored to its premarket family haven.[20] *The Island* certainly supplies us with images of childishness violated by a corrupt political economy. It fetishizes the fetal curl of developing clones in their plastic sacs and the wondering naïveté of each "product" as it is led away for "harvesting." It also relieves this pain—and rewards our vicarious participation in it—by delivering its victim-heroes into a space beyond economic subjection: the final shot reveals Lincoln and Jordan back aboard their dream boat surrounded by white light. But here the child—and his virtuous blankness—is not just a victim of commodification but also its outcome. That is, rather than staging a retreat to a prepolitical, premarket condition of innocence and wholeness, *The Island* locates these in a postmarket denouement. Freedom is accessed through the market's power to wipe us clean and make us new.

For all of its absurdity, *The Island* is remarkable for its hyperliteral statement of the problematic that this book has traced through the nineteenth century—the impossibility of imagining private selfhood and its democratic entitlements without the framing context of property and market relations. Preceding chapters have explored how this paradox haunts U.S. privacy discourse throughout the nineteenth century, generating narratives of alienation and reunification, dispossession and reappropriation, invasion and elimination, exile and belonging. We have seen that over time these narratives become increasingly self-conscious and self-referential, increasingly apt to acknowledge the dependence of privacy upon its difference from property. *The Island* marks a point at which this acknowledgment has become fully overt, and also blandly un-self-aware. It also presents a case in which the promise of private selfhood no longer emerges nostalgically, through a recursive affirmation of lost origins. *The Island* rejects nostalgia. Although Lincoln tracks down his sponsor, he kills and replaces him: purity supplants originality. *Renovatio* is the name of the yacht from Lincoln's dream of self-(non)possession—the same yacht on which he and Jordan reappear in the final shot—and the film extends the metaphor of rebirth by routing each escape from the clone factory through a long, vaginal tunnel. First Lincoln and Jordan, then the entire clone population emerge from this birth canal to confront the real world with exaggerated wonder and defenselessness: a crowd of white-garbed white people who gaze about themselves in awe while Djimon Honsou, playing the descendent of African slavery, stands apart with a grin and a thumbs-up. World music builds to crescendo. This is the rebirth of a polis, free, pure, manufactured, and adorable. To trope this escape as a birth is, of course, to suggest that it marks not a restoration of but a progression toward freedom. The same suggestion applies to Lincoln's usurpation of Tom's life. Although this death punishes Tom for his sexual and capitalist incontinence, it also makes good on his contract with Merrick Corporation by delivering his body into perfection. By bringing the hostile worlds of commodification and noncommodification into contact—into crisis—Tom has successfully arranged for their separation and his own self-(non)-possession.

By adding the logic of progression—or procreation—to the old story of imperiled privacy, *The Island* enhances its power to reconcile the tensions between democratic and capitalist frameworks. Not only does it picture a freedom from property relations that is achieved *through* property relations, it also presents an image of property relations that is deeply reassuring. In *Retheorizing Commodification*, Joan Williams and Viviana Zelizer point out that the hostile worlds paradigm obscures the diverse and hybrid character of commodity relations—including the ways that noncommodifying care ethics and interpersonal intimacy inform them—to create a falsely grim, dehumanized picture.[21] In *The Island*, however, it becomes apparent that this same binary opposition can also be reassuring. As we have seen, the film imagines marketization as a kind of creative violence that penetrates white male individuality in order to beget wholeness and inviolability. More, it recasts the movement of capitalism as monolithic, abstract, and inward, suppressing the chaotic and centrifugal effects of expanding industrial economies that ravage natural landscapes, regional economies, and third world populations. In this film about rampant commodification and market growth, globalization somehow never comes up. All of the action occurs explicitly within a national context, and—once Lincoln escapes from the colony, where corporate and political power disastrously coincide—the U.S. state, like the individual, is conveyed into freedom from market interests. When Dr. Merrick recalls his abortive experiments with isolated body parts, he explains that "without consciousness, human experience, emotion... the organs fail." Merrick's admission is clearly intended as testimony to the sacrosanct nature of human life, even at the tissue level. Hence the grim satisfaction with which Lincoln announces that even an "insurance policy has feelings and dreams." What this detail really illustrates, of course, is a political economy in which human personality is reduced to scaffolding for the commodified laboring body and the "feelings and dreams" of private selfhood amount to nothing more than false consciousness. It never occurs to the film's creators that we live in a world where conscious bodies *are* used for spare parts on a vast scale to fuel industrial capitalism and the wars waged on its behalf.[22] Here the existential dispossession of the transcendent—and therefore white, male, property-holding, and American—individual displaces the epidemic exploitation of the world's poor. The politics of class, race, and gender enter the film only as metaphors to facilitate the forward movement into unfreedom, or "slavery," required to set Lincoln free.

When Lincoln and Jordan first learn that they are clones, their informant breaks it to them by saying, "You're not real. Not a real person like me." For Bay, this is the moment that "sets up the whole dilemma in the movie." As he explains in his DVD commentary, "What I'm saying in this movie is 'Yes, they have souls,' and 'Yes, they are people.'... Who deserves to live, the human or the clone?" Although this impassioned stance on clone identity politics seems premature, the decision Bay demands from us is important: human or clone, original or copy, free or owned, which account of ourselves should survive? In a different context, this question might imply a refusal of Romantic anticapitalism—an incipient commodity manifesto, or a proposal to explore what freedom and belonging could look like without a hostile worlds genesis. But Bay would rather be a god than a product.[23]

Thus his film exemplifies the limiting perspective of privacy crises—in the twenty-first century as in the nineteenth—that insist on an either/or world, indulging a fantasy of absolute subjection (clone as slave) in order to generate a fantasy of perfect emancipation and transcendence (clone as soul). This is a narrative with little to say about "humans" who struggle against and within capitalist culture and material necessity, inhabiting bodies that are both pure and corrupt, free and subjected. Their story will require a different narrative, and a different question.

NOTES

CHAPTER 1: INTRODUCTION

1. Samuel D. Warren and Louis D. Brandeis, "The Right to Privacy: The Implicit Made Explicit," in *Philosophical Dimensions of Privacy: An Anthology*, ed. Ferdinand David Schoeman (Cambridge: Cambridge University Press, 1984), 76–77. All subsequent quotations from this essay are from this source and cited parenthetically in the text.
2. See David W. Leebron, "The Right to Privacy's Place in the Intellectual History of Tort Law," *Case Western Reserve Law Review* 41:3 (1991), 769–810; Robert C. Post, "Rereading Warren and Brandeis: Privacy, Property, and Appropriation," *Case Western Reserve Law Review* 41:3 (1991), 647–81.
3. "The Point of View," *Scribner's Magazine* 9:2 (February 1891), 261; John Gilmer Speed, "The Right of Privacy," *North American Review* 163:476 (July 1896), 64.
4. E. L. Godkin, "The Rights of the Citizen, Part IV: To His Own Reputation," *Scribner's Magazine* 8:1 (July 1890), 65.
5. Ouida, "The Penalities of a Well-Known Name," *North American Review* 154:427 (June 1892), 738.
6. Ibid., 739.
7. See Neal Gabler, *Life: The Movie: How Entertainment Conquered Reality* (New York: Vintage, 2000); Richard Schickel, *Intimate Strangers: The Culture of Celebrity in America* (Chicago: Ivan R. Dee, 2000). For an early and influential version of this argument see Richard Sennett on the dangers of "absolute communicativeness" and the overexposure of personality that takes place at the expense of public reason: *The Fall of Public Man* (New York: W. W. Norton, 1974), 262.
8. See Christopher Lasch, *Haven in a Heartless World: The Family Besieged* (New York: Basic Books, 1977); Eli Zaretsky, *Capitalism, the Family and Personal Life* (New York: Harper & Row, 1976); and Stephanie Coontz, *The Social Origins of Private Life: A History of American Families, 1600–1900* (London: Verso, 1988) on the presence of the state in the home—especially of working-class and poor people—and on its interarticulation with market capitalism. For an excellent overview of the

changing dynamics of seclusion and surveillance in early nineteenth-century America, see Milette Shamir, *Inexpressible Privacy: The Interior Life of Antebellum American Literature* (Philadelphia: University of Pennsylvania Press, 2006), chapter 4.

9. "Novel Writing," *North American Review* 25:56 (July 1827), 208; "The Artist, Merchant and Statesman," *U.S. Democratic Review* 17:89 (November 1845), 340; Richard Grant White, "The Pest of the Period," *The Galaxy* 9:1 (January 1870), 102.
10. John Proffat, "The Law of Newspaper Libel," *North American Review* 131:285 (August 1880), 110.
11. Richard Grant White, "Language According to Sample," *The Galaxy* 15:1 (January 1873), 60. Both *undisprivacied* and *disprivacied* had appeared in a poems by James Russell Lowell.
12. Prominent examples include Shamir, *Inexpressible Privacy*; Louis Renza, *Edgar Allan Poe, Wallace Stevens, and the Poetics of American Privacy* (Baton Rouge: Louisiana State University Press, 2002); Brook Thomas, "The Construction of Privacy in and around *The Bostonians*," *American Literature* 64 (1992), 719–47; Joel Pfister, *The Production of Personal Life: Class, Gender and the Psychological in Hawthorne's Fiction* (Stanford, CA: Stanford University Press, 1991); and Gordon Hutner, *Secrets and Sympathy: Forms of Disclosure in Hawthorne's Novels* (Athens: University of Georgia Press, 1988).
13. For a recent example, see Shamir, *Inexpressible Privacy*, 2.
14. See Shirley Samuels, ed., *The Culture of Sentiment: Race, Gender, and Sentimentality in Nineteenth-Century America* (New York: Oxford University Press, 1992); Bruce Burgett, *Sentimental Bodies: Sex, Gender, and Citizenship in the Early Republic* (Princeton, NJ: Princeton University Press, 2001); Glenn Hendler and Mary Chapman, eds., *Sentimental Men: Masculinity and the Politics of Affect in American Culture* (Berkeley: University of California Press, 1999); Glenn Hendler, *Public Sentiments: Structures of Feeling in Nineteenth-Century American Literature* (Chapel Hill: University of North Carolina Press, 2001).
15. Peter Coviello, *Intimacy in America: Dreams of Affiliation in Antebellum Literature* (Minneapolis: University of Minnesota Press, 2005).
16. Lauren Berlant and Michael Warner, "Sex in Public," in *Intimacy*, ed. Lauren Berlant (Chicago: University of Chicago Press, 2000), 311.
17. See for example, Stacey Margolis, *The Public Life of Privacy in Nineteenth-Century American Literature* (Durham, NC: Duke University Press, 2005). In her study, Margolis persuasively argues that during the nineteenth century, "private intention and feeling" became less relevant to the individual's identity than the "social effects" he creates (2). To pursue this thesis, however, Margolis disengages privacy from publicity and rules out the possibility that the former could be a function of the latter. By her account, public effect "subordinates" and "eclipses" privacy in nineteenth-century values, and a character who accesses his "real

and innermost self" via public mediation is said to "have . . . no privacy" (1–4).

18. Shamir, *Inexpressible Privacy*, 14. Shamir cautions that by too thoroughly dismantling the liberal subject "we put ourselves in danger of losing sight of that nontradable, publicly nonnegotiable dimension of subjective difference that even those social groups most oppressed by liberal hegemony were (and are) unwilling to forgo completely" (14).
19. Ibid., 104.
20. The absence of this component from Elizabeth Dillon's analysis in *The Gender of Freedom: Fictions of Liberalism and the Literary Public Sphere* (Stanford, CA: Stanford University Press, 2004) illustrates my claim. Dillon forcefully establishes that "privacy . . . is constructed and articulated in the public sphere. The privacy of women is the product not of women's seclusion within their homes, but of a public articulation and valuation of women's domestic position" (4). Yet she does not theorize this process of "articulation and valuation" in any detail, or explain how it is that particular representations come to signify privacy. This omission tacitly frames (white) womanhood as always already private within the liberal social contract, and plays out in certain of Dillon's arguments where publicity seems not to produce but merely to reinforce the preestablished privacy value of white womanhood. For example, in Dillon's theorization of what she terms "open sociality," a mode of publicity wherein "private identity is avowedly produced in public" rather than renaturalized as a domain that stands prior to and separate from the public (195–96), it is unclear what private identity means—what encodes it as such in the absence of a framing narrative of a priority? To explore this question, I look at how privacy's public display relies upon effects of irony, anxiety, or ironic anxiety by which writers hyperbolize the way that privacy draws its meaning from its difference from—its performed intolerance for—publicity.
21. Shamir, *Inexpressible Privacy*, 18–19. These references to British law are often couched in calls for emulating America's parent nation, and expressing its Anglo-Saxon racial origin.
22. What I refer to here is the iconic action of privacy tropes, similar to the effect that Michael Warner has identified in public displays of heterosexual intimacy that encode utopian and universalized value and instantiate zones of heteronormative public culture: see "Zones of Privacy," in *What's Left of Theory: New Work on the Politics of Literary Theory*, ed. Judith Butler, John Guillory, and Kendall Thomas (New York: Routledge, 2000), 75–113.
23. Quoted in Shamir, *Inexpressible Privacy*, 108.
24. In *Romances of the Republic*, Shirley Samuels explains that privacy is what Foucault would describe as both instrument and model: that is, its quality of separation from the public-political domain makes it discernible as a resource to the public-political domain, and as an exemplar of a more pure and virtuous public-political domain; *Romances of the Republic:*

Women, the Family, and Violence in the Literature of the Early American Nation (New York: Oxford University Press, 1996).

25. Speed, "The Right of Privacy," 64, 65.
26. *Griswold v. Connecticut*, 381 U.S. 479 (June 7, 1965).
27. Wendy Brown, "The Power of Rights," *The Boston Review: A Political and Literary Forum* 18:3 (June–August 1993); Lauren Berlant, "The Subject of True Feeling" in *Feminist Consequences: Theory for the New Century*, ed. Elisabeth Bronfen and Misha Kavka (New York: Columbia University Press, 2001), 127.
28. Even Warren and Brandeis conclude by acknowledging that the boundary they aim to legalize is impossible to determine by "fixed formula" and requires "an elasticity which shall take account of the varying circumstances of each case" ("The Right to Privacy," 86–89). Legal scholars have since come to describe this essay as a defining moment of undefinition, a key point of reference in the contentious status of legal privacy—both civil and constitutional—that lies at the heart of today's most controversial issues, including reproductive rights, marriage, and civil liberties. As Diane Zimmerman puts it, the essay "has retained just enough life to give it nuisance value"; "Musings on a Famous Law Review Article: The Shadow of Substance," *Case Western Reserve Law Review* 41:3 (1991), 823.
29. Patricia Williams, *The Alchemy of Race and Rights* (Cambridge: Harvard University Press, 1991), 164.
30. See Lasch, *Haven in a Heartless World*; Zaretsky, *Capitalism, The Family and Personal Life*; Coontz, *The Social Origins of Private Life*.
31. See Amy Dru Stanley, *From Bondage to Contract: Wage Labor, Marriage and the Market in the Age of Slave Emancipation* (Cambridge: Cambridge University Press, 1998), chapter 1; Thomas, "The Construction of Privacy in and around *The Bostonians*," 16; Shamir, *Inexpressible Privacy*, chapter 4.
32. Pamela Haag puts this transition at the close of the nineteenth century, arguing that the locus of freedom transferred from market to home in conjunction with changing notions of heterosexual consent. More recently, Elizabeth Dillon has placed the origins of "modern liberalism" in the contexts of colonial gender politics. Pamela Haag, *Consent: Sexual Rights and the Transformation of American Liberalism* (Ithaca: Cornell University Press, 1999), 75–79; Dillon, *The Gender of Freedom*.
33. Speed, "The Right of Privacy," 64.
34. Godkin, "The Rights of the Citizen," 67.
35. "Liberal selfhood," observes Shamir, "is constructed both on the premise of private property and through the denial of property." *Inexpressible Privacy*, 14.
36. Many contemporary legal theorists still argue that privacy is reducible to other torts for libel, property, assault. See Ferdinand Schoeman, "Privacy: Philosophical Dimensions of the Literature," in his *Philosophical*

Dimensions of Privacy: An Anthology (Cambridge: Cambridge University Press, 1984), 16–17.

37. See Post, "Rereading Warren and Brandeis."
38. For a classic analysis of this theory, see C. B. Macpherson, *The Political Theory of Possessive Individualism* (New York: Oxford University Press, 1962).
39. See Hannah Arendt, *The Human Condition* (Chicago: University of Chicago Press, 1958); and *On Revolution* (New York: Viking Press, 1965).
40. M. G., "The Photographic Nuisance," *The Nation* 1286 (February 1890), 154.
41. "The Point of View," 261; Harry Kalven Jr., "Privacy in Tort Law—Were Warren and Brandeis Wrong?" *Law and Contemporary Problems* 31 (1966), 334.
42. Nancy Isenberg, *Sex and Citizenship in Antebellum America* (Chapel Hill: University of North Carolina Press, 1998), 117.
43. Godkin, "The Rights of the Citizen," 65.
44. John Durand, "French Domestic Life and Its Lessons," *Atlantic Monthly* 48:286 (August 1881), 166.
45. John Burroughs, "House Building," *Scribner's Monthly* 11:3 (January 1876), 334–35.
46. Linda Kerber, *Women of the Republic: Intellect and Ideology in Revolutionary America* (Chapel Hill: University of North Carolina Press, 1997); Lynn Hunt, *The Family Romance of the French Revolution* (Berkeley: University of California Press, 1993); Samuels, *Romances of the Republic*; Shirley Samuels, *Facing America: Iconography and the Civil War* (New York: Oxford University Press, 2004); Lauren Berlant, *The Anatomy of National Fantasy: Hawthorne, Utopia, and Everyday Life* (Chicago: University of Chicago Press, 1991).
47. Dillon, *The Gender of Freedom*, 20.
48. Ibid., 204.
49. White, "The Pest of the Period," 110.
50. Ibid., 110–11. A similar criticism of women's disregard for the barrier between privacy and public discourse appears in an 1894 issue of *Scribner's*, where a writer ridicules an "intending hostess" for "sending a reporter to her dressmaker and her caterer for an account of her dress and a list of her viands." "The Point of View," *Scribner's Magazine* 15:4 (January 1894), 526.
51. Two recent and important exceptions are Shamir's *Inexpressible Privacy* and Peter Coviello's *Intimacy in America*, both of which inform my own analysis. Neither study, however, gives sustained attention to gender and race intersectionality.
52. Karen Sánchez-Eppler, *Touching Liberty: Abolition, Feminism, and the Politics of the Body* (Berkeley: University of California Press, 1993); Stanley, *From Bondage to Contract*.
53. Ouida, "The Penalities of a Well-Known Name," 738.

54. This is a logic that Walter Benn Michaels finds epitomized in *Uncle Tom's Cabin* by the character of Topsy, an enslaved child who has no parental origins (she claims to have "nebber been born") and has been raised by a speculator. Michaels, *The Gold Standard and the Logic of Naturalism* (Berkeley: University of California Press, 1987), 103–4.
55. Coviello, *Intimacy in America*, chapter 2.
56. Ibid., 29, 53.
57. "The Barbarism of Slavery: Speech of Honorable Charles Sumner, on the bill for the admission of Kansas as a free state, in the United States Senate," June 4, 1860. Quoted in Stanley, *From Bondage to Contract*, 24.
58. See George M. Fredrickson, *The Black Image in the White Mind: The Debate on Afro-American Character and Destiny, 1817–1914* (Hanover: Wesleyan University Press, 1971), chapter 1.
59. See Saidiya Hartman, *Scenes of Subjection: Terror, Slavery, and Self-Making in Nineteenth-Century America* (New York: Oxford University Press), chapter 5.
60. Godkin, "The Rights of the Citizen," 65.
61. Charles D. Meigs, *Address Delivered before the Union League of Philadelphia, October 31, 1864* (Philadelphia: Collins Printer, 1864), 18.
62. See Shamir for a related discussion of how interior design pattern books were another mechanism for installing and cashing in on the U.S. citizen's desire for privacy: *Inexpressible Privacy*, 3.
63. Harriet Jacobs, *Incidents in the Life of a Slave Girl, Written by Herself* (Cambridge: Harvard University Press, 1987), 1.
64. For a discussion of Jacobs's production of privacy, see Burgett, *Sentimental Bodies*, chapter 6.
65. Caroline M. Churchill, *"Little Sheaves" gathered while gleaning after reapers. Being letters of travel commencing in 1870, and ending in 1873* (San Francisco, 1874).
66. "The Privacy of the Dead," *The Living Age* 93:1199 (May 25, 1867), 535. For discussion of similar disavowals, see Ann Fabian, *The Unvarnished Truth: Personal Narratives in Nineteenth-Century America* (Berkeley: University of California Press, 2000), chapter 2; and Scott Casper, *Constructing American Lives: Biography and Culture in Nineteenth-Century America* (Chapel Hill: University of North Carolina Press, 1999), 61.
67. Zaretsky, *Capitalism, the Family and Private Life*, 14–15.
68. William Dean Howells, "Autobiography, a New Form of Literature," *Harpers Monthly Magazine* 119 (1909), 798; Stephen Arch, *After Franklin: The Emergence of Autobiography in Post-Revolutionary America, 1780–1830* (Hanover: University Press of New England, 2001), 15, 47.
69. Raymond Williams, *The Long Revolution* (New York: Columbia University Press, 1961).
70. Richard Grant White, "The Pest of the Period," 106–7.
71. Mrs. Amelia E. Barr, "The Servant-Girl's Point of View," *North American Review* 154:427 (June 1892), 730.

72. Casper demonstrates that class distinctions were reinforced in the differing market strategies used for midcentury life writing. While the highbrow publication of privacy revealed the authentic inner man, middle-brow privacy was an instrument of moral didacticism, and lowbrow privacy was the stuff of sensationalism: *Constructing American Lives*, 5–6.
73. Fabian, *The Unvarnished Truth*, 35.
74. James Russell Lowell, "Fable for Critics," in *Critical Essays on Margaret Fuller*, ed. Joel Myerson (Boston: G.K. Hall, 1980), 64.
75. Anonymous, "Vanity *versus* Philosophy. Margaret Fuller Ossoli," in *Critical Essays on Margaret Fuller*, ed. Joel Myerson (Boston: G. K. Hall, 1980), 89.
76. Ralph Waldo Emerson, James Freeman Clarke, and William Ellery Channing, eds., *Memoirs of Margaret Fuller Ossoli* (Boston: Phillips, Sampson and Company, 1852), I.61, II.9.
77. Shamir, *Inexpressible Privacy*, 139.
78. Ibid., 144.
79. Nell Irvin Painter, *Sojourner Truth: A Life, a Symbol* (New York: W. W. Norton, 1996), chapter 18.
80. See ibid., 197.
81. Coviello, *Intimacy in America*, 2–3.
82. "Notes by the Road," *American Whig Review* 3:2 (February 1846), 150.
83. The perceived legitimacy of this claim persists into the twenty-first century. In the furor over Dick Cheney's quail hunting accident in February 2006, the press focused less on the fact that the vice president had shot a friend in the face (after a drink) than on his failure to immediately inform the public, repeatedly asserting that as vice president, he had no privileged claim to the facts of the event.
84. "Biographical Mania," *New York Mirror, and Ladies Literary Gazette* 7 (May 15, 1830), 359.
85. See Casper, *Constructing American Lives*, 96–97.
86. "The Privacy of the Dead," *The Living Age* 93:1199 (May 25, 1867), 537.
87. Ibid., 536.
88. "The Point of View," *Scribner's Magazine*, 261; Charles C. Binney, "Why Private Grounds Should Be Enclosed," *Garden and Forest* 3:148 (December 24, 1890), 626.

CHAPTER 2: TARNISHED ICONS, SHINING LIVES

1. Margaret Fuller, *Summer on the Lakes* (1843), in *The Essential Margaret Fuller*, ed. Jeffrey Steele (New Brunswick, NJ: Rutgers University Press, 1992), 69–225. All subsequent quotations from this text are from this source and cited parenthetically in the text.

2. Jeffrey Steele cautions against overreading the relation between Fuller and Mariana, pointing out that Fuller refers to herself as a separate character in the Mariana episode. He finds that *Summer* is suffused with "textual irony that detached Fuller from total identification" with her varying voices and personae in *Summer*; Steele, *Transfiguring America: Myth, Ideology, and Mourning in Margaret Fuller's Writing* (Columbia: University of Missouri Press, 2001), 137. For a discussion of the differing theories on the significance of Mariana's death in relation to Fuller's self-presentation, see Susan Gilmore, "Margaret Fuller 'Receiving' the 'Indians,'" in *Margaret Fuller's Cultural Critique: Her Age and Legacy*, ed. Fritz Fleischmann (New York: Peter Lang, 2000), 191–227. For Gilmore, the death stands for Fuller's rejection of an eastern self cultivated according to constraining gender conventions, a "self she wished to leave behind" (191–92).
3. The way Weld is referenced via negative comparison echoes interestingly with the typological opening in *Of Plymouth Plantation*, where Bradford recounts how his band of colonists is denied even the comforts of Mount Pisgah. The allusion seems to place Mariana in the line of martyred nation builders.
4. Margaret Fuller, *Woman in the Nineteenth Century* (1845), ed. Larry J. Reynolds (New York: Norton Critical Editions, 1998), 6. All subsequent quotations from this text are from this source and cited parenthetically in the text.
5. As Julie Ellison puts this, "Fuller thinks through all ethical issues in terms of character" and envisions the energies of revolution as "most often transmitted as part of a program of self-definition" in *Delicate Subjects: Romanticism, Gender, and the Ethics of Understanding* (Ithaca, NY: Cornell University Press, 1990), 218, 227.
6. Another medium of iconicity for Fuller is the embodied performance of personality, as both Sandra Gustafson and Julie Ellison demonstrate in their discussions of Fuller's self-presentation in the Conversations series she ran for women. Gustafson, "Choosing a Medium: Margaret Fuller and the Forms of Sentiment," *American Quarterly* 47:1 (March 1995), 48; Ellison, *Delicate Subjects*, 237, 240–60. Mariana's story combines the two modes and suggests they are indivisible for Fuller. She wanted self-presentation to function as a kind of text—a sign for something beyond itself. Yet she also wanted textual biography to mimic the immediacy of embodied self-publication, and deployed (auto)biography less as diachronic narrative than as a synchronic image of law through personality. As Emerson put it, describing his own plans for *Representative Men*, "to draw characters, not write lives"; quoted in F. O. Matthiessen, *American Renaissance: Art and Expression in the Age of Emerson and Whitman* (London: Oxford University Press, 1941), 71.
7. Margaret Fuller, "Self-Definitions" (1840), in Steele, *The Essential Margaret Fuller*, 6; and *Woman*, 6.

8. See especially Ellison, *Delicate Subjects*; and Christina Zwarg, *Feminist Conversations: Fuller, Emerson, and the Play of Reading* (Ithaca, NY: Cornell University Press, 1995), 102. Zwarg is most interested in how Fuller's portrayal of reading emphasizes the contingency of epistemology and the relativity of historic truth. She makes the important point that travel and reading are synonymous processes in *Summer*. Conversely, my argument focuses on the foundationalist dimension of Fuller's reading/recognition model—the way its movement through truths is teleological, insistently oriented toward Truth. As I read Fuller, reading/recognition takes Fuller traveling through juxtaposed frames of contingent meaning, but finally aligns with national millennial destiny.
9. G. W. F. Hegel, *Phenomenology of Spirit* (1806; Oxford University Press, 1979). For authoritative studies of Hegelian recognition, see Robert R. Williams, *Hegel's Ethics of Recognition* (Berkeley: University of California Press, 1997); and Axel Honneth, *The Struggle for Recognition: The Moral Grammar of Social Conflicts* (Cambridge: Polity Press, 1995), 31.
10. These images reveal the influence of her friend William Ellery Channing and his notion of self-cultivation as an "unfolding." See William Ellery Channing, "Self-Culture," in *William Ellery Channing, Selected Writings*, ed. David Robinson (New York: Paulist Press, 1985).
11. Charles Taylor, "The Politics of Recognition," in *Multiculturalism: Examining the Politics of Recognition* (Princeton, NJ: University of Princeton Press, 1994), 31–32.
12. Ralph Waldo Emerson, *The Journals and Miscellaneous Notebooks of Ralph Waldo Emerson*, ed. William H. Gilman, Ralph H. Orth, et al. (Cambridge: Harvard University Press, 1960–1982), 7:342.
13. Ralph Waldo Emerson, "The American Scholar" (1849) and *Representative Men* (1850), in *Essays and Lectures*, ed. Joel Porte (New York: Library of America, 1983), 620–21. All subsequent quotations from Emerson's essays and lecture refer to this source and are cited parenthetically in the text.
14. In addition to identifying self-publication with social reform, Emerson links the individual's act of self-publication to his own self-actualization. In "The Poet" (1844) he writes, sounding almost Arendtian, "The man is only half himself, the other half is his expression," and in the "Divinity School Address" (1849) he stresses not only the importance of finding but also the necessity of outwardly manifesting one's own relation to divinity—"if utterance is denied, the thought lies like a burden on the man" (*Essays and Lectures*, 448, 83).
15. Both Zwarg and Gustafson argue that Fuller's attention to the creative power of spectators leads her to adopt a materialist-constructivist framework for identity (Gustafson, "Choosing a Medium," 50; Zwarg, *Feminist Conversations*, 108).
16. I use the term *misrecognition* in the Hegelian sense, to describe the failure or denial of recognition, and the resulting distortion of identity that

this imposes on particular subjects. I do not intentionally evoke Lacan, although his concept of misrecognition—where the subject mistakes the unity of the mirrored image for himself—resonates interestingly with Fuller's ideas about the transformative influence of spectacle upon self-identity.

17. See Nancy Fraser, "Rethinking Recognition," *New Left Review* 3 (May–June 2000), 107–20; Nancy Fraser and Axel Honneth, *Redistribution or Recognition? A Political-Philosophical Exchange* (London: Verso, 2003); Seyla Benhabib, "The Generalized and the Concrete Other: The Kohlberg-Gilligan Controversy and Feminist Theory," in *Feminism as Critique: On the Politics of Gender*, ed. Seyla Benhabib and Drucilla Cornell (Minneapolis: University of Minnesota Press); Seyla Benhabib, *The Claims of Culture: Equality and Diversity in the Global Era* (Princeton, NJ: Princeton University Press, 2002); Seyla Benhabib, *Multiculturalism: Examining the Politics of Recognition* (Princeton, NJ: Princeton University Press, 1994).
18. See, for example, Carolyn Sorisio, *Fleshing Out America: Race, Gender, and the Politics of the Body in American Literature, 1833–1879* (Athens: University of Georgia Press, 2002).
19. Ellison, *Delicate Subjects*, 10, 223–24.
20. Christopher Newfield, *The Emerson Effect: Individualism and Submission in America* (Chicago: University of Chicago Press, 1996).
21. Ellison, *Delicate Subjects*, 245.
22. Letter to W. H. Channing, July 1841, quoted in ibid., 244.
23. Margaret Fuller, "Fourth of July," in *Margaret Fuller, Critic: Writings from the New-York Tribune, 1844–1846*, ed. Judith Mattson Bean and Joel Myerson (New York: Columbia University Press, 2000), 149–50.
24. See Henry David Thoreau, "Civil Disobedience" (1849), in *Walden and Civil Disobedience* (New York: Penguin, 1983), 383–413; Ralph Waldo Emerson, "Fugitive Slave Law" (1854), in *Essays and Lectures.*
25. In Mariana, this process focuses on her excessive and racialized corporeality; as Ellison writes, Mariana's cultural critique is "conveyed through the theatrical rebellion of her body, and it is on the body, also, that her rejection by her peers is inscribed," *Delicate Subjects*, 231.
26. Margaret Fuller, "Self-Definitions" (1840), in Steele, *The Essential Margaret Fuller*, 11. All further quotations from Fuller's journal refer to this source and are cited parenthetically in the text.
27. Phillipe Lejeune, *On Autobiography* (Minneapolis: University of Minnesota Press, 1989); Michel Foucault, "What Is an Author," in *The Foucault Reader*, ed. Paul Rabinow (New York: Pantheon Books, 1984), 101–20.
28. Margaret Fuller, "Autobiographical Romance" (1840), in Steele, *The Essential Margaret Fuller*, 24–25. All further quotations from Fuller's autobiography refer to this source and are cited parenthetically in the text.

29. Carole Pateman, *The Sexual Contract* (Stanford, CA: Stanford University Press, 1988).
30. Jean Jacques Rousseau, *The Social Contract* (New York: Penguin Classics, 1968), 49.
31. For a contemporary example, see Steele, *Transfiguring America*, 11, 29.
32. To the extent that Fuller's portrayal of the Roman American does pose a critique of American masculinity, it is deeply compassionate. This is an important point, often overlooked in Fuller scholarship that tends to read her work as feminist in the most limiting, antimale sense (Zwarg a crucial exception here).
33. Virgil, *The Aeneid*, trans. Robert Fitzgerald (New York: Random House, 1985), 67, lines 61–66.
34. Dante, *The Inferno of Dante*, trans. Robert Pinsky (New York: Farrar, Straus and Giroux, 1994).
35. Many critics note the homoerotic overtones of the Kilshaw episode and cite it as an example of what Carroll Smith-Rosenberg calls Romantic Friendship and describes as an intense mode of same-sex intimacy that preceded the codification of homosexual identity by turn-of-the-century sexologists in "The Female World of Love and Ritual: Relations between Women in Nineteenth-Century America," *Signs: Journal of Women in Culture and Society* I:1 (1975), 1–29. For a particularly rich consideration of Fuller in this light, see Mary Wood, "'With a Ready Eye': Margaret Fuller and Lesbianism in Nineteenth-Century American Literature," *American Literature: A Journal of Literary History, Criticism, and Bibliography* 65:1 (1993), 1–18. Making such a connection helps get at the ambiguous status of bodies as both material and immaterial and sites of both sameness and difference in Fuller's memory of Kilshaw. But it also threatens to overemphasize the significance of the same-sex dimension. As we shall see, Fuller continues to develop her theory of utopian intimacy in *Summer* and *Woman*, and there she idealizes heterosexual complementarity.
36. On Fuller's own anxiety about this problem, see Margaret Vanderhaar Allen, "[A Classic of Feminist Literature]," in Reynolds, *Woman in the Nineteenth Century*, 240; and Sorisio, *Fleshing Out America*, 146–47. Zwarg sees Fuller trying to mask or downplay the risqué aspect of her subject, *Feminist Conversations*, 173–74.
37. These appeared in *The Dial* under Fuller's editorship from July 1840 to April 1842.
38. Friends are like spheres, Emerson argues in "Experience," only able to touch at a single point and therefore utterly misrecognizing a tiny part for the whole. In "Friendship" and "Self-Reliance," he warns that our heroes and friends always become our idols, hypostatized versions of the (always, again, limited) ideal we have projected onto them and therefore obstacles to our continued self-becoming.

39. For analyses of how the ethic of possessive individualism organizes social identity and cross-difference relations in nineteenth-century U.S. discourse, see Phillip Fisher, *Hard Facts: Setting and Form in the American Novel* (New York: Oxford University Press, 1985); Gillian Brown, *Domestic Individualism: Imagining Self in Nineteenth-Century America* (Berkeley: University of California Press, 1990); and Lori Merish, *Sentimental Materialism: Gender, Commodity Culture and Nineteenth-Century American Literature* (Durham: Duke University Press, 2000).
40. Charles Taylor, "The Politics of Recognition," 28.
41. The two important exceptions here are Zwarg, *Feminist Conversations* (see especially 108, 124, 169–70), and Sorisio, *Fleshing Out America*, chapter 5, who examine how Fuller uses the "tragic narrative" of vanishing Indians to explore and revise the construct of gender difference.
42. It is important to note that Fuller returns to the Sappho and Eloisa scholars later in the text, to reimagine them as aspiring to true recognition, true marriage with Woman. They are developmental figures, consistent with Fuller's use of a Hegelian dialectical "struggle" for recognition.
43. Ralph Waldo Emerson, "An Address to the Senior Class in Divinity College, Cambridge, July 15, 1838," in *Essays and Lectures*, 73–92; Theodore Parker, "A Discourse of the Transient and Permanent in Christianity" (1841), in *Transcendentalism: A Reader*, ed. Joel Myerson (New York: Oxford University Press, 2000), 340–66. For a related analysis of spectacles, spectators, and power, see Ellison, *Delicate Subjects*, on romantic desire and gendered analytical aggression (11, 217).
44. Lauren Berlant, *The Anatomy of National Fantasy: Hawthorne, Utopia, and Everyday Life* (Chicago: University of Chicago Press, 1991). For work on the iconic function of white womanhood in nineteenth-century public discourse, see also Joan Landes, *Visualizing the Nation: Gender, Representation, and Revolution in Eighteenth-Century France* (London: Palgrave, 2001); Mary P. Ryan, *Women in Public: Between Banners and Ballots, 1825–1880* (Baltimore: Johns Hopkins University Press, 1990); and Shirley Samuels, *Romances of the Republic: Women, the Family, and Violence in the Literature of the Early American Nation* (New York: Oxford University Press, 1996).
45. Steele, *Transfiguring America*, 6. In this psychological biography of Fuller, Steele analyzes Fuller's own idolatrous fixation on male authority figures, beginning with her father, and traces the process by which she learns to break this destructive attachment. He attributes the term to Bronson Alcott.
46. Emerson et al., *Memoirs of Margaret Fuller Ossoli*, I.229; and Bell Gale Chevigny, *The Woman and the Myth: Margaret Fuller's Life and Writings* (New York: Feminist Press, 1986), 61.
47. Cynthia Davis makes a similar point in her discussion of differing representations of embodiment in Thoreau, Emerson, and Fuller: "Fuller attempts not just to interrogate but to distill Transcendental and gendered

views of human nature in order to blend the best of both. Specifically, she attempts to retain nature as a category of identity and an experiential base for women as well as men, while she simultaneously bemoans conventional, naturalized definitions of gender. In sum, she seeks to sever gender from nature in order to facilitate the definition of 'woman' as unqualified soul"; "Margaret Fuller, Body and Soul," *American Literature: A Journal of Literary History, Criticism, and Bibliography* 71:1 (March 1999), 41.

48. In *Summer* this occurs when the bodies of Native Americans are presented as tragic, damaged, and constraining in ways that overtly recall similar representations of white female bodies. Thus, the tragic body that burdens the Seeress reappears in the "defaced figures" and "broken and degraded condition" of Indians (222).
49. This racial logic of idolatry again refracts parts of Emerson's original concept. Paranoid about the overwhelming "magnetism" of great men, Emerson warns us not to make them idols and become "possessed by" them. The trope of slavery is repeatedly part of this warning (indeed, the notion of idolatry is racialized from its emergence in the miracles controversy, where he repeatedly characterizes it as "oriental"). In his lecture on the fugitive slave law, Emerson reflects upon how Daniel Webster's public speaking style "enslaves" its audience, a conceit that conflates the effect of Webster's magnetism with the way that Webster's compromise bill implicates U.S. citizens in actual slavery. With Fuller, for whom the unfreedom of the idolater is less compelling than that of the idol (and who, as we have seen, is much more confident of the benevolent, authenticating effects of spectacular selves upon their audience), enslavement becomes a way to think about how the object of the misrecognizing gaze becomes trapped in history because too identified with her idol status. In a sense, she imagines women as part of their own enslaved audience.
50. Nancy Fraser, "Rethinking Recognition," 110.
51. For a related argument, see David Peritz, "Toward a Deliberative and Democratic Response to Multicultural Politics: Post-Rawlsian Reflections on Benhabib's *The Claims of Culture*," *Constellations* 11:2 (2004), 266–90.
52. Lauren Berlant and Michael Warner, "Sex in Public," in *Intimacy*, ed. Lauren Berlant (Chicago: University of Chicago Press, 2000), 313.
53. This reflects the way Fuller generally refigures the violent contact zones of her era with a vision of bloodless amalgamation in *Summer*. For instance, Fuller affirms racialist thinking about Native Americans by writing "nature seems, like all else, to declare, that this race is fated to perish. Those of mixed blood fade early, and are not generally a fine race. They lose what is best in either type, rather than enhance the value of each, by mingling" (188). But she seeks to ameliorate this "fated" genocide with a proposal for cultural integration: "Ere they depart, I wish there might be some masterly attempt to reproduce, in art or literature, what is proper to them, a kind of beauty and grandeur, which few of the every-day crowd

have hearts to feel, yet which ought to leave in the world its monuments, to inspire the thought of genius through all ages" (189). Here, appropriation of a strategically disembodied native culture into white publicity erases the embodied "departure" that enables it; it also figures a kind of imaginative progeneration such as we found in the earlier passage, with the Indian monuments spawning the inspiration and genius of those who remain. See Nicole Tonkovitch, "Traveling in the West, Writing in the Library: Margaret Fuller's *Summer on the Lakes*," *Legacy: A Journal of American Women Writers* 10:2 (1993), 80–83, and Sorisio, *Fleshing Out America*, 164, for more on Fuller's agreement with racist ethnological arguments, including theories on the biological impossibility of racial amalgamation.

54. Amy Kaplan, *The Anarchy of Empire in the Making of U.S. Culture* (Cambridge: Harvard University Press, 2002).
55. Ellison, *Delicate Subjects*, 273.
56. Quoted in Stephanie Coontz, *The Social Origins of Private Life: A History of American Families, 1600–1900* (New York: Verso, 1988), 214. Fuller was well versed in such arguments. "The passions, like fire, are a bad master," she writes in *Woman*, "but confine them to the hearth and the altar, and they give life to the social economy, and make each sacrifice meet for heaven" (91). For more on this representation of marriage, see Coontz, 213–15; and Nancy Isenberg, *Sex and Citizenship in Antebellum America* (Chapel Hill: University of North Carolina Press, 1998), 44, 178.
57. Coontz, *The Social Origins of Private Life*, 215.
58. Elise Lemire, *"Miscegenation": Making Race in America* (Philadelphia: University of Pennsylvania Press, 2002), chapter 3.
59. See especially Bell Gale Chevigny, "To the Edges of Ideology: Margaret Fuller's Centrifugal Evolution," in *Woman in the Nineteenth Century: An Authoritative Text, Backgrounds, and Criticism*, ed. Larry J. Reynolds (New York: W. W. Norton, 1998) on dialectics; Zwarg, *Feminist Conversations*, on dialogue and "double reading" (3–8). Particularly significant in this context is Zwarg's claim that Fuller juxtaposes essentialist and poststructuralist frames of identity in a way that resists prioritizing one over the other or even synthesizing them together.
60. In a variation on this theme, Fuller opens *Summer on the Lakes* with an apology for its failure to encapsulate the great meaning of the New World:

    Had the scholar means to tell
    How grew the vine of bitter-sweet,
    What made the path for truant feet,
    Winter nights would quickly pass,
    Gazing on the magic glass
    O'er which the new-world shadows pass;

But, in fault of wizard spell,
Moderns their tale can only tell
In dull words, with a poor reed
Breaking at each time of need. (69)

As the enjambment in line 11 suggests, she attributes her failure in part to the subjective limits of epistemology: it is only her tale she can tell, only autobiography. The conceit frames *Summer*, itself, as a shining life strategy even while questioning that strategy's power.

61. One, of course, is Mariana, whose story of tragic constraint generates Fuller's vision for the future utopian union of America and her American. Zwarg suggests that, like Fourier, Fuller values unusual people as transition figures—hence her emphasis on Mariana, the Seeress of Prevorst, and Black Hawk—but also understands their special vulnerability to retaliation and containment. Mariana, writes Zwarg, is "what might be called the vanishing American woman," *Feminist Conversations*, 109.
62. Thus, when Fuller offers us our first glimpse of Indians from her boat on Lake Michigan—"Their blanketed forms, in listless groups or stealing along the bank, with a lounge and a stride so different in its wildness from the rudeness of the white settler"—it is directly juxtaposed in shot–reverse shot sequence with a portrait of her fellow travelers, "almost all New Englanders, seeking their fortunes." Of the latter she writes, "They had brought with them their habits of calculation...all talking not of what they should do, but of what they should get in the new scene. It was to them a prospect, not of the unfolding nobler energies, but of more ease, and larger accumulation" (80). This pairing underscores the limits of cross-cultural reading, illustrating misrecognition under the regime of manifest destiny and the capitalism that drives it.
63. Zwarg, *Feminist Conversations*, 108.
64. The passage begins with yet another racial trope: "By men in this country, as by the Jews, when Moses was leading them to the promised land, every thing has been done that inherited depravity could do, to hinder the promise of heaven from its fulfilment" (13). Fuller's analogy is to the Jews who prevent their own progress to the promised land by stopping to worship their false idol.
65. This suggests an effect I have elsewhere described as racialist exceptionalism, where the unfreedom of blacks (and here "reds" as well) becomes meaningful and beneficial as the occasion for America's city upon a hill of freedom in "Harriet Beecher Stowe, Caroline Lee Hentz, Herman Melville and American Racialist Exceptionalism," in *A Companion to American Fiction, 1780–1865*, ed. Shirley Samuels (London: Blackwell, 2004), 365–77.
66. This marriage takes place in a utopian space of private relations. It also requires that space in order to be imagined: "In private life, I am assured by men who are not so sustained and occupied by the worship of pure

beauty, that . . . many men feel that no temptation can be too strong for the will of man, if he invokes the aid of the Spirit instead of seeking extenuation from the brute alliances of his nature" (80–81).

67. Alys Eve Weinbaum, *Wayward Reproductions: Genealogies of Race and Nation in Transatlantic Modern Thought* (Durham, NC: Duke University Press, 2004), 5–6.
68. Zwarg, *Feminist Conversations*, 168–70.
69. Berlant and Warner, "Sex in Public," 37.
70. Ibid., 37.

CHAPTER 3: STOWE'S TRUTHS

1. Harriet Beecher Stowe, "Sojourner Truth: The Libyan Sibyl" (1863), in *Narrative of Sojourner Truth: A Bondswoman of Olden Time Emancipated by the New York Legislature in the Early Part of the Present Century with a History of Labors and Correspondence Drawn from Her Book of Life* (Chicago: Johnson, 1970), 116. All subsequent quotations from this essay are from this source and cited parenthetically in the text.
2. A list of the most prominent includes Stowe, Olive Gilbert, Frances Gage, Frances Titus, and Elizabeth Cady Stanton. See chapter 1 for a discussion of Truth's own manipulations and uses of the Truth Myth. For other discussions of Truth's strategic self-constructions and their relation to representations by other writers, see Nell Irvin Painter, *Sojourner Truth: A Life, a Symbol* (New York: W. W. Norton, 1996), chapter 20; Christina Accomando, *"The Regulations of Robbers": Legal Fictions of Slavery and Resistance* (Columbus: Ohio State University Press, 2001), 6–7, chapter 3; Lori Merish, *Sentimental Materialism: Gender, Commodity Culture, and Nineteenth-Century American Literature* (Durham, NC: Duke University Press, 2000), 216–28; and Erlene Stetson and Linda David, *Glorying in Tribulation: The Lifework of Sojourner Truth* (Lansing: Michigan State University Press, 1994).
3. Painter, *Sojourner Truth*, 158.
4. Patricia J. Williams, *Alchemy of Race and Rights: Diary of a Law Professor* (Cambridge: Harvard University Press, 1991), 183.
5. See Eric Lott, *Love and Theft: Blackface Minstrelsy and the American Working Class* (New York: Oxford University Press, 1995); Karen Sánchez-Eppler, *Touching Liberty: Abolition, Feminism, and the Politics of the Body* (Berkeley: University of California Press, 1993); Jean Fagan Yellin, *Women and Sisters: The Anti-Slavery Feminists in American Culture* (New Haven, CT: Yale University Press, 1992); Robyn Wiegman, *American Anatomies: Theorizing Race and Gender* (Durham, NC: Duke University Press, 1995); Paul Gilmore, *The Genuine Article: Race, Mass Culture and American Literary Manhood* (Durham, NC: Duke University Press, 2002).

6. "How the Proclamation Works in Virginia," *The Chicago Tribune*, January 16, 1863, 3.
7. See especially Gillian Brown, *Domestic Individualism: Imagining Self in Nineteenth-Century America* (Berkeley: University of California Press, 1992).
8. Hannah Arendt, *The Human Condition* (Chicago: University of Chicago Press, 1958); and *On Revolution* (New York: Viking Press, 1965).
9. Alexis de Tocqueville, *Democracy in America* (New York: Everyman's Library, 1994), II.164, 214.
10. Bruce Burgett, *Sentimental Bodies: Sex, Gender, and Citizenship in the Early Republic* (Princeton, NJ: Princeton University Press, 2001), 20; see chapter 1 for a summary of this debate among Americanist historians and cultural critics.
11. Christopher Castiglia, "Abolition's Racial Interiors and the Making of White Civic Depth," *American Literary History* 14:1 (Spring 2002), 38.
12. Elizabeth Young, *Disarming the Nation: Women's Writing and the American Civil War* (Chicago: University of Chicago Press, 1999); Naomi Sofer, *Making the "America of Art": Cultural Nationalism and Nineteenth-Century Women Writers* (Columbus: Ohio State University Press, 2005).
13. Margaret Fuller, *Woman in the Nineteenth Century* (New York: W. W. Norton, 1998). See chapter 1 for a discussion of how critics represented Fuller's public persona.
14. In her preface to *The Culture of Sentiment*, Shirley Samuels writes, "The masculine national body, the 'sinews of a new nation,' is opposed to the feminine—and to slavery. But at the same time women were responsible for managing the relation between national embodiment and national bodies." *The Culture of Sentiment: Race, Gender, and Sentimentality in Nineteenth-Century America* (New York: Oxford University Press, 1992), 4.
15. Painter, *Sojourner Truth*, 181. A stark example can be found in Elizabeth Cady Stanton's many references to Truth as advocate for the American Woman's Suffrage Association even after that group had begun defining itself against black suffrage in infamously racist terms. See Rosalyn Terborg-Penn, *African American Women in the Struggle for the Vote, 1850–1920* (Bloomington: Indiana University Press, 1998).
16. Hortense Spillers, "Mama's Baby, Papa's Maybe: An American Grammar Book," in *African American Literary Theory: A Reader*, ed. Winston Napier (New York: New York University Press, 2000), 260.
17. Accomando, *"The Regulations of Robbers,"* 79.
18. See Carleton Mabee, *Sojourner Truth: Slave, Prophet, Legend* (New York: New York University Press, 1993), 52.
19. Sánchez-Eppler, *Touching Liberty*, 48–49.
20. Olive Gilbert, *Narrative of Sojourner Truth*, ed. Mary Washington (New York: Vintage Books, 1993), 8. All subsequent quotations from Gilbert are from this edition and cited parenthetically in the text.

21. Quoted in Painter, *Sojourner Truth*, 166–68.
22. Painter describes Truth as resistant to this association with mobs. Recounting Truth's early experiences of moral reform among the New York underclass, she writes: "Isabella did not take well to the work. The difficulty grew out of conflicting assumptions about Isabella's position relative to the ladies and the prostitutes. She did not lump herself with the people at the bottom" while her white fellow reformers "probably assumed... that poor, black Isabella would have a special rapport with the downtrodden" (45–46).
23. Young, *Disarming the Nation*, 29–30.
24. For diverging opinions see Painter, *Sojourner Truth*; and Mabee, *Sojourner Truth: Slave, Prophet, Legend.*
25. Anonymous, *The Daily Picayune*, March 22, 1853.
26. Caroline Lee Hentz, *The Planter's Northern Bride* (Chapel Hill: University of North Carolina Press, 1970), 27, 240–41.
27. Anonymous, *The Daily Picayune*, March 22, 1853.
28. Hentz, *Northern Bride*, 265.
29. Ibid., 172.
30. Ibid., 109, 202.
31. Ibid., 392.
32. Anonymous, *The Daily Picayune*, May 29, 1853.
33. Anonymous, *The Daily Picayune*, June 8, 1853.
34. Harriet Beecher Stowe, *Dred: A Tale of the Great Dismal Swamp* (New York: Penguin, 2000), 89. All subsequent quotations from this novel are from this edition and cited parenthetically in the text.
35. Merish, *Sentimental Materialism*, 156.
36. For a full account of Kinmont's theory on "romantic racialism" and Stowe's relation to it, see George Frederickson, *The Black Image in the White Mind: The Debate on Afro-American Character and Destiny, 1817–1914* (Middlebury, VT: Wesleyan University Press, 1987), 97–129.
37. Maria Karafilis, "Spaces of Democracy in Harriet Beecher Stowe's *Dred*," *American Quarterly* 55:3 (Autumn 1999), 38.
38. In her notes Stowe acknowledges that her titular character also refers to Dred Scott. Her narrator adds that Dred is "a name not unusual among the slaves, and generally given to those of great physical force" (208).
39. Abraham Lincoln, "Speech on the Kansas-Nebraska Act, October 16, 1854," in *Lincoln's Speeches Reconsidered*, ed. John Channing Briggs (Baltimore: Johns Hopkins University Press, 2005), 75–76.
40. For more on how representations of grotesque, racialized embodiment were used to discredit opposing political interests, see Elise Lemire, *"Miscegenation": Making Race in America* (Philadelphia: University of Pennsylvania Press, 2002). The majority of such uses were against Lincoln and other Republican candidates before and after the war. See chapter 4 for a discussion of how Reconstruction Democrats deployed grotesque racist

caricatures of enfranchised blacks as a symbol of the self-interest of the radical Republicans who championed them.

41. For a related discussion of racial tropes and the market economy, see Gilmore, *The Genuine Article*, 2. Gilmore argues that blackness figures simultaneously as ontological "truth" and authenticity, and as a mutable, transferable commodity.
42. Stowe's first description of the swamp makes the echo especially clear: "regions of hopeless disorder, where the abundant growth and vegetation of nature, sucking up its forces from the humid soil, seems to rejoice in a savage exuberance, and bid defiance to all human efforts either to penetrate or subdue" (209).
43. Gregg Crane, "Dangerous Sentiments: Sympathy, Rights, and Revolution in Stowe's Antislavery Novels," *Nineteenth-Century Literature* 51:2 (September 1996), 176–204, 180.
44. Even Harry—who, like his mixed-race counterpart from *Uncle Tom*, George Harris, speaks like a lawyer and argues from democratic principles—cries out at one point to his sister/master, Nina, "I could serve you to the last drop of my blood! but I hate everybody else! I hate your country! I hate your laws!" (146). Given that Harry emigrates to Canada with the other escaped slaves, his outcry registers less as immanent critique than self-exemption. For a more detailed analysis of these and other scenes of "cross-reading" in *Dred*, see Gail Smith, "Reading with the Other: Hermeneutics and the Politics of Difference in Stowe's *Dred*," *American Literature* 69:2 (June 1997), 289–313.
45. Castiglia makes a similar point when he argues that the project of moral sympathy was to transform the privileged subject who extends sympathy rather than the condition of that sympathy's object; "Abolition's Racial Interiors," 38.
46. For a reading of *Dred*'s exceptionalist logic as framed by discourse on benevolent nationalism, see Susan M. Ryan, "Charity Begins at Home: Stowe's Antislavery Novels and the Forms of Benevolent Citizenship," *American Literature* 72:4 (December 2000), 751–82.
47. Many critics have pointed to the way that structures of sympathetic possession mimic those of slavery, and Cindy Weinstein has rightly pointed out that by hyperbolizing that similarity we risk repeating the arguments of proslavery that likewise found no difference between freedom and slavery; *Family, Kinship and Sympathy in Nineteenth-Century American Literature* (Cambridge: Cambridge University Press, 2005). Here, the danger of conflating the two types of possession is that it obscures the possibility that Stowe self-consciously intends the similarity.
48. Where I read the Canadian colony as a supplement that extends and corrects U.S. democracy, other critics have tended to see the relations as either entirely disjunct or continuous. Ryan and Robert Levine interpret its proximity as an attempt by Stowe to remedy her much-criticized colonization plot from *Uncle Tom's Cabin*; Ryan, "Charity Begins at Home";

Robert Levine, "The African-American Presence in Stowe's *Dred*," in *Criticism and the Colorline: Desegregating American Literary Studies*, ed. Henry B. Wonham (New Brunswick, NJ: Rutgers University Press, 1996). Conversely, Karafilis reads both the Canadian and the swamp colonies as spaces that "reterritorializ[e]" the democratic imaginary, disassociating it from the political and geographical context of U.S. nationalism. In relation to deterritorialized democracies, we might think also of Castiglia's arguments about the "citizen-form" of abolition that disengaged citizenship from the corrupt institutions of nation-state and attached it, instead, to God; "Abolition's Racial Interiors," 39–41.

49. *New Orleans Crescent*, cited in Thomas F. Gossett, *Uncle Tom's Cabin and American Culture* (Dallas: Southern Methodist University Press, 1985), 190; Anonymous, *The Daily Picayune*, March 22, 1853.
50. Anonymous, *The Southern Literary Messenger*, June 1853, 322.
51. Anonymous, *The Daily Picayune*, February 11, 1853.
52. Anonymous, *The Daily Picayune*, October 8, 1852.
53. See Young, *Disarming the Nation*, 54–55; and Diane Roberts, *Myth of Aunt Jemima: Representations of Race and Region* (New York: Routledge, 1994).
54. Stowe questions the power of sympathy upon moral as well as political action in *Dred*, when she describes the type who "melted in tears over [sentimental narratives], indulged in the luxury of sentimental grief, and derived some comfort, from the exercise, to go on in ways of sin" (472).
55. For a discussion of sympathetic strategy as antidemocratic and coercive, see Elizabeth Barnes, *States of Sympathy: Seduction and Democracy in the American Novel* (New York: Columbia University Press, 1997). For an argument that explores sympathy as more varied and adaptable in its imagined effects, see Weinstein, *Family, Kinship and Sympathy.*
56. Quoted in Mark V. Tushnet, *Slave Law in the American South: State v. Mann in History and Literature* (Lawrence: University Press of Kansas, 2003), 265.
57. See especially Crane, "Dangerous Sentiments." Stowe's tone of authorial respect is particularly audible when the speech is contrasted with the self-interested theories of power she puts in the mouths of slaveholders like Tom Gordon and Mr. Jekyl (169, 386).
58. See Arendt, *On Revolution.*
59. Crane, "Dangerous Sentiments," 181.
60. For a very different reading of the aestheticization of black bodies in *Dred*, see Sánchez-Eppler, *Touching Liberty*, 29–30.
61. For an example, see "The Two Cabins," *The Daily Picayune*, New Orleans, February 24, 1853.
62. Sofer, *Making the "America of Art,"* 5.
63. For a related analysis of this impasse and Stowe's solution, see Crane, "Dangerous Sentiments." I am especially interested in his discussion of the debate between Senator and Mrs. Bird—representing slave law

versus moral sentiment. Pointing out that it is not Mrs. Bird (Stowe's voice) but the senator who sets private morality in opposition to public law, Crane argues that Stowe envisions a dialogue between the two that maintains their distinction but allows them to shape each other (188–90).

64. Robert Stepto makes a similar argument regarding *Uncle Tom's Cabin*, tracing Stowe's reliance on black abolitionist writing to forge her own refutation of proslavery arguments in "Sharing the Thunder: The Literary Exchanges of Harriet Beecher Stowe, Henry Bibb, and Frederick Douglass," in *New Essays on Uncle Tom's Cabin*, ed. Eric J. Sundquist (Cambridge: Cambridge University Press, 1986).
65. An important exception here is Stowe's inclusion of Nat Turner's confession as an appendix, with many of Thomas Gray's asides removed. See Levine, "The African-American Presence in Stowe's *Dred*," for a discussion of this strategy.
66. Ibid., 173.
67. Describing the court appearance through which Truth reclaimed custody of her son, Gilbert dwells on how Truth becomes confused over the swearing in and attempts to whisper to the Bible; Gilbert comments, in one of her frequent gestures of editorialization, "She took a lawful oath, as far as the outward ceremony could make it one. All can judge how far she understood its spirit and meaning" (34). The gloss concisely delineates a boundary between Truth and the public "all" who are bound together by their understanding of the "lawful oath" and their ability to inhabit the abstractions of text, law, contract, and ceremony.
68. Once the emancipation date for New York State was established, it was illegal to sell slaves into states where slavery would continue to be legal. See Painter, *Sojourner Truth*, for a detailed account of the case.
69. Castiglia, "Abolition's Racial Interiors," 37.
70. Important here is that the orphans are both black and white, a fact emphasized by Stowe's narrator. Ryan finds a utopian image of coracial community in Milly's household. I do not disagree, but nor do I not find that this group outweighs the racial differential so carefully established in Canada. More, there is the fact that Milly initially shares this household with Old Tiff and the orphaned offspring of Sue. When it is discovered that the children have inherited the Virginia fortune, they become Clayton's wards, suggesting that coraciality only works below the poverty line and that the apotheosis into incorporeal freedom (effected by the inheritance) renders the children white.
71. See Amy Dru Stanley, *From Bondage to Contract: Wage Labor, Marriage, and the Market in the Era of Slave Emancipation* (Cambridge: Cambridge University Press, 1998), chapter 3.
72. Quoted in ibid., 106.
73. Ibid., 104. Another vivid image in this category of surplus white embodiment was that of the maimed and helpless war veteran. See Shirley

Samuels, *Facing America: Iconography and the Civil War* (New York: Oxford University Press, 2004).

74. Saidiya Hartman, *Scenes of Subjection: Terror, Slavery, and Self-Making in Nineteenth-Century America* (New York: Oxford University Press), 121.
75. Ibid., 125–26.
76. Ryan, "Charity Begins at Home," 758–59.
77. Harriet Beecher Stowe, "The Education of Freedmen," *North American Review* 128:271 (June 1879), 613, 605.
78. See Pamela Haag, *Consent: Sexual Rights and the Transformation of American Liberalism* (Ithaca, NY: Cornell University Press, 1999), chapter 2.
79. On the emergence of a new hierarchy of literary genres, outlets, and readerships, see Lawrence Buell, *New England Literary Culture: From Revolution through Renaissance* (Cambridge: Cambridge University Press, 1989); Richard Brodhead, *Cultures of Letters: Scenes of Reading and Writing in Nineteenth-Century America* (Chicago: University of Chicago Press, 1994); and Lawrence Levine, *Highbrow/Lowbrow: The Emergence of Cultural Hierarchy in America* (Cambridge: Harvard University Press, 1988). See Sofer, *Making the "America of Art,"* chapter 1; and Joan Hedrick, *Harriet Beecher Stowe, a Life* (New York: Oxford University Press, 1994), for discussions of Stowe's specific relation to it.
80. Nathaniel Hawthorne, *The Marble Faun* (New York: Oxford University Press, 2002). All subsequent quotations from this novel are from this edition and cited parenthetically in the text.
81. This dynamic actually precedes Augustus, going back to Cleopatra's own strategies of public self-display (which included stamping her image on the national currency), which encouraged an economy of nationalist identification via her maternal image. See Guy Weill Goudchaux, "Was Cleopatra Beautiful? The Conflicting Answers of Numismatics," in *Cleopatra of Egypt: From History to Myth*, ed. Susan Walker and Peter Higgs (Princeton, NJ: Princeton University Press), 210–73.
82. Cleopatra is a site of multivalent representations, not all of them in keeping with the tradition from which Story works. Her intellect and erudition were often emphasized on stage—most famously by Sarah Bernhardt in the 1890s and, in a performance Stowe might have seen, by Isabella Glynn in 1847. Reina Green has shown that in England Cleopatra was strongly associated with Elizabeth I and reappropriated as a figure for womanly resolve and even marital fidelity, once her suicide was refigured as an act of devotion to Anthony; Reina Green, "Eroticizing Virtue: The Role of Cleopatra in Early Modern Drama," in *Women as Sites of Culture: Women's Roles in Cultural Formation from the Renaissance to the Twentieth Century*, ed. Susan Shifrin (London: Ashgate, 2002). For more on the Cleopatra myth in nineteenth-century culture, see Mary Hamer, *Signs of Cleopatra: History, Politics, Representation* (New York: Routledge, 1993); and Mary Hamer, "Black *and* White? Viewing Cleopatra in 1862," in *The*

Victorians and Race, ed. Shearer West (London: Ashgate Scholar Press, 1996), 53–67.

83. Hamer, "Black *and* White?" 55.
84. See Hartman, *Scenes of Subjection*, chapter 5.
85. Ann Fabian, *The Unvarnished Truth: Personal Narratives in Nineteenth-Century America* (Berkeley: University of California Press, 2000), chapter 3.
86. Quoted in Painter, *Sojourner Truth*, 166, 168.
87. William Lloyd Garrison, "Preface," in *Narrative of the Life of Frederick Douglass, an American Slave* (New York: Signet Classic, 1997), 7–8.
88. Other critics find a dialogic or collaborative structure in the interaction of these two speakers, even differentiating their styles as oral and textual, and ascribing to them what one might expect—an opposition between black authenticity/presence and white inauthenticity/absence (e.g., Stetson and David, *Glorying in Tribulation*, 59; and Accomando, *"The Regulations of Robbers,"* 69). Such interpretations present some sticky problems. One is the danger of commodifying an "authentic black oral" in a manner that reinscribes Gilbert's strategy by reifying a voice that precedes and thereby becomes a means of constituting a public register. Also, although it is important to recognize the value of orality in black writing, it is equally crucial that the "absence" of textuality would convey not inauthenticity but legitimacy to the audience Gilbert addresses. Recall the famous moment in Douglass's *Narrative* where he describes himself at the writing table, fitting his pen into the "cracks" cut in his feet by slavery: Douglass also deploys the authority of "testifying scars," but—in a way unavailable to the illiterate Truth—he never relinquishes his authority to determine their public meaning.
89. See Hedrick, *Harriet Beecher Stowe*, 362–74, for Stowe's ambivalence about woman's suffrage.
90. Painter, *Sojourner Truth*, 154.
91. Evident here, as well, is the dynamic that Lawrence Levine identifies in *Highbrow/Lowbrow*, wherein the move toward enforcing a highbrow cultural standard occurs in response to postbellum changes and volatility within previously established social orders.
92. Levine, "The African American Presence," 173; Peter Gibian, "The Politics of the Parlor," talk delivered November 2004, American Studies Association, Atlanta, Georgia.
93. Painter, *Sojourner Truth*, 154.
94. The reference is to the title of Lott's 1995 study of blackface minstrelsy.
95. This reference is especially interesting given Hawthorne's invocation of "L'Allegro" in the studio scene from *The Marble Faun*.
96. Virgil, *The Aeneid*, vi: 98.
97. Gage corrects the error in her Akron essay one month later.
98. Hamer, "Black *and* White?" 59–60. In *"The Regulations of Robbers,"* Accomando points out that Story undertook the Sibyl as a portrait of essential African character (77).

99. Hamer, "Black *and* White?" 61.
100. In "Reading with the Other," Gail Smith argues that after 1856 "Stowe increasingly shows men needing to read like women, but not vice versa" (306).
101. Yellin, *Women and Sisters*, 82.
102. Robyn Weigman, "Intimate Publics: Race, Property, and Personhood," *American Literature: A Journal of Literary History, Criticism, and Bibliography* 74:4 (December 2002), 860. For the history and analysis of forced sterilization, Norplant, and welfare reform in relation to black women, see Dorothy Roberts, *Killing the Black Body: Race, Reproduction, and the Meaning of Liberty* (New York: Vintage Books, 1997); and Williams, *Alchemy of Race and Rights*, 219.
103. Toni Morrison, "The Talk of the Town," *New Yorker*, October 5, 1998, 32.
104. Congress, House, Representative Jesse Jackson Jr. of Illinois, H. Res. 611, 105th Cong., 2nd sess., *Congressional Record* 144:154 (December 18, 1998), p. H11809.
105. Neal Gabler, "Doing Away with Public Life," *Economic Times* (March 1999).
106. Frederick Moten with B. Jenkins, "The Return of the Oppressed," in *Our Monica, Ourselves: The Clinton Affair and the National Interest*, ed. Lauren Berlant and Lisa Duggan (New York: New York University Press, 2001), 150.
107. *All Politics*, CNN, August 30, 1998; "There Is No Case for Impeachment," *Chicago Tribune*, December 17, 1998, 30.
108. Morrison, "The Talk of the Town," 32.
109. Quoted in David Corn, "Capitol Losses," *Nation* 267:11 (November 1998), 6.
110. Reprinted in the *New York Times*, August 18, 1998, A12.
111. On the intersection of privacy rights, DOMA, and the Clinton impeachment, see Phillip Brian Harper, "Preface," in *Private Affairs: Critical Ventures in the Culture of Social Relations* (New York: New York University Press), 1999. On the intersection of privacy rights, PRWA, and the Clinton impeachment, see Katha Pollitt, "Subject to Debate: September Thong," *Nation* 267:10 (October 5, 1998), 10.
112. Moten, "The Return," 146–47.
113. See, for example, Loren Glass, "Publicizing the President's Privates," *Postmodern Culture*, 9:3 (1999).
114. At the impeachment hearings, Representative David Obey (D-WI) asked, "What [have we] done to our own children, to the President's privacy and dignity (and that of Monica Lewinsky) and even to the dignity of the nation itself by the placement of that report on the internet?" *Congressional Record* 144:154 (December 18, 1998), p. H11813.
115. Morrison, "The Talk of the Town," 32.

1. Andrew Johnson, "Veto of the Civil Rights Bill, March 27, 1866: to the Senate of the United States," in *Handbook of Politics for 1868*, ed. Edward McPherson, clerk of the house of representatives of the United States (Washington City: Philp and Solomons, 1868), 75. All subsequent quotations from this speech are from this source and cited parenthetically in the text.

   Johnson quotes here from *Commentaries on American Law*, a text by the late New York Supreme Court judge James Kent that had become a touchstone for conservative legal thought. For analysis of Kent's *Commentaries on American Law* and its impact on midcentury political and legal discourse concerning race relations, see John Theodore Horton, *James Kent: A Study in Conservatism, 1763–1847* (New York: Da Capo, 1969), 264–306.
2. Hans L. Trefousse describes Johnson's rage upon learning, while in Washington, that black troops had been lodged in his Nashville home. Immediately sexualizing this contact between white domesticity and black subjects, Johnson assumed his home was being run as a brothel. Trefousse, *Andrew Johnson: A Biography* (New York: W. W. Norton, 1989), 225. For more on Johnson's particular obsession with miscegenation, see Eric Foner, *A Short History of Reconstruction, 1863–1877* (New York: Harper & Row, 1990), 84; and LaWanda Cox, *Freedom, Racism, and Reconstruction: Collected Writings of LaWanda Cox*, ed. Donald G. Nieman (Athens: University of Georgia Press, 1997), 109.
3. Quoted in Cox, *Freedom, Racism, and Reconstruction*, 48.
4. For full accounts and analyses of Johnson's differences with Congress over Reconstruction, see Trefousse, *Andrew Johnson*; W. E. B. DuBois, *Black Reconstruction in America: An Essay Toward a History of the Part Which Black Folk Played in the Attempt to Reconstruct Democracy in America, 1860–1880* (New York: Russell and Russell, 1935); and Foner, *A Short History*. For more on debates about the meaning of freedom in the period between the Thirteenth and Fourteenth Amendments, see in addition to the above, Amy Dru Stanley, *From Bondage to Contract: Wage Labor, Marriage, and the Market in the Age of Slave Emancipation* (New York: Cambridge University Press, 1998); Frank McGlynn and Seymour Drescher, *The Meaning of Freedom: Economics, Politics, and Culture after Slavery* (Pittsburgh: University of Pittsburgh Press, 1992); and Julie Saville, *The Work of Reconstruction: From Slave to Wage Labor in South Carolina, 1860–1870* (New York: Cambridge University Press, 1994).
5. Lora Romero, *Home Fronts: Domesticity and Its Critics in the Antebellum United States* (Durham, NC: Duke University Press, 1997), 4.
6. Nina Baym, *Woman's Fiction: A Guide to Novels by and about Women in America, 1820–70* (Urbana: University of Illinois Press, 1993), 27. Jane

Tompkins, *Sensational Designs: The Cultural Work of American Fiction, 1790–1860* (New York: Oxford University Press, 1985).

7. For a materialist history of the emergence of middle-class domestic ideology, see Stephanie Coontz, *The Social Origins of Private Life: A History of American Families, 1600–1900* (London: Verso, 1988); and Stuart Blumin, *The Emergence of the Middle Class: Social Experience in the American City, 1760–1900* (Cambridge: Cambridge University Press, 1989). For historiography that focuses on the status of women within this emergence, see Nancy Cott, *The Bonds of Womanhood: "Woman's Sphere" in New England, 1780–1835* (New Haven, CT: Yale University Press, 1977); and Barbara Welter, "The Cult of True Womanhood: 1820–1860," *American Quarterly* 18 (1966), 151–74. For literary history in relation to these developments, see Joel Pfister, *The Production of Personal Life: Class, Gender, and the Psychological in Hawthorne's Fiction* (Stanford, CA: Stanford University Press, 1991); Gillian Brown, *Domestic Individualism: Imagining Self in Nineteenth-Century America* (Berkeley: University of California Press, 1990); and Milette Shamir, *Inexpressible Privacy: The Interior Life of Antebellum American Literature* (Philadelphia: University of Pennsylvania Press, 2006).
8. See Elise Lemire, *"Miscegenation": Making Race in America* (Philadelphia: University of Pennsylvania Press, 2002).
9. Catharine Maria Sedgwick, "20 February 1831," in *The Power of Her Sympathy: The Autobiography and Journal of Catharine Maria Sedgwick*, ed. Mary Kelley (Boston: Massachusetts Historical Society, 1993), 129.
10. Toni Morrison, "The Talk of the Town," *New Yorker*, October 5, 1998, 32.
11. Frances Smith Foster, *Written by Herself: Literary Productions by African American Women, 1746–1892* (Bloomington: Indiana University Press, 1993), 119.
12. For other arguments that focus on this aspect of Keckley's text, see William Andrews, "The Changing Moral Discourse of Nineteenth-Century African American Women's Autobiography: Harriet Jacobs and Elizabeth Keckley," in *De/Colonizing the Subject: The Politics of Gender in Women's Autobiography*, ed. Sidonie Smith (Minneapolis: University of Minnesota Press, 1992), 225–41; and Xiomara Santamarina, "Behind the Scenes of Black Labor: Elizabeth Keckley and the Scandal of Publicity," *Feminist Studies* 28:3 (Fall 2002), 514–37.
13. Jennifer Fleischner, *Mastering Slavery: Memory, Family, and Identity in Women's Slave Narratives* (New York: New York University Press, 1996), 99; Johnnie M. Stover, "African American 'Mother Tongue' Resistance in Nineteenth-Century Postbellum Black Women's Autobiography: Elizabeth Keckley and Susie King Taylor," *a/b: Auto/Biography Studies* 18:1 (Summer 2003), 127.
14. Fleischner, *Mastering Slavery*, 99.
15. For an excellent analysis of Jacobs's treatment of privacy, see Bruce Burgett, *Sentimental Bodies: Sex, Gender, and Citizenship in the Early*

Republic (Princeton, NJ: Princeton University Press, 1998), chapter 6. As Burgett demonstrates, Jacobs also uses a combination of personal disclosure and conspicuous silence to mark a textual zone of privacy she may claim as her own. Rafia Zafar and Lynn Domina both suggest that Keckley's pointed reticence functions similarly. See Rafia Zafar, *We Wear a Mask: African American Women Write American Literature, 1760–1870* (New York: Columbia University Press), 155–57; Lynn Domina, "I Was Re-elected President: Elizabeth Keckley as Quintessential Patriot in *Behind the Scenes: Thirty Years a Slave and Four Years in the White House*," in *Women's Life-Writing: Finding Voice/Building Community*, ed. Linda S. Coleman (Bowling Green, OH: Bowling Green State University Popular Press, 1997), 145.

16. *The Citizen* [New York], April 18, 1868, quoted in Jennifer Fleischner, *Mrs. Lincoln and Mrs. Keckley: The Remarkable Story of the Friendship between a First Lady and a Former Slave* (New York: Broadway Books, 2003), 316. *New York Citizen*, quoted in Foster, *Written by Herself*, 128.
17. Elizabeth Keckley, *Behind the Scenes: Thirty Years a Slave and Four Years in the White House* (New York: Oxford University Press, 1988), 290. All subsequent quotations from this autobiography are from this edition and cited parenthetically in the text.
18. *The World* [New York], October 6, 1867. For a more detailed account of the scandal, see Fleischner, *Mrs. Lincoln and Mrs. Keckley*; Jean H. Baker, *Mary Todd Lincoln: A Biography* (New York: W. W. Norton, 1987); Honoré Willsie Morrow, *An Appreciation of the Wife of Abraham Lincoln* (New York: William Morrow, 1928); and Ruth Painter Randall, *Mary Lincoln: Biography of a Marriage* (Boston: Little, Brown, 1953).
19. *The Republican* [Springfield, MA], October 3, 1867.
20. *The Democrat* [Rochester], October 5, 1867.
21. For an account of Mary's class-inflected reception in Washington, see Fleischner, *Mrs. Lincoln and Mrs. Keckley*, chapter 9.
22. Baker, *Mary Todd Lincoln*, 190.
23. The pairing of "body natural" and "body politic," which Claude Lefort uses to distinguish the politician's physical body from his symbolic one, comes from Ernst Kantorowicz's seminal study, *The King's Two Bodies: A Study in Mediaeval Political Theology* (Princeton, NJ: Princeton University Press, 1957).
24. Claude Lefort, "The Image of the Body in Totalitarianism," in *Political Forms of Modern Society*, ed. John B. Thompson (Cambridge: MIT Press, 1986), 303.
25. *The Republican* [Springfield, MA], October 3, 1867.
26. David Herbert Donald, "'This Damned Old House': The Lincolns in the White House," in *The White House: The First Two Hundred Years*, ed. Frank Friedel and William Pencak (Boston: Northeastern University Press, 1994), 55.

27. Donald, "This Damned Old House," 54. Other presidents shared Lincoln's sentiment. Andrew Jackson was compelled to escape his presidential home by way of a window to escape being crushed during his inauguration celebration. Harry Truman looked back on his term in office saying, "It seems like there was always somebody for supper." Daniel J. Boorstin, "Roles of the President's House," in ibid., 10.
28. Boorstin, "Roles," 8.
29. Lincoln was often accused of modeling herself after Empress Eugénie Napoleon—the very image of a feminized usurpation of power; see, for example, "The Truth about Mrs. Lincoln," *The Independent*, August 10, 1882. This was not always a pejorative comparison, for Lincoln could also be praised for "giving life and character to the White House, as the 'rosy Empress' who won all hearts by her queenly manners" in *The Statesman* [Ohio], October 8, 1867.
30. Boorstin, "Roles," 12.
31. Betty Boyd Caroli, *First Ladies*, expanded ed. (New York: Oxford University Press, 1995), 62.
32. Quoted in Baker, *Mary Todd Lincoln*, 277. Strangely enough, in the late 1990s the Lincolns and their property appeared again at the center of this problem of self-interest and political iconography. In "renting out" the Lincoln Bedroom to potential campaign contributors, President Bill Clinton was perceived as using the nation's property as capital for his own political investments.
33. Mary Lincoln remained in the news for years as an object of ridicule and censure. The publicity probably influenced Congress's failure to authorize an adequate pension for her. She lived on very little money and grew increasingly preoccupied with both her own financial debts and the nation's debt to her. Near the end of her life Lincoln was subjected by her son Robert to an insanity trial and briefly committed to an asylum.
34. Lefort, "The Image of the Body," 305.
35. Ibid., 298.
36. *The Argus* [Albany], July 17, 1882.
37. Quoted in Baker, *Mary Todd Lincoln*, 185.
38. The granting of political appointments as a mode of bestowing personal and political favor was openly practiced during both Lincoln's and Johnson's administrations when first the war and then Reconstruction left open a plethora of political offices and drew an "unprecedented" number of patronage seekers. See William Searle, *The President's House: A History*, Volume 1 (Washington, DC: White House Historical Association, 1986), 364.
39. Baker, *Mary Todd Lincoln*, 277, 201.
40. Andrew Johnson, "Veto of the Civil Rights Bill," 78.
41. Throughout the Civil Rights and Freedmen's Bureau veto speeches, Johnson repeatedly reminds Congress of the great need for labor on Southern plantations, assuring them that "there is no danger that the exceedingly great

demand for labor will not operate in favor of the laborer." Andrew Johnson, "Veto of the Freedmen's Bureau Bill, February 19, 1866: to the Senate of the United States," in *Handbook of Politics for 1868*, ed. Edward McPherson, clerk of the house of representatives of the United States (Washington City: Philp and Solomons, 1868), 71.

42. Foner argues that economic autonomy was still the prevailing ideal of democratic identity, so that, well into the period when free labor rhetoric was widespread, free labor was still often opposed to autonomy and land ownership as a form of dependency and servility. The two reconcile to some extent with the notion that free labor is not a permanent status but a means of climbing to economic independence; Eric Foner, *Free Soil, Free Labor, Free Men: The Ideology of the Republican Party before the Civil War* (New York: Oxford University Press, 1995), 16–18.
43. Andrew Johnson, "First Inaugural Address. October 17, 1853," in *The Papers of Andrew Johnson, Volume 2 (1852–1857)*, ed. LeRoy P. Graf and Ralph W. Haskins (Knoxville: University of Tennessee Press, 1967).
44. For instance, it was generally true, as Johnson points out, that the ex-slave possessed "a perfect right to change his place of abode...if...he [did] not find in one community or State a mode of life suited to his desires, or proper remuneration for his labor." However, this right was all but negated by the common practice of paying workers only once a year. In this situation, a worker could not simply "move to...where labor [was] more esteemed and better rewarded" as Johnson suggests ("Veto of the Freedmen's Bureau Bill," 70–71). In fact, some states required freedmen to take work from previous owners before accepting another offer. In a nation that located freedom in obligation by consent rather than subjection, many blacks found themselves working for the very whites they had previously addressed as master (and were often beaten for refusing to continue this form of address). For more on the white supremacist agenda in free labor discourse, see Foner, *Free Soil*; and Stanley, *From Bondage to Contract*. For more on the black codes see DuBois, *Black Reconstruction*; Foner, *A Short History*; and Eugene Genovese, *Roll, Jordan, Roll: The World the Slaves Made* (New York. Vintage Books, 1976).
45. Indeed, Johnson foresaw this possibility: "While we ought to do our best to bring them...up to our present level...in doing so, we should, at the same time raise our own intellectual status so that the relative position of the two races would be the same" (quoted in Trefousse, *Andrew Johnson*, 236).
46. Quoted in ibid., 236.
47. For a full summary of the pamphlet and discussion of reactions, see Sidney Kaplan, "The Miscegenation Issue in the Election of 1864," *Journal of Negro History* 34 (1949), 274–343. For accounts of how postbellum racial politics took form in new and newly enforced laws against interracial marriage, see Peter W. Bardaglio, "'Shamefull Matches': The Regulation of Interracial Sex and Marriage in the South before 1900,"

in *Sex, Love, Race: Crossing Boundaries in North American History*, ed. Martha Hodes (New York: New York University Press, 1999), 112–38; and Peggy Pascoe, "Miscegenation Law, Court Cases, and Ideologies of 'Race'," in Hodes, *Sex, Love, Race*, 464–90. For analysis of antimiscegenist rhetoric in protests against black suffrage, see Martha Hodes, "The Sexualization of Reconstruction Politics: White Women and Black Men in the South after the Civil War," in *American Sexual Politics: Sex, Gender, and Race since the Civil War*, ed. John C. Fout and Maura Shaw Tantillo (Chicago: University of Chicago Press, 1993), 59–74; and Lemire, *"Miscegenation."*

48. Keckley's book was actually published during Andrew Johnson's impeachment trial. Jennifer Fleischner points out that its appearance during this time of intense national instability added to the hostile reception.

49. The radical Republicans dumped women's political rights from their platform as they turned their efforts from abolition to black male suffrage. As for the rights of black women in specific, speakers like William Lloyd Garrison listed "mastery over a wife" among the rights owed to black men. Following their abandonment by the Republicans, the white organizers of the female suffragist movement debated whether or not to include black women in their interest group. Elizabeth Cady Stanton, among others, offered increasingly racist rationales for a white-only women's movement and, in 1869, this issue precipitated the split of female suffrage organizers into two separate groups—Stanton's National Woman Suffrage Association and Lucy Stone's American Woman Suffrage Association. For an alternative analysis of black women's "neither one nor the other" status in representational politics as it applies to Keckley, see Elizabeth Young, *Disarming the Nation: Women's Writing and the American Civil War* (Chicago: University of Chicago Press, 1999), 109–11.

50. Foner, *A Short History*, 38. Karen Sánchez-Eppler points out that even a text like *Uncle Tom's Cabin*, which claims domesticity as a site for utopian politics and freedom, still constructs that domesticity and that freedom as "predicated upon the absence of black bodies: Tom's 'victory' wins him the freedom of heaven; George, Eliza, and the rest find theirs only in Liberia"; Sánchez-Eppler, *Touching Liberty: Abolition, Feminism, and the Politics of the Body* (Berkeley: University of California Press, 1993), 48. For one of the earliest and best discussions of how portrayals of black women in domestic fiction serve to reinforce images of white domestic virtue, see Hazel Carby, *Reconstructing Womanhood: The Emergence of the Afro-American Woman Novelist* (New York: Oxford University Press, 1987).

51. Laura Wexler, *Tender Violence: Domestic Visions in an Age of U.S. Imperialism* (Chapel Hill: University of North Carolina Press, 2000), 101.

52. Zafar, *We Wear a Mask*, 156.

53. Sánchez-Eppler argues along similar lines concerning the relation between black bodies and domesticity in Harriet Jacobs's *Incidents in the Life of a*

Slave Girl. She writes, "[Jacobs] locates freedom in feminized spaces; but while she haunts these houses, she cannot occupy them. In her effort to escape, her body literally lines the floors and ceilings of houses, just as in servitude her body and its labor sustains the Southern home.... Slavery can create the private, domestic realm precisely because the slave has no privacy and no claim on domestic space or domestic utterance"; *Touching Liberty*, 87–88.

54. The book was also published under the alternative titles *White House Revelations or Behind the Scenes* and *Behind the Scenes, the Great Sensational Disclosures, by Mrs. Keckley*; see John E. Washington, *They Knew Lincoln* (New York: E. P. Dutton, 1942), 231–34.
55. For more on the veil image in slave narratives, see Zafar, *We Wear a Mask*; and Robert B. Stepto, *From behind the Veil: A Study of Afro-American Narrative* (Urbana: University of Illinois Press, 1979). For more on the significance of the veil image in Keckley, see Young, *Disarming the Nation*; and Zafar.
56. See Foster, "Autobiography after Emancipation," and Young for arguments that emphasize this strategy of self-authorization.
57. Houston A. Baker, "Autobiographical Acts and the Voice of the Southern Slave," in *The Slave's Narrative*, ed. Charles T. Davis and Henry Louis Gates Jr. (New York: Oxford University Press, 1985), 242–61. This could be particularly so for women, whose enslavement was made to speak for unfreedoms other than their own in the rhetoric of white female abolitionist-suffragists, as Karen Sánchez-Eppler shows in *Touching Liberty*. Chapter 3, this volume, examines this strategy in relation to Sojourner Truth and Harriet Beecher Stowe.
58. Ben Slote, "Revising Freely: Frederick Douglass and the Politics of Disembodiment," *a/b: Auto/Biographical Studies* 11:1 (1996), 20.
59. See Ryan Simmons for a related argument about Keckley's strategy of framing texts within other texts so as to reveal the situatedness of meaning and subvert "received ways of reading" (28, 30–30), in "Naming Names: *Clotel* and *Behind the Scenes*," *CLA Journal* 153:1 (September 1999), 19–37.
60. Andrews, "The Changing Moral Discourse," 227.
61. Ibid., 233.
62. Harriet Jacobs, *Incidents in the Life of a Slave Girl, Written by Herself* (Cambridge: Harvard University Press, 1987), 199. Another contrasting example is to be found in Douglass's argument concerning the ethics of slaves stealing from their masters. He insists that slavery negates the recognized standards of honesty and respect for property; Frederick Douglass, *My Bondage and My Freedom* (New York: Penguin, 2003), 139–40.
63. Frances Smith Foster, "Autobiography after Emancipation: The Example of Elizabeth Keckley," in *Multi-Cultural Autobiography: American Lives*, ed. James Robert Payne (Knoxville: University of Tennessee Press, 1992), 49.

64. See Saidiya Hartman, *Scenes of Subjection: Terror, Slavery, and Self-Making in Nineteenth-Century America* (New York: Oxford University Press).
65. See William Andrews, "Introduction," in *Sisters of the Spirit: Three Black Women's Autobiographies of the Nineteenth Century* (Bloomington: Indiana University Press, 1986), 1–22.
66. This theme bears out in personal contexts, as well, such as her marriage to "Mr. Keckley," where her disappointments and his dissipation are emblematized in the fact that he has claimed to be free but turns out to be enslaved (50).
67. For an example, see Domina, "I Was Re-elected President," 142.
68. Johnson, "Veto of the Freedmen's Bureau Bill," 70.
69. Jacobs, *Incidents in the Life*, 45.
70. Lauren Berlant, *The Queen of America Goes to Washington City: Essays on Sex and Citizenship* (Durham, NC: Duke University Press, 1997), 225.
71. Ibid., 226.
72. Ibid.
73. See Stanley, *From Bondage to Contract*, 48–50. Here again, comparison between *Behind the Scenes* and *Incidents* points to basic differences between antebellum and postbellum narrative strategies. Jacobs's narrative dwells heavily upon notions of domesticity and motherhood to foreground similarities (and therefore discrepancies) between her identity and the "true womanood" of her white readers. In contrast, Keckley scarcely mentions the death of her son, George, although she provides a lengthy account of Willie Lincoln's death and Mary's grief over it.
74. *The Democrat* [Rochester], October 5, 1867.
75. For alternative accounts of Keckley's rhetorical strategy concerning the clothing and the figure of the First Lady, see Young, *Disarming the Nation*, 126–133; and Zafar, *We Wear a Mask*.
76. Santamarina, "Behind the Scenes of Black Labor," 531.
77. Washington, *They Knew Lincoln*, 213. Keckley also eventually managed, as Mary did not, to sell her own collection of Lincoln memorabilia, including the bloodstained cloak Mary had worn on the night of the assassination (Fleischner, *Mrs. Lincoln and Mrs. Keckley*, 323).
78. Betsy Kickley [D. Ottolengul]. *Behind the Seams: By a Nigger Woman Who Took In Work from Mrs. Lincoln and Mrs. Davis* (New York: National News Company, 1868), 5. All subsequent quotations are from this edition and cited parenthetically in the text.
79. Years later, it would even be rumored that Elizabeth Keckley had never existed and that *Behind the Scenes* had been authored by the abolitionist Jane Swisshelm (Fleischner, *Mrs. Lincoln and Mrs. Keckley*, 335).
80. Eric Lott, *Love and Theft: Blackface Minstrelsy and the American Working Class* (New York: Oxford University Press, 1993), 138.

81. Andrew Johnson, "Veto of the Civil Rights Bill," 75. In fact George was not "weighed down" by his African blood. Records show that he passed for white as a student at Wilberforce University and as a Union soldier. In both cases, Keckley's son registered as George Kirkland, taking the name of his white father after years of using his mother's last name. His action later enabled Keckley to receive a war pension by claiming she had been married to her dead son's father (Washington, *They Knew Lincoln*, 208–9).

CHAPTER 5: THE COST OF SELF IN TWO ALCOTT UTOPIAS

1. Samuel D. Warren and Louis D. Brandeis, "The Right to Privacy: The Implicit Made Explicit," in *Philosophical Dimensions of Privacy: An Anthology*, ed. Ferdinand David Schoeman (Cambridge: Cambridge University Press, 1984), 81. All subsequent quotations from this essay are from this source and cited parenthetically in the text.
2. Louisa May Alcott, *Little Men: Life at Plumfield with Jo's Boys* (New York: Signet Books, 1987), 327. All subsequent quotations from this novel are from this edition and cited parenthetically in the text.
3. For an overview of U.S. social evolutionary discourse, see Richard Hofstadter, *Social Darwinism in American Thought* (Boston: Beacon Press, 1991). For work on the diversity of Darwinistic adaptations, see Greta Jones, *Social Darwinism and English Thought: The Interaction between Biological and Social Theory* (Brighton, UK: Harvester Press, 1980).
4. John Fiske, *The Destiny of Man Viewed in Light of His Origin* (Boston: Houghton Mifflin, 1899), 100.
5. J. V. Sears, "Housekeeping Hereafter," *Atlantic Monthly* 48:287 (September 1881), 331.
6. Ibid., 334–38.
7. Ouida, "The Penalties of a Well-Known Name," *North Atlantic Review* 154:427 (June 1892), 734.
8. Ibid., 736–39.
9. E. L. Godkin, "The Rights of the Citizen to His Own Reputation," *Scribner's Magazine* 8:1 (July 1890), 65. Apparently this theory took root. Forty years later, Zora Neale Hurston would similarly assert the absence of the concept of privacy in black culture: "It is said that Negroes keep nothing secret, that they have no reserve. This ought not to seem strange when one considers that we are an outdoor people accustomed to communal life. Add this to all-permeating drama and you have the explanation." See Hurston, "Characteristics of Negro Expression," in *African American Literary Theory: A Reader*, ed. Winston Napier (New York: New York University Press, 2000), 39.

10. John Gilmer Speed, "The Right of Privacy," *North Atlantic Review* 163:476 (July 1896), 74.
11. Sears, "Housekeeping Hereafter," 331.
12. Anonymous, "The Right to Be Let Alone," *Atlantic Monthly* 67:401 (March 1891), 429.
13. See Claudia Durst Johnson, " 'Transcendental Wild Oats' or the Cost of an Idea," *American Transcendental Quarterly* 12:1 (March 1998), 45–64.
14. Louisa May Alcott, *Jo's Boys, or How They Turned Out* (New York: Bantam Books, 1995), 35. All subsequent quotations from this novel are from this edition and cited parenthetically in the text.
15. Quoted in Sheryl A. Englund, "Reading the Author in *Little Women*: A Biography of a Book," *American Transcendentalist Quarterly* 12:3 (September 1998), 204.
16. Ibid., 206. See Englund for an excellent analysis of nineteenth- and twentieth-century marketing strategies in relation to the autobiographical claims of Alcott's fiction. On Alcott's hate of publicity, see Martha Saxton, *Louisa May Alcott: A Modern Biography* (New York: Farrar, Straus and Giroux, 1995), 315, 349.
17. John Seeley Hart, *The Female Prose Writers of America* (Philadelphia: Butler, 1855), 5–6.
18. Richard Brodhead, *Cultures of Letters: Scenes of Reading and Writing in Nineteenth-Century America* (Chicago: University of Chicago Press, 1993), 70.
19. Herman Melville, *Pierre: or, the Ambiguities* (New York: Penguin, 1996), 250.
20. Gillian Brown, *Domestic Individualism: Imagining Self in Nineteenth-Century America* (Berkeley: University of California Press, 1990), chapter 5.
21. See Amy Dru Stanley, *From Bondage to Contract: Wage Labor, Marriage, and the Market in the Age of Slave Emancipation* (Cambridge: Cambridge University Press, 1995), 84–86. As Stanley explains, disputes over labor contracts raised "questions that were metaphysical as well as moral and economic—about the nature of the human essence, about autonomy and alienation, about the relation of self ownership, labor, and time" (86).
22. Brodhead, *Cultures of Letters*, 70.
23. This passage quotes almost directly from an entry in Alcott's journal about installing a furnace at Orchard House for the comfort of her dying mother. Louisa May Alcott, "December 1871," in *The Journals of Louisa May Alcott*, ed. Joel Myerson, Daniel Shealy, and Madeleine B. Stern (Boston: Little, Brown, 1989), 179–80.
24. Edna Cheney, *Louisa May Alcott: Life, Letters and Journals* (Boston: Little, Brown, 1928), iv.
25. Caroline Levander, "The Science of Sentiment: The Evolution of the Bourgeois Child in Nineteenth-Century American Narrative," *Modern Language Studies* 30:1 (Spring 2000), 27–44; Maude Hines, "Missionary Positions: Taming the Savage Girl in Louisa May Alcott's *Jack and Jill*," *The Lion and the Unicorn* 23:3 (1999), 373–94.

26. Elizabeth Young, *Disarming the Nation: Women's Writing and the American Civil War* (Chicago: University of Chicago Press, 1992), 72.
27. See Stanley, *From Bondage to Contract*, 8; and Stephanie Coontz, *The Social Origins of Private Life: A History of American Families, 1600–1900* (London: Verso, 1988), 128–30.
28. Coontz, *The Social Origins of Private Life*, 165–66.
29. William B. Scott, *In Pursuit of Happiness: American Conceptions of Property from the Seventeenth to the Twentieth Century* (Bloomington: Indiana University Press, 1977), 10.
30. See Coontz, *The Social Origins of Private Life*, 79.
31. Thomas Jefferson, "Letter to Correa de Serra, 1814," in *The Writings of Thomas Jefferson, Volume 19*, ed. Andrew A. Lipscomb and Albert Ellery Bergh (Washington, DC: Memorial Edition, 1903–4), 210.
32. Charles Sellers, *The Market Revolution: Jacksonian America, 1815–1846* (Oxford: Oxford University Press, 1991), 43–47.
33. Alexis de Tocqueville, *Democracy in America* (New York: Alfred A. Knopf, 1945), II.122.
34. Henry David Thoreau, *Walden and Civil Disobedience* (New York: Penguin, 1983), 47. See also Emerson's distinction between the farmer's property in his farm and the poet's "property in the horizon": Ralph Waldo Emerson, "Nature," *Essays and Lectures*, ed. Joel Porte (New York: Library of America, 1983), 9.
35. Quoted in Mark Holloway, *Heavens on Earth: Utopian Communities in America, 1680–1880* (New York: Dover Publications, 1966), 104.
36. Charles Lane and A. Bronson Alcott, "The Consociate Family Life," in *Transcendentalism: A Reader*, ed. Joel Myerson (Oxford: Oxford University Press, 2000), 439. All subsequent quotations from this text are from this source and cited parenthetically in the text.
37. Amos Bronson Alcott, "July 21, 1842," in *The Journals of Bronson Alcott*, ed. Odell Shepard (Boston: Little, Brown, 1938), 165.
38. Quoted in Richard Francis, *Transcendental Utopias: Individual and Community at Brook Farm, Fruitlands, and Walden* (Ithaca: Cornell University Press, 1997), 151. In the same journal entry, Alcott links this effect of false mirroring to empiricism, which he describes as "the half-visaged theories of materialism...the one-eyed philosophy of Experience—substituting effects for causes, and solving all mysteries by outward observation" (in Francis, *Transcendental Utopias*, 32–33). Mistaking the material world for the whole of existence, the empiricist becomes too enamored of his own power to act upon and shape it. He comes to mistake human agency for the highest power. This is both an over- and underestimation of himself. It is also a self-perpetuating trap. As Richard Francis puts it in his analysis of Alcott's philosophy, "man makes his presence felt on the external world and then is impressed by the evidence of his own manipulation of that world; consequently, instead of taking his superiority for granted, he becomes subservient to, and tries to learn from, the environment which he has, in part, created" (ibid., 151–52).

39. Louisa May Alcott, "Transcendental Wild Oats," in *Alternative Alcott*, ed. Elaine Showalter (New Brunswick, NJ: Rutgers University Press, 1988), 366. Although the character who speaks these lines (Timon Lion) represents Charles Lane rather than Bronson Alcott (Abel Lamb) in Louisa's parable, the ideas are more typical of the latter. Jean Pfaelzer finds that Alcott revises history significantly in "Transcendental Wild Oats" by attributing many of Bronson's actions and attitudes to Charles Lane, making him the villain and her father the innocent idealist. Jean Pfaelzer, "The Sentimental Promise and the Utopian Myth: Rebecca Harding Davis's 'The Harmonists' and Louisa May Alcott's 'Transcendental Wild Oats,'" *American Transcendental Quarterly* 3 (March 1989), 85–99.
40. See chapter 2 for a discussion of these ideas in the writing of Margaret Fuller.
41. Amos Bronson Alcott, "Days from a Diary," *Dial* 2 (April 1842), 426.
42. Alcott, "Transcendental Wild Oats," 365.
43. In "Consociate Family Life," Bronson writes: "As to Property, we discover...its just disposal...in its entire absorption into the New Spirit" (Lane and Alcott, "The Consociate Family Life," 438).
44. Francis, *Transcendental Utopias*, 141.
45. Alcott, "Transcendental Wild Oats," 377.
46. Amos Bronson Alcott, *Concord Days* (Philadelphia: Albert Saifer, 1872), 3–4.
47. Quoted in Helen Deese, "Alcott's Conversations on the Transcendentalists: The Record of Caroline Dall," *American Literature* 60:1 (March 1988), 18.
48. Louisa May Alcott, *Journals*, 47.
49. See Brodhead, *Cultures of Letters*, for his influential discussion of how "disciplinary intimacy" is exemplified in this and other Alcott methods, which he finds representative of middle-class antebellum family practice generally. See Young for a discussion of the gendered dynamics of disciplinary intimacy in the Alcott family: *Disarming the Nation*, 77–78.
50. Louisa May Alcott, *Journals*, 45.
51. In 1874 Abba bequeathed her diary to Louisa, intending—surmises Martha Saxton—that its contents should become another resource for Louisa's fiction.
52. Louisa May Alcott, *Journals*, 73.
53. For more about Bronson Alcott's abolitionism, see Sarah Elbert, "Introduction," in her *Louisa May Alcott on Race, Sex, and Slavery* (Boston: Northeastern University Press, 1997), xxi.
54. Bronson also conflated slavery with "the subjugation" of wage labor: "From the state of serfdom to the receipt of wages, may be a step in human progress; but it is certainly full time for taking a new step out of the hiring system" (Lane and Alcott, "The Consociate Family Life," 439). Most other communitarians were also antislavery activists and several promoted black self-improvement and assimilation. In every case, this

attempt focused on property. Owen made blacks fellow holders in community property. Frances Wright encouraged (still enslaved) blacks at the Nashoba Commune to earn money toward freedom. Many famous black abolitionists joined communes; Frederick Douglass, Sojourner Truth, and David Ruggles were all at Northhampton Association.

55. Elbert, "Introduction," xv–xvi.
56. Odell Shepard, *Pedlar's Progress: The Life of Bronson Alcott* (Boston: Little, Brown, 1937), 127.
57. Abigail May Alcott, "August 26, 1843," in *The Journals of Bronson Alcott*, 154–55.
58. Lane and Alcott, "The Consociate Family Life," 438.
59. Elbert, "Introduction," xxvi.
60. Ibid., ix.
61. Plumfield also references Temple School and features many of Bronson's pedagogical techniques—including, most famously, his method of requiring misbehaving students to inflict their prescribed punishment upon him. Louisa herself described *Little Men* as an attempt to vindicate her father's reputation as an educator and encouraged attempts to reissue *Record of a School* along with it (see Saxton, *Louisa May Alcott*, 313).
62. Young, *Disarming America*, 102.
63. Tocqueville, *Democracy in America*, II.122–23.
64. Elbert, "Introduction," ix.
65. Louisa May Alcott, *Little Women; or Meg, Jo, Beth, and Amy* (Boston: Roberts Brothers, 1868–69), 370.
66. See for example Janice M. Alberghene, "Autobiography and the Boundaries of Interpretation: On Reading *Little Women* and *The Living Is Easy*," in *Little Women and the Feminist Imagination: Criticism, Controversy, Personal Essays*, ed. Alberghene and Beverly Lyon Clark (New York: Garland, 1999), 347–76.
67. See Hines, "Missionary Positions."
68. Ibid.; John W. Crowley, "Little Women and the Boy-Book," *New England Quarterly* 58:3 (September 1985), 384–99; Levander, "The Science of Sentiment."
69. Levander, "The Science of Sentiment," 42.
70. Young, *Disarming the Nation*, 72.
71. Alcott, *Little Women*, 369.
72. Michael Moon, "Nineteenth-Century Discourse on Childhood Gender Training: The Case of Louisa May Alcott's *Little Men* and *Jo's Boys*," in *Queer Representations: Reading Lives Reading Cultures*, ed. Martin Duberman (New York: New York University Press, 1997), 210.
73. As Gregory Eiselein points out, "Alcott saturates *Little Men* with contradiction, paradox, and intertwined opposites" to "engender new meaning...and generate insights that are often surprising, unexpectedly delightful, and ultimately indicative of Alcott's larger views about socialization, education, and morality" (3, 7), in "Contradiction in Louisa

May Alcott's *Little Men*," *New England Quarterly* 78:1 (March 2005), 3–25.

74. Herbert Spencer, "Property," in *The Evolution of Society: Selections from* Principles of Sociology, ed. Robert L. Carneiro (Chicago: University of Chicago Press, 1967), 195. Here Spencer differs from other evolutionary thinkers, who believed the primitive personality indifferent to property. Pointing out that even dogs protect their master's belongings, he argues that savages and children exhibit a "less developed" understanding of ownership, based upon physical (vs. abstract legal) possession and not inattentive to the rights of others.
75. The best known case of this strategy, the Dawes Act, occurred several decades after the writing of *Little Men*. However, the practice begins during the colonial era. See Sellers, *The Market Revolution*, 7–8.
76. This realignment of ownership with racial integration rather than subjugation suggests a new way to read the title of Alcott's 1863 story, "My Contraband." Many critics find this title odd for the way it resonates with slavery; see, for example, Mark Patterson, "Racial Sacrifice and Citizenship: The Construction of Masculinity in Louisa May Alcott's 'The Brothers,'" *Studies in American Fiction* 25:2 (Autumn 1997), 150–51. In light of *Little Men*, however, Nurse Dane's possessive claim to Robert Dane might be better understood as an act of accommodation and amalgamation.
77. Brodhead, *Cultures of Letters*, 70.
78. Louisa May Alcott, "To John Seely Hart, September 13, 1871," in *The Selected Letters of Louisa May Alcott*, ed. Joel Myerson, Daniel Shealy, and Madeleine Stern (Boston: Little, Brown, 1987), 160.
79. See Coontz, *The Social Origins of Private Life*, 293; and Stanley, *From Bondage to Contract*, 149.
80. Eric Sundquist, "Mark Twain and Homer Plessy," *Representations, Special Issue: America Reconstructed, 1840–90* 24 (Fall 1988), 108.
81. See Thomas F. Gossett, *Uncle Tom's Cabin and American Culture* (Dallas: Southern Methodist University Press, 1985).
82. William Graham Sumner, "The Forgotten Man," in *Selected Essays of William Graham Sumner: Social Darwinism* (Englewood Cliffs, NJ: Prentice Hall, 1963), 129.
83. Sundquist, "Mark Twain and Homer Plessy"; Amy Robinson, "Forms of Appearance and Value: Homer Plessy and the Politics of Privacy," in *Performance and Cultural Politics*, ed. Elin Diamond (London: Routledge, 1996), 237–61.
84. Albion Tourgée, "Brief for Homer A. Plessy," in *The Thin Disguise: Turning Point in Negro History; Plessy v Ferguson; A Documentary Presentation, 1864–96*, ed. Otto H. Olsen (New York: Humanities Press, 1967), 83.
85. Henry Billings Brown, *Plessy v. Ferguson*, 163 U.S. 537 (1896), in ibid., 110–11.
86. Robinson, "Forms of Appearance and Value," 238.
87. Brown, *Plessy v. Ferguson*, 109.

88. Sundquist, "Mark Twain and Homer Plessy," 103.
89. For a contrasting reading of isolation and loss in *Jo's Boys*, see Gregory Eiselein, "Modernity and Louisa May Alcott's *Jo's Boys*," *Children's Literature* 34 (2006), 83–108.
90. Ibid., 93.
91. Louisa May Alcott, *Journals*, 183.
92. These ladies also reflect the gendered construction of mass culture, such as we see in *Pierre* or in Henry James's famous invective against female readers. Jo complains that girls are always the worst invaders of her intimacy and privacy (49), and Dan calls Teddy "curious as a girl" when the boy pries into his secrets with annoying persistence (316).
93. Here I am thinking of Elizabeth Young's work on how Alcott and others use Civil War themes to represent the conflicting impulses of white womanhood and female authorship (see Young, *Disarming the Nation*). Dan also represents Jo/Alcott's limited ability as headmistress/author to counter the increasingly constricted national space of white middle-class belonging. Dan imagines himself creating a new utopian community called Dansville where he will convert "black sheep" like himself into good men; but the plan is never realized.
94. In *Jack and Jill*, Jill exhibits stoicism that is similarly racialized, pathologized, and admired all at once, when she bears great pain "with the courage of a little Indian"; see Hines, "Missionary Positions," 379.
95. Levander, "The Science of Sentiment," 34.
96. Also suggesting Alcott's ambivalence here is that Jo's opposition to Dan's reticence perfectly recapitulates the demands placed on her as authoress. She is faulted "if she decline[s] to open her heart to [readers]" and faulted again "if she [finds] it impossible to answer the piles of letters sent to her" (38).
97. Young, *Disarming the Nation*, 104.
98. Moon, "Nineteenth-Century Discourse on Child Gender Training," 214.
99. Ibid.
100. Eiselein also notes the incestuous implications of Laurie and Bess's relationship, but reads the episode as an expression of Alcott's desire to protect Bess's freedom, allowing her to pursue her "artistic career" and find a different (and gender-ambiguous) "mate" later on; Eiselein, "Modernity and Louisa May Alcott's *Jo's Boys*," 88.

CHAPTER 6: EPILOGUE

1. Samuel D. Warren and Louis D. Brandeis, "The Right to Privacy: The Implicit Made Explicit," in *Philosophical Dimensions of Privacy: An Anthology*, ed. Ferdinand David Schoeman (Cambridge: Cambridge University Press, 1984), 75–103.

2. Miranda Joseph, "The Multivalent Commodity: On the Supplementarity of Value and Values," in *Retheorizing Commodification: Cases and Readings in Law and Culture*, ed. Joan C. Williams and Martha M. Ertman (New York: New York University Press, 2005), 383–401. For more discussions of the "hostile worlds" paradigm, see other contributions to this same collection, especially Martha M. Ertman and Joan C. Williams, "Preface: Freedom, Equality, and the Many Features of Commodification," 1–43; and Joan C. Williams and Viviana A. Zelizer, "To Commodify or Not to Commodify, That Is *Not* the Question," 362–83.
3. See Williams and Zelizer, "To Commodify," 364–66.
4. The President's Council on Bioethics, "Executive Summary: Human Cloning and Human Dignity: An Ethical Inquiry," http://www.bioethics.gov/reports/cloningreport/.
5. "Overview," Electronic Privacy Information Center (EPIC), http://www.epic.org/privacy/genetic/.
6. E. Donald Shapiro and Michelle L. Weinberg, "DNA Data Banking: The Dangerous Erosion of Privacy," *Cleveland State Law Review* 38:455 (1990), 476.
7. Priscilla Wald, "What's in a Cell?: John Moore's Spleen and the Language of Bioslavery," *New Literary History* 36:2 (2005), 219.
8. "Use of DNA for Detection and Treatment of Disease," EPIC website, http://www.epic.org/.
9. A good starting place on the extensive scholarship in this area is Paul Brodwin's edited collection, *Biotechnology and Culture: Bodies, Anxieties, Ethics* (Bloomington: Indiana University Press, 2000). See especially the essays collected in part II, "Maternity in Question."
10. On black prisoners and DNA privacy rights, see Kristina Rooker, "DNA and Privacy," University of Dayton, http://academic.udayton.edu/health/05bioethics/00rooker.htm. On race and the reproductive market, see Robyn Weigman, "Intimate Publics: Race, Property, and Personhood," *American Literature: A Journal of Literary History, Criticism, and Bibliography* 74:4 (December 2002), 859–86; Patricia Williams, *The Alchemy of Race and Rights: Diary of a Law Professor* (Cambridge: Harvard University Press, 1991), 224; and Dorothy Roberts, *Killing the Black Body: Race, Reproduction, and the Meaning of Liberty* (New York: Vintage, 1997). On bioprospecting, see Wald, "What's in a Cell?" 221–22; and Debra Harry, "Patenting of Life and Its Implications for Indigenous Peoples," Indigenous Peoples Council on Biocolonialism, January 1995, http://www.ipcb.org/publications/briefing_papers/files/patents.html; and Vandana Shiva, *Biopiracy: The Plunder of Nature and Knowledge* (Boston: South End Press, 1997).
11. Weigman, "Intimate Publics."
12. The President's Council on Bioethics, 5.
13. Wald's discussion in "What's in a Cell?" of historical displacement in representations of the bioslavery trope is particularly astute.

14. Rachel Reitsleff, "*The Island*," *Cinescape*, July 22, 2005.
15. Margaret Fuller, "Self-Definitions," in *The Essential Margaret Fuller*, ed. Jeffrey Steele (New Brunswick: Rutgers University Press, 1992), 11. Interestingly, the film even interprets this development as a privacy invasion—"What are you doing in my house?" Tom Lincoln demands, when first confronted by Lincoln Six Echo, and the Merrick public relations representative describes it as a "home invasion."
16. "Director's Commentary," *The Island*, DVD (Warner Home Video, 2006).
17. Dennis Lim, "DimClone," *Village Voice*, July 19, 2005.
18. Alys Weinbaum, "Coda: Gene/alogies for a New Millennium," in *Wayward Reproductions: Genealogies of Race and Nation in Transatlantic Modern Thought* (Durham. NC: Duke University Press, 2004).
19. Lauren Berlant, "The Subject of True Feeling: Pain, Privacy, and Politics," in *Feminist Consequences: Theory for the New Century*, ed. Elisabeth Bronfen and Misha Kavka (New York: Columbia University Press, 2001), 130–31.
20. Lauren Berlant, "The Subject of True Feeling," 128.
21. Williams and Zelizer, "To Commodify," 366.
22. Interestingly, this very point is the focus of Kazuo Ishiguro's novel, *Never Let Me Go*, published just months before *The Island*'s release.
23. The reference is to Donna Haraway's essay "A Cyborg Manifesto: Science, Technology, and Socialist-Feminism in the Late Twentieth Century" (in *Simians, Cyborgs and Women: The Reinvention of Nature* [New York: Routledge, 1991], 149–81).

INDEX